"We Will Be Citizens"

ALSO EDITED BY JAMES FISHER

*Tony Kushner: New Essays on the Art
and Politics of the Plays* (McFarland, 2006)

"We Will Be Citizens"
New Essays on Gay and Lesbian Theatre

Edited by
JAMES FISHER

McFarland & Company, Inc., Publishers
Jefferson, North Carolina, and London

LIBRARY OF CONGRESS ONLINE CATALOG DATA

"We will be citizens" : new essays on gay and lesbian theatre / edited by James Fisher.
    p.   cm.
    Includes bibliographical references and index.

    ISBN 978-0-7864-3418-3
    softcover : 50# alkaline paper

    1. American drama — 20th century — History and criticism. 2. Homosexuality in literature. 3. Gay men in literature. 4. Lesbians in literature. 5. Gays' writings, American — History and criticism. 6. Homosexuality and literature — United States — History — 20thcentury. 7. Theater — United States — History — 20th century. I. Fisher, James. II. Title.
PS338.H66W49   2009
809'.93353 — dc22   2008044264

British Library cataloguing data are available

©2008 James Fisher. All rights reserved

No part of this book may be reproduced or transmitted in any form or by any means, electronic or mechanical, including photocopying or recording, or by any information storage and retrieval system, without permission in writing from the publisher.

On the cover: Tyler Reilly and Elizabeth Aspenlieder in *Angels in America*, directed by Jason Southerland and Nancy Curran Willis, photograph by Dalyn Miller (courtesy Boston Theatre Works)

Manufactured in the United States of America

McFarland & Company, Inc., Publishers
  Box 611, Jefferson, North Carolina 28640
    www.mcfarlandpub.com

To two of my brothers,
Scott L. Fisher and Daniel R. Fisher

Table of Contents

Introduction
  James Fisher 1

From Tolerance to Liberation: Gay Drama in the Mainstream from *Torch Song Trilogy* and *The Normal Heart* to *Angels in America, Love! Valour! Compassion!* and *Take Me Out*
  James Fisher 7

Mainsteam Theatre, Mass Media, and the 1985 Premiere of *The Normal Heart*: Negotiating Forces between Emergent and Dominant Ideologies
  Jacob Juntunen 32

"Not Just Any Woman": Bradford Louryk, a Legacy of Charles Ludlam and the Ridiculous Theatre for the Twenty-First Century
  Sean F. Edgecomb 56

Mamet, Homophobia, and Chicago Politics
  Charles Eliot Mehler 79

No Tragedy: Queer Evil in the Metaphysical Comedies of Nicky Silver
  Jordan Schildcrout 90

Gay and Lesbian Theatre for Young People or the Representation of "Troubled Youth"
  Manon van de Water and Annie Giannini 103

Crossing the Border: Irish Drama and the Queer American Character
  David Cregan 123

Lisa Kron: Facing and Placing Lesbian Identity on New York Stages
  Leslie Atkins Durham 141

The Last Gay Man: *Raised in Captivity* and *Hurrah at Last*
  Robert F. Gross 158

The Soundplay's the Thing: A Formal Analysis of John (aka
  Lypsinka) Epperson's Queer Performance Texts
    Joe E. Jeffreys   177

The (Fe)Male Gays: Split Britches and the Redressing of
  Dyke Camp
    Paul Menard   185

"Ladies and Gentlemen, People Die": The Uncomfortable
  Performances of Kiki and Herb
    James Wilson   194

Notes on Contributors   213
Index   217

Introduction

"We Will Be Citizens": New Essays on Gay and Lesbian Theatre is intended not as a thorough critical analysis or history of the emergence of gay and lesbian contributions to the American stage, but instead as a select sampling of the diversity of work by a select group of playwrights and performers, particularly since the late 1960s, who have chosen to center part or all of their achievement on depictions of the experiences and social progress of homosexuals in the United States. This volume takes its title from the final speech of Tony Kushner's two-play epic *Angels in America* (New York: Theatre Communications Group, 1995), in which its central character, Prior Walter, a gay man dying of AIDS, insists that homosexuals are an undeniable fact of American life despite a long tradition of oppression. And, as such, they do not ask for but demand the rights of full and equal citizenship. "We won't die secret deaths anymore" (280), Prior insists, and despite the harrowing tragedies of AIDS and its profound impact on the gay community, much progress has been achieved in the last decades of the twentieth century. As Michael Kinsley writes in "The Quiet Gay Revolution" in the June 25, 2007 issue of *Time* magazine, "On no issue is history moving faster than on 'gay rights'.... The work is not finished, of course, but what took black Americans more than a century, gays have accomplished in two or three decades.... Twenty years from now, maybe sooner, gays will have it all" (22).

Kinsley's assertion might have seemed overly optimistic only a short while ago—in the early 1990s—at the time Kushner crafted Prior's speech, but in the first years of the new millennium, as societal debate centers on the issue of "gay marriage," it is clear that a majority of Americans are far more accepting of homosexuals than was true at the time Kushner wrote his play. Without question, many obstacles, like gay marriage, remain to be resolved, and homophobia persists, but gay men and women now experience greater equality and much of the acceptance Prior demanded for them.

Many reasons may be identified for this evolution of American attitudes; central among them is the unprecedented rise of gay and lesbian theatre and drama since the late 1960s. In this, the mainstream American stage—usually dismissive of overtly politicized drama—has succeeded in framing the discussion of gay rights and, in the process, has progressed the debate on homosexuals in American life. However, despite Kinsley's optimism, it took time.

Gay characters can be located in U.S. drama from its beginnings, although prior to the mid-twentieth century homosexuals in plays are rarely identified as such and until the late 1960s, gay lives—and the cultural issues they faced—were rarely if ever evident. This began to change after World War II, almost exclusively through conflicted depictions of gays in the Broadway plays of Tennessee Williams until the burgeoning Off and Off Off Broadway movements of the late 1950s provided experimental venues within which playwrights could explore with greater freedom such previously taboo topics. With the popular and commercial success of Mart Crowley's *The Boys in the Band* on Broadway in 1968, gay male characters (soon to be followed by lesbians) moved to center stage, as did an increasingly serious, diverse, and frank examination of the moral, spiritual, and political issues raised by the emergence of homosexuals from the nation's closet. And by the early 1980s, gay characters and themes were seen with increasing frequency in drama and film (and occasionally prime-time television), but with the appearance of AIDS, first referred to as "gay cancer," homosexuality became a dominant—if not *the* dominant—topic in serious American drama. An intense rise in homophobia beginning with the first AIDS cases was the downside of greater visibility for gays, although in both society and, particularly, in the theatre—images of gays broadened and deepened.

Precisely defining the meaning of gay theatre and drama is a slippery slope, but in the case of this collection of essays the term will be understood simply to mean any play or performance in which the author or performer—whether gay or straight, man or woman—chooses to centrally explore an aspect of the homosexual experience in theatrical terms. The resultant "queering" of American theatre resulting from gay activism, along with the evolution of several remarkably varied generations of gay and lesbian writers and actors, has produced an era of gay-themed theatre since the late 1960s, and this volume is an attempt to explore but a small portion of the bounty of that period, which, it should be stressed, continues unabated. With the onset of AIDS in the early 1980s, gay drama increasingly and more overtly explored the serious questions inherent in being homosexual in America and, to a significant extent, gay drama has dominated American stages in the last twenty years. Most gay dramas achieving mainstream acclaim have been by and about gay men, with other gay sub-groups—lesbians in particular—making strides in Off and Off Off Broadway theatres.

The stage in America has traditionally been a welcoming environment for explorations of difference, a place where marginalized or oppressed "others" are able to give voice to their struggles. Gays and lesbians found in the theatre a means of expressing their hidden lives; the stage proved to be a venue in which pleas for tolerance and demands for equality could be heard, and what academics refer to as "teaching moments" could educate both sympathetic and hostile audiences.

Kushner's *Angels* was a battle cry, a dramatic completion of the themes and purposes of earlier gay plays: "We will be citizens," Prior insisted in *Angels*, "The time has come" (280). Indeed, it had, and among other things, Kushner's two *Angels* plays in their entirety celebrate that notion of sociopolitical arrival while, at the same time, acknowledge the continuing struggle toward full citizenship and offer a commemoration of the sacrifices, and tragedies, of the past. These essays will explore the various ways and means by which dramatists and performers have chronicled gay and lesbian experiences in American life, with particular emphasis on developments since the late 1960s, and the path by which, at least on stage, gays and lesbians moved toward their full citizenship.

The history of this journey is among the most compelling and significant stories of the late twentieth century. The most intense period of the crusade for homosexual rights stretches from the end of World War II to the present. This struggle is set against a background of societal homophobia profoundly exacerbated in the era of AIDS and, like most tectonic shifts in the American landscape, it has proven to be fodder for great theatre. Gay and lesbian characters and their stories finally moved into the cultural mainstream just as real-life homosexuals broke through into the consciousness of a society that at best had previously ignored them — and at worst persecuted them. It is no coincidence that as the Stonewall riot, a seminal event in the gay rights movement, occurred, Crowley's *The Boys in the Band* was offering its view of gay life on a Broadway stage not very far away. Such intersections of reality and illusion would occur frequently, as it did a generation later when Moisés Kaufman's *The Laramie Project* was created to reflect the harrowing reality of events surrounding the brutal murder of gay college student Matthew Shepherd.

The Boys in the Band introduced Broadway audiences to homosexual life and the dilemmas facing gay men living within the American family, setting the stage for similar theatrical explorations of the homosexual experience, although it took nearly a decade before another groundbreaking gay drama appeared on Broadway. Fervent tolerance pleas in Harvey Fierstein's *Torch Song Trilogy* and William Hoffman's *As Is* in the late 1970s and early 1980s appeared in tandem with celebrations of gay "fabulousness" and camp in Charles Ludlam's Theatre of the Ridiculous productions in Off and Off Off Broadway theatres before Fierstein's *Torch Song Trilogy* achieved acclaim and popularity sufficient enough to bring it to Broadway. When the initial horrors of the AIDS epidemic emerged shortly thereafter, gay plays and performers transitioned to expressing angry indictments of American society's homophobia and to reveal the widespread impact of AIDS. This was most memorably seen in works as diverse as gay activist Larry Kramer's semi-autobiographical drama *The Normal Heart* in the mid–1980s to Terrence McNally's wistful, near-elegiac Pulitzer Prize–winning *Love! Valour! Compassion!* in the mid–1990s. As the millennium approached, many gay and lesbian dramatists followed McNally's lead with lighter works that inspired a broad range of gay- and lesbian-themed plays, from the farcical satires by Christopher Durang and Paul Rudnick to the unnerving humor mixed with pathos lesbian dramatist Paula Vogel brought to the grim subject of pedophilia in *How I Learned to Drive*. In the same period, numerous performance artists adopted dark or satiric tones that matched Kramer's fiercely critical polemics.

Perhaps the most important gay-themed work of the 1990s, Kushner's *Angels in America*, subtitled "a gay fantasia on national themes," took gay and lesbian drama to another level. Inspired by many sources, not least of which were the diverse range of gay plays that had preceded his, from Fierstein's assimilationist comedy to Kramer's rage-filled assaults on the American conscience, Kushner was able to transcend the typical structures of gay drama of the 1980s through a merger of boldly theatricalized flights of history, politics, and imagination in the two *Angels* plays. Ambitious beyond all reasonable expectations, *Angels* set a high bar for the gay and lesbian dramatists who emerged in the next decade, inspiring such writers as Richard Greenberg, Naomi Wallace, Craig Lucas, Nicky Silver, Suzan-Lori Parks, and many others. Greenberg's 2002 hit Broadway play *Take Me Out*, queered baseball, the national pastime, to be followed by the 2005 Academy Award-winning film *Brokeback Mountain*, which exposed homosexuality among cowboys, a last icon of hyper-masculine heterosexuality. American drama had been dominated by plays dealing with homosexuality for decades by the time *Take Me Out* (and *Brokeback Mountain*) appeared and the social changes reflected proved to be, as Kinsley writes, more rapid than anyone might expect. And the dramatic manifestations do not even begin to include the numerous performers— some of whom are chronicled in this collection — bringing facets of gay and lesbian life to the fore. All of which suggests that the significance of homosexual theatre merits much more scholarly attention than it has received in the direction of exploring and acknowledging trends and assessing the lasting value of the growing canon of gay-themed dramatic works, productions, and performances, whether overtly political or not, which have contributed to major changes in American theatre specifically, and American culture in general.

Providing perspectives on the historical progress of gays and lesbians is an obvious goal of this volume. While not attempting a sweeping chronological history of gay and lesbian theatre and drama in America, the contributors to this collection illuminate the experience of gays and lesbians as society continues to reckon with the changes that have occurred since the 1960s and the continuing debate of the social, religious, and political issues of homosexual life in the United States in the twenty-first century.

The essays featured in *"We Will Be Citizens"* are, as previously noted, an eclectic sampling of scholarship reflecting the remarkable diversity of gay- and lesbian-themed American plays, playwrights, and performers. Beginning with my own survey of gay drama from the late 1960s through the early twenty-first century, the volume's contributors focus more specifically on single artists and works. Jacob Juntunen insightfully illuminates the controversial debut of Larry Kramer's *The Normal Heart*, a landmark work indicting a range of socio-political forces at the dawn of the AIDS crisis while Sean F. Edgecomb explores the work of Bradford Louryk, a "legacy" of the late Charles Ludlam and the Ridiculous Theatre who carries forth Ludlam's unique approach into the twenty-first century. Other playwrights, gay and straight, are emphasized in several essays. For example, Jordan Schildcrout dissects the "metaphysical comedies" of Nicky Silver, while Robert F. Gross also considers Silver's work by focusing on *Raised in Captivity*, pointing up its thematic connections to Richard Greenberg's *Hurrah at Last*. Charles Eliot Mehler traces depictions of homophobia in David Mamet's gritty Chicago plays, Leslie Atkins Durham examines the complexities of "lesbian identity" in the works of Lisa Kron, and David Cregan reflects on the evolution of "queer" American characters by stepping outside the national border to find a unique perspective of such figures residing in Irish drama. Some essential gay and lesbian performers are also scrutinized, with Joe E. Jeffreys' consideration of the drag performances of Lypsinka (Joe Epperson), Paul Menard's exploration of the "dyke camp" style of Split Britches, and James Wilson's study of the ways in which performance artists Kiki and Herb destabilize traditional views of drag and gay camp. Finally, Manon van de Water and her student, Annie Giannini, collaborate to provide a rare view of gay- and lesbian-themed plays for young audiences. The diversity of these essays mirrors the diversity of gay theatre and drama in millennial America and it is likely that some illumination about the unknowable future of gay theatre and drama may be found among these worthy contributions to the field of gay studies.

The contributors to this collection are similarly diverse in experience and accomplishment, representing the realms of both traditional scholarship and ephemeral performance. This seems particularly appropriate since the history of gay and lesbian theatre has been conveyed and defined by groundbreaking scholars while dramatists and performers have inspired the development of gay literature and drama and, more importantly, all have shaped and influenced the national conversation on the subject. Both well-known and emerging voices of gay theatre and drama in the United States are chronicled herein, and the authors of these essays direct readers toward these singular artists and their accomplishments. As editor of the volume, I am deeply grateful for their efforts, and also for their good will and patience. Sincere thanks are due to my theatre colleagues and students at the University of North Carolina at Greensboro. Appreciation is also owed to several individuals and institutions, including Peter Frederick, David Garrett Izzo, Philip C. Kolin, Kaizaad Navroze Kotwal, Tony Kushner, Felicia Hardison Londré, Diane and Jamey Norton, Warren Rosenberg, Laurence Senelick, Bert Stern, and former coworkers at Wabash College. My wife, Dana Warner Fisher, and our children Daniel and Anna, provided love and support as always, and I am also appreciative of other family members, particularly my mother, Mae H. Fisher, and departed friends including Kenneth Kloth, Erminie C. Leonardis, John C. Swan, and Lauren K. Woods.

From Tolerance to Liberation

Gay Drama in the Mainstream from
Torch Song Trilogy *and* The Normal Heart
to Angels in America, Love! Valour!
Compassion! *and* Take Me Out

JAMES FISHER

In arguably the most iconic of the many gay-themed plays to emerge in late twentieth-century American drama, *Angels in America*, its playwright Tony Kushner ends his nearly seven-hour, two-play epic with a proclamation from his central character, Prior Walter, a gentle gay man dying of AIDS: "We won't die secret deaths anymore. The world only spins forward. We will be citizens. The time has come" (Kushner 280). Prior's insistence brought an era of extraordinary gay plays to a hard-won zenith, reflecting vast changes in the American cultural landscape and, particularly, the depiction of gays on stage. Overt depictions of homosexuals were rare in American drama prior to the 1960s, and until the late 1970s they appeared mostly in either peripheral (and usually stereotyped) roles in mainstream plays or on Off and Off Off Broadway stages. It is the purpose of this essay to trace the evolution of gay characters and gay-themed drama on Broadway from the seminal work, Mart Crowley's *The Boys in the Band* (1968), to recent plays. Focusing on Broadway obviously eliminates many worthy gay plays that found life in Off and Off Off Broadway theatres, but an examination of the mainstream provides an undeniable barometer of evolving American attitudes, and the plays reflect the rapid and remarkable changes of the past half-century.

The term *gay drama*, which typically refers to plays written by or about homosexuals, was coined in the mid–twentieth century in the same period various other marginalized groups—women, African-Americans, Latinos—similarly sought liberation from oppressive social constraints denying opportunity and equality for the demographic within American life. That the earliest serious homosexual-themed plays—or plays with prominent gay characters—were, in essence, pleas for tolerance is thus not surprising. The tale of mainstream gay drama since World War II is one of a journey out of the closet that led from such tolerance pleas to liberation and activism, from requests for acceptance to demands for equality and, ultimately, a permanent altering of the social contract. Heteronormative America is coming to an end, millennial dramatists insist in their plays, and in tandem with this knowledge, demands for equality recede only because early twenty-first century gay playwrights and performers assume its existence. Their gay characters and themes reflect the vast changes in American society's relationship with homosexuality that began in the mid–twentieth century, in fringe theatres and moving to the mainstream in the late 1970s and beyond.

The journey has proven to be a long and slow one, and although it can be argued, as Michael Kinsley does in a recent magazine essay, that "on no issue is history moving faster than on 'gay rights'" (Kinsley 22), that journey has yet to reach its conclusion. The movement toward liberation and acceptance has been complex, fraught with perils, and studded with tragedy, yet the emergence of gays from the shadows of American life has re-energized American drama in ways few other social movements have ever done. Drama in the United States, particularly within the commercial mainstream venues on Broadway, has often seemed particularly resistant to overtly politicized plays, yet in the area of homosexual drama — from early gay tolerance plays to current liberated works — audiences have been surprisingly receptive, despite occasional controversies mostly generated by fundamentalist religions, the extreme political right wing, and resistant conservative critics.

The wellspring of the public's acceptance of gay-themed plays, which undoubtedly began with the Broadway success of Crowley's *The Boys in the Band*, came from Off and Off Off Broadway plays by a range of dramatists in preceding decades, particularly the 1950s and 1960s. However, it was not until the late 1970s that a steady flow of gay-themed plays found a wide audience on Broadway, although it can be argued, and should certainly be noted, that a gay sensibility, often present in drama dating from the dawn of time, imbued much American (and European) drama since the late nineteenth century. Homosexual men, lesbians, bisexuals, and transgendered individuals are traditionally grouped together under the all-encompassing label of "gay" within the realm of drama, although in recent decades the term has come to refer to a gay sensibility — "fabulousness" as Kushner has proudly referred to it — meaning simply a collective means of viewing the world through the lens of gay culture. With the onset of the AIDS epidemic in the early 1980s, gay plays, which were at that particular moment finding greater mainstream acceptance, shifted to more overtly explore serious questions inherent in the dilemma of being homosexual in homophobic America blaming gays for AIDS, while to a significant extent, gay drama and its themes provided an arena in which issues surrounding AIDS — and gay life in general — could be explored or debated.

Until the 1990s, most gay dramas achieving mainstream acclaim were by or about homosexual men, with lesbian, bisexual, and transgender writers making strides in Off and Off Off Broadway theatres. Alfred Kazin writes, "'The love that dare not speak its name' (in the nineteenth century) cannot, in the twentieth, shut up" (Kazin 38), but the emergence of a vigorous gay drama on American stages demonstrates, among other things, that much remains to be said on a subject about which the stage has been silent for too long and about which American society still has many conflicts to be resolved. Without question, however, gay drama is a reflection of the extraordinary changes that Kinsley posits have occurred with such speed in recent decades. Reflecting on the history of homosexuals in American theatre, Kushner, whose *Angels in America* was arguably the most acclaimed "gay drama" of the late twentieth century, believes that "there's a natural proclivity for gay people — who historically have often spent their lives hiding — to feel an affinity for the extended make-believe and donning of roles that is part of theatre. It's reverberant with some of the central facts of our lives" (Blanchard 42). Kushner identifies at least one of the reasons homosexuals find refuge and a necessary means of expression in drama, though even in theatre homosexuals were traditionally as consigned to the "closet" as gays were in other walks of American life.

Prior to the mid–twentieth century, openly gay dramatists or explorations of the subject in drama were strictly taboo in America, although many gay dramatists were at work, including Clyde Fitch, a close friend and possible lover of Oscar Wilde, and Avery Hopwood, the most popular purveyor of bourgeois stage farces in the 1910s and 1920s. Perhaps the first American play to feature overt depictions of homosexuality, Mae West's *The Drag* (1927), written under West's pen name Jane Mast, generated so much controversy that it closed prior to completing a pre–Broadway tour. West's exploitive play, which features an on-stage drag ball, set the stage for her next, *The Pleasure Man* (1928), which also included gay characters. West was a small part of a generation of writers and artists working in the 1920s inclined to delve, albeit tentatively, into previously taboo subjects, ranging from sexuality and interracial marriage to politics and women's rights. West aimed for titillation and sensationalism in service of a general goal of sexual liberation, while on a more serious level other dramatists experimented tentatively. The leading American playwright of the period, Eugene O'Neill, may have featured a gay character in his Pulitzer Prize-winning *Strange Interlude* (1928), although it is not explicitly stated that Charles Marsden, a sexually ambivalent dandy resistant to hyper-masculine peers, is a closeted homosexual. Like many dramatists, O'Neill sought veiled means to express such characters, but the times did not help. In New York, local authorities sought successfully to outlaw any depiction of what was unspecifically categorized as "sex degeneracy, or sex perversion" on stages from 1927 to 1967. Playwrights were obliged to approach the subject with caution, but plays featuring gay characters or themes sometimes found acceptance, including British dramatist Mordaunt Shairp's *The Green Bay Tree* (1933), which had a Broadway success, Lillian Hellman's admired *The Children's Hour* (1934), and a range of plays written after World War II by Tennessee Williams, with other dramatists tentatively following his lead in sexualizing the American stage.

Williams' importance as the transitional figure of early gay drama in the United States cannot be overstated, for he moved the stage from virtually complete avoidance of the topic to at least an uneasy contemplation of sexuality, including homosexuals and their hidden lives. In short, Williams began the process of liberating sexuality — and homosexuality in particular — from the realm of stage taboos. Williams' plays, particularly his earliest in the 1930s and 1940s, are understandably ambivalent on the question of homosexuality, but over time his gay characters become more visible, transgressive, and diverse. In an interview, Williams stressed, "Sexuality is part of my work, of course, because sexuality is a part of my life and everyone's life. I see no essential difference between the love of two men for each other and the love of a man for a woman; no essential difference, and that's why I've examined both" (Berkvist 101). Williams' characters, gay or straight, deeply feel the absence of love and exhibit a profound need for some sort of deeper connection, but as a rule Williams was writing about love, not the boundaries of gender. Constraints on depictions of sexuality in Williams' time meant that his sexually confused characters— gay, straight, or something in between — are inherently fugitives from mainstream society. They can only be fulfilled through transgression against its rigid strictures and these transgressions come, in the final analysis, at great, often tragic, personal cost.

Williams' frequent attention to matters of sexuality broke down barriers, encouraging early 1950s playwrights to follow his lead. Robert Anderson's *Tea and Sympathy* (1953), a major Broadway (and cinematic) success, is a well-crafted drama with ideas of homosexuality firmly rooted in bourgeois, conformist attitudes of 1950s America. However, its popularity suggests that audiences were at least willing to entertain the subject of homosexuality — and, perhaps, to make a tentative visit to alien territory. The play's depiction of Tom Lee, a sensitive young man brutally treated by fellow students and a homophobic, hyper-masculine headmaster at a private school, is certainly relevant to the experience of closeted homosexuals, but when Anderson's play seems to suggest that Tom can be "saved" from a homosexual life through an encounter with the headmaster's unhappy wife who takes Tom to bed to prove his (hetero) manhood, the play starkly reflects distorted attitudes that now seem, at best, quaint if not downright mendacious. Throughout the 1950s, other playwrights occasionally treated gay characters and issues, but often not in their most visible work. For example, William Inge, a newspaperman who turned to playwriting after being inspired by Williams, features gay characters in his lesser-known one-acts, including *The Boy in the Basement* (1962), in which an undertaker's assistant secretly attracted to a local youth is forced to receive the boy's body after a fatal accident. The man's emotional reaction to the death of the object of his unspoken affection reveals the secret sufferings of closeted gay men in a sympathetic light. Inge similarly dealt with the subject in another aptly named one-act, *The Tiny Closet* (1959), but in his major dramas, he generally avoided homosexuality, although most of his plays excoriate small-mindedness, bigotry in any form, and offer sympathetic portraits of those failing to fit into the strictly observed moral (or, more appropriately, moralizing) constraints of Middle American small-town values.

Homosexual characters and themes found fuller voice through the racial divisions of the Civil Rights era in *The Toilet* (1964) by LeRoi Jones (Amiri Baraka), a savage depiction of the impact of bigotry set in a high school lavatory. In the same period, the early plays of Edward Albee, most particularly *Everything in the Garden* (1964), followed Williams' lead, but almost all gay-themed drama was to be found exclusively in Off Broadway theatres. Straight dramatists of the period also occasionally explored issues of male sexuality, including Arthur Miller in *A View from the Bridge* (1955), in which a violent male-on-male kiss sets in motion the downfall of homophobic longshoreman Eddie Carbone, but homosexuality and gay characters were still restricted to the periphery on American stages from the mid–1950s to the mid–1960s.

As previously noted, the generally accepted breakthrough gay play, *The Boys in the Band*, simultaneously won praise for depicting more realistic images of homosexuals and criticism for presenting outmoded stereotypes of gays. The play's lasting value may be its warning against a closeted life — or attempts by gay men to hide behind a public façade of a "straight" life — and in comparatively progressive images of the gay lifestyle and the particular dilemmas facing effeminate gays unable to conceal their sexual orientation. The critical appreciation and commercial success of *The Boys in the Band* on stage, and in a subsequent film version, encouraged serious and more varied depictions of gay life, although stereotypes continued to abound. Occasionally, more complex, realistic portrayals of gay relationships appeared, as in Lanford Wilson's critically applauded *5th of July* (1978), a drama exploring the disillusionments of the Vietnam generation, and Wilson, a gay writer, often featured homosexuals in the large canon of his plays from the early 1960s, again mostly in Off Broadway theatres. In that period, Off Broadway proved fertile ground for openly gay dramatists and plays featuring homosexual characters and themes. Caffe Cino in Greenwich Village is an example of one such forum and, following the Stonewall riot in June 1969, Off Broadway gay dramatists became more activist in responding to homosexual concerns and in deconstructing gender and sexual stereotypes. Robert Patrick, one of the playwrights emerging from Caffe Cino, won some critical acclaim in Off and Off Off Broadway theatres before resisting its growing commercialization. However, Patrick's most acclaimed play, *Kennedy's Children* (1974), ironically became his most visible work when it was produced in large commercial theatres in England and the U.S. Most of Patrick's prolific output was presented in small venues and chronicled the history and evolution of gay lives more frankly than seemed possible in mainstream theatres prior to the late 1970s.

Profound changes were in the offing during the 1970s as gay dramatists presented more diverse images of gay characters. Drag actor/playwright Charles Ludlam and his Ridiculous Theatrical Company created camp spoofs of popular culture reflecting a far more confident gay sensibility. In his adaptation of Dumas' *Camille* (1974) and his own Gothic farce, *The Mystery of Irma Vep* (1984), among numerous others, Ludlam smashed stereotypes and exploited clichés from art, Hollywood movies, and nineteenth-century romantic theatre for their inherent humor and theatricality. Ludlam's work found a comfortable home in Off Broadway theatres, but on the other end of the spectrum, actor/playwright Harvey Fierstein was among the first gay dramatists after Crowley to make the seemingly impossible leap from the cultural fringes into the Broadway mainstream. Fierstein's *Torch Song Trilogy* (1981), three connected one-acts he had honed Off Broadway for several years in the 1970s, coupled attitudes from the growing "gay pride" movement with a realistic depiction of the personal life of a drag performer struggling to find love and acceptance in a still-homophobic society prior to AIDS. This plea for tolerance proved surprisingly resonant with Broadway audiences and led to a long run and a film adaptation scripted by (and starring) Fierstein.

Fierstein's theatrical ambitions bloomed while he was studying at the Pratt Institute, where he began writing plays including *In Search of the Cobra Jewels* (1972), *Freaky Pussy* (1974), and *Flatbush Tosca* (1975), the last of which was produced by the New York City Theater Ensemble. A 1975 play, *Cannibals Just Don't Know No Better*, remains unproduced, but when he centered attention on the semi-autobiographical character of Arnold Beckoff, a young Jewish gay man who works as a drag queen, Fierstein found his voice as a humanistic spokesman for homosexual tolerance. *The International Stud* (1976), *Fugue in a Nursery* (1979), and *Widows and Children First!* (1979) — the three plays making up *Torch Song Trilogy*— underscore the need for love as independent of gender or moral conceptions and constraints in any era. Fierstein's alter-ego Arnold is a tough but vulnerable survivor despite his fears, and a character demonstrating significant personal integrity. A true forerunner of Kushner's Prior Walter, Arnold is similarly indomitable and hopeful in the face of numerous disappointments and considerable personal tragedy.

The International Stud finds Arnold working as a drag performer (using the stage name "Virginia Hamm," selected after discarding such previous pseudonyms as "Kitty Litter, Bang Bang LaDesh, Bertha Venation" [Fierstein 16] 17). Arnold is abandoned by Ed, his bisexual lover, for a woman, and responds with equal parts bemusement, wistfulness, and more than a touch of irony:

> I think my biggest problem is being young and beautiful. It is my biggest problem because I have never been young and beautiful. More importantly, I will never be young and beautiful. Oh, I've been beautiful. And God knows I've been young. But never the twain have met. Not so's anyone would notice anyway [Fierstein 13–14].

Despite his outrageous "on-stage" persona, Arnold is a gentle man and succinctly states his desire for a loving relationship, although there are other failed affairs in his past:

> In my life I have slept with more men than are named and/or numbered in the Bible (Old and New Testaments put together). But in all those beds not once has someone said, "Arnold, I love you..." that I could believe. So, I ask myself, "Do you really care?" And the only honest answer I can give myself is, "Yes, I care." I care because ... [*catches himself*] I care a great deal. But not enough [Fierstein 17].

Ed cannot quite let go of his relationship with Arnold when he becomes intimately involved with Laurel, in what Arnold calls, "a sudden burst of heterosexuality" (Fierstein 29). Tellingly, Arnold's concern is for fairness to Laurel, a vulnerable and intelligent young woman, who apparently is not consciously aware of Ed's bisexual nature. Arnold asks Ed, "Don't you think she has a right to know what she's letting herself in for? [*no response*] What's the matter? Catch your tongue in the closet door?" (Fierstein 29). Ed continues to ignore Arnold's warnings and pretends to be proud of his move into the "straight" world, but Arnold insists, "How can sleeping with a woman make you proud of yourself if you know you'd rather be with a man? How can you ever get any respect from anyone if you won't be yourself? There's no you to respect!" (Fierstein 31). In spite of the warnings, Ed goes to Laurel, and Arnold, feeling abandoned, turns to impersonal sexual encounters at a gay bar. In this, Fierstein seems poised to explain homosexual promiscuity as a direct result of the exclusion of gays from "normal" heterosexual relationships, while also demonstrating the need for commitment, as when Ed returns to visit Arnold in his dressing room, and, in tears, insists that "I'm so scared. I need you" (Fierstein 43). As the play ends, Arnold is left pondering how to handle the situation with Ed, feeling that

> maybe he's treating me just the way I want him to. Maybe I use him to give me that tragic Torch Singer status that I admire so in others. If that's true ... then he's my International Stud. Wouldn't that just be a kick in the rubber parts? I love him. That's for sure. [*fighting back tears*] But do I love him enough? What's enough? [Fierstein 44].

Arnold's personal story continues in *Fugue in a Nursery*, in which Laurel has learned of Ed's bisexuality and she calls to invite Arnold and his new lover, Alan, to visit at Ed's farm in upstate New York. Arnold resists the visit, but Alan insists and from this point the rest of the play takes place in a huge circular bed, underscoring the shifting relationships. Laurel, hoping to get a sense of Ed's true feelings for Arnold, pretends to be excited about the visit ("Imagine being hostess to your lover's ex and his new boyfriend. Now if that isn't civilized then what is? It's downright Noël Coward" [Fierstein 52]), but Arnold remains wary, recognizing that such civility comes at a price that includes tremendous emotional pitfalls. He is especially sensitive about the age difference between him (nearly 40) and Alan (18) and Ed is not pleased about Alan's presence initially ("It's that damned kid. This was going to be a beautiful weekend. The three of us together. I thought ... that have the two of you here together ... that I'd be able to put a period on that whole section of my life." [Fierstein 60]), but the foursome pairs off in different groupings, allowing Fierstein to explore varied gay and straight views of love and sex. Arnold and Ed reminisce about their relationship, with Ed telling Arnold, "You were always a homosexual chauvinist. To you everyone's either gay or in the closet" (Fierstein 69). Arnold, still searching for a lasting and meaningful relationship, ruminates on contemporary life: "When an affair hits the skids you shed it like last year's fashion and head back to the streets. There are plenty more where that one came from. And that, my ex-husband, is what I call the miracle of modern sex" (Fierstein 70). Pre–AIDS sex, one might add, because such attitudes would radically change with the onset of the AIDS epidemic. Ed and Alan have a fleeting sexual encounter that leads to confrontations between the two pairs of lovers, with new understanding in both relationships. Laurel later visits Arnold at the club where she hears him sing a torch song, and he explains that his affection for such songs is "about taking all that misery and making it into something.... Anyway, the audiences like it. I guess getting hurt is one thing we all have in common" (Fierstein 97), underscoring Fierstein's two-way tolerance plea. As the play ends, Arnold and Alan have solidified their relationship ("As married as two men can illegally get" [Fierstein 97]) and Laurel contemplates the possibility of marriage with Ed.

Widows and Children First! is set five years later as Arnold is trying to cope with the murder of Alan, who has been beaten to death by anti-gay thugs. He is also attempting to win long-denied acceptance from his "Ma," a situation that has been forced by his plan to raise David, a troubled teenager he and Alan were in the process of adopting. Ed is sleeping on Arnold's couch while he and Laurel, who have been married, are enduring a separation, and Arnold elicits Ed's support in facing his mother. As Arnold puts it, when Alan died "I was expected to observe the same vow of silence about him as she had about my father. So we've learned to make meaningful conversation from the weather, general health and my brother's marital status. I never even told her how Alan was killed" (Fierstein 117). Fierstein depicts Arnold's anxiety about his mother's judgment in both comic and serious ways. Curious about Ed's presence, Ma disapprovingly asks if he is "a friend-friend or a euphemism friend?" to which Arnold replies, "He used to be a euphemism, now he's just a friend" (Fierstein 124). Ma unexpectedly meets David before Arnold can explain why the boy is living with him. When David impulsively announces "I'm his son" (Fierstein 131), Ma takes the news badly, but Arnold insists that adopting David "is not a crazy thing. It's a wonderful thing that I'm very proud of" (Fierstein 142). When Arnold compares his feelings about missing Alan to Ma's for her late husband, she explodes with rage: "What loss did you have? You fooled around with some boy...? Where do you come to compare that to a marriage of thirty-five years?" (Fierstein 144). Arnold loses his temper, as well:

> Listen, Ma, you had it easy. You have thirty-five years to remember, I have five. You had your children and friends to comfort you, I had me! My friends didn't want to hear about it. They said, "What're you gripin' about? At least you had a lover." 'Cause everybody knows that queers don't love. How dare I? You had it easy, Ma. You lost your husband in a nice clean hospital, I lost mine out there. They killed him there on the street. Twenty-three years old laying dead on the street. Killed by a bunch of kids with baseball bats [Fierstein 145].

Resolving not to talk about Alan, Arnold and Ma painfully try to resolve their differences over David. She sarcastically wonders what Arnold knows about raising children, to which he replies, "What's to know? Whenever I have a problem I simply imagine how you would solve it, and do the opposite" (Fierstein 148). When Ma learns that David is gay and has been placed with

Arnold as a positive role model, she concludes, "The world has gone completely mad and I'm heading south for the summer" (Fierstein 149).

This line is key to understanding Fierstein's plea for tolerance, which he sees as a path running both directions. He concedes that Ma, and those of her generation sharing her traditional values, find the socio-sexual landscape changing more quickly than they can absorb (no less accept) and, in fact, that they may never be able (or willing) to fully embrace the revised social contract that Fierstein's Arnold represents. Ma is a decent woman who cannot revise her views (which are coupled with her deep-seated disappointment in producing a homosexual son), and by making Arnold such a thoroughly sympathetic figure, Fierstein makes clear that decency dictates that both sides have no choice but to find common ground wherever possible. Time, it is presumed, will take care of the rest.

Ma has expressed her dissenting opinions, but Arnold, speaking from a position typical of characters central to tolerance plays, makes his views just as clear, noting that he has worked hard to achieve independence so "I don't have to ask anyone for anything. There is nothing I need from anyone except love and respect. And anyone who can't give me those two things has no place in my life" (Fierstein 152). Ma, upset by the gauntlet that Arnold has thrown down, prepares to leave while he tries once more to share his dilemma with her — and to reconcile their differences: "Alan loved all my faults; my temper, my bitchiness, my fat.... He looked for faults to love. And Ed? Ed loves the rest. And really, who needs to be loved for their virtues? Anyway, it's easier to love someone who's dead; they make so few mistakes" (Fierstein 172). Ma is touched (it is, after all, a necessary element in a tolerance play for the antagonist to be changed or vanquished) and advises that his feelings for Alan "won't ever go away," that remembering "becomes part of you, like wearing a ring or a pair of glasses. You get used to it and it's good ... because it makes sure you don't forget" (Fierstein 172). Although Ma has softened slightly, she leaves with no true resolution except that she cannot change Arnold or alter his choices (a situation reflecting mainstream societal attitudes of the time and the sense that change is happening even if members of that society are not prepared for or receptive to those changes) and Arnold is left to ponder the future.

When *Torch Song Trilogy* finally moved to Broadway in June 1982 for a successful run at the Little Theatre, more significant battles than those of a homosexual son's acceptance by his mother were in the offing. With the arrival of AIDS and a fuller comprehension of its ultimate toll on the gay community — and American society in general — plays like *Torch Song Trilogy* were rendered moot. Fierstein, like many of his contemporaries, suffered personal losses and grimly understood society's failings. As an "out" celebrity, Fierstein became deeply engaged in political activism and charitable causes surrounding the AIDS crisis, and the subject of AIDS began to become more central to his playwriting, as it necessarily did for other gay dramatists in this period. It was now impossible to write about the subject of homosexuality in contemporary American life without factoring in AIDS and the ways in which the culture responded (or failed to respond) to it.

Fierstein's next production, *Spookhouse*, which had been written earlier than *Torch Song Trilogy*, had a brief run and garnered little significant critical attention despite the success of *Torch Song Trilogy*. Fierstein found success again with his libretto for *La Cage aux Folles*, a lavish musical comedy based on the popular French screen farce of the same name which, in turn, had been based on Jean Poiret's play (Fierstein was not involved with the later film, *The Birdcage* [1996], which was also suggested by the same source). With music and lyrics by the venerable Jerry Herman (*Hello, Dolly! Mame*, and *Mack and Mabel*), and under the direction of gay dramatist and director Arthur Laurents, *La Cage aux Folles* achieved an impressive 1,761 performances in New York and emerged as a groundbreaking work. It was the first Broadway musical to feature as its romantic duo a pair of middle-aged gay men and its success may have been due, in part, to a perceived need for a life-affirming gay-themed entertainment in the face of the mounting horrors of AIDS.

La Cage aux Folles has all the trappings of a traditional farce with the addition of the "fabulousness" of gay nightlife. Set in a transvestite nightclub run by Georges and starring his longtime lover, Albin, *La Cage* pits its non-traditional protagonists against the ultra-conservative parents of a young woman engaged to Georges' grown son, who has been raised by Georges and Albin. Fearing the engagement will end when the girl's parents find out, it is decided that Albin should absent himself. However, he instead shows up in drag pretending to be the boy's "mother," leading to a series of typically farcical confusions. As the ruse falls apart, the son acknowledges that Albin has, in fact, been a true parent to him and all are reconciled. Audiences embraced the show's uplifting message, which mirrored the humanism of *Torch Song Trilogy*. At the same time, Fierstein did not shy away from a more confrontational depiction of gay life in the age of AIDS. The messages inherent in Fierstein's next dramatic effort, *Safe Sex*, first produced in 1987 at the La Mama Experimental Theatre, were couched in the context of the distressing times.

Like *Torch Song Trilogy*, *Safe Sex* consists of three one-act plays, *Manny and Jake*, *Safe Sex*, and *On Tidy Endings*, all connected by a central theme: the impact of AIDS on both homosexuals and heterosexuals. *Manny and Jake* depicts an AIDS sufferer debating new dating rules with a potential lover; *Safe Sex* dramatizes a man who fears intimacy and uses his HIV status to continue his isolation; and *On Tidy Endings*, regarded by critics as the strongest of the three plays, portrays an intense encounter between the widow and gay lover of a man who has recently died of AIDS. Five years into the AIDS crisis, *Safe Sex* reflects a playwright angered by the slow response of mainstream America to the mounting death toll. No simple plea for tolerance is evident in *Safe Sex*—Fierstein leaves behind the tone (if not the dramatic structure) of *Torch Song Trilogy* and the joy of *La Cage aux Folles*, both of which offered optimistic visions of a society with the potential to embrace the gay "other," toward a reflection of the rage growing in the homosexual community and leading to the fiery polemics of Larry Kramer's *The Normal Heart* (1985).

Indeed, by the mid–1980s darker views of the homosexual experience began to dominate even as Fierstein scored his initial success with *Torch Song Trilogy*. Martin Sherman's grim period drama, *Bent* (1978), emphasizes the tragic fate of homosexuals during the Holocaust, and by the time it reached Broadway in the early 1980s, parallels between that era and the homophobic response to AIDS in contemporary American society were unmistakable. Charles Ludlam's death in the mid–1980s was only one among many prominent theatre artists early in the crisis that took on metaphorical significance as the next transition in gay drama fully emerged. Depictions of the personal struggles of gays and divisive social questions inflamed by AIDS became a theatrical cottage industry during the 1980s and into the 1990s. William Hoffman's *As Is* (1985) plunged into the personal horrors of AIDS before it was recognized by most as the international epidemic it would become, but no playwright in the 1980s addressed AIDS and its attendant issues as directly as Kramer.

The Normal Heart is no less than a scathing indictment of American society's failure to respond to AIDS, reflecting Kramer's vigorous—and often frustrating—off-stage activism. A successful screenwriter (the Academy Award-winning *Women in Love*) and novelist (*Faggots*), Kramer had written his first Off Broadway play, *Sissies' Scrapbook*, in 1973. Semi-autobiographical, *Sissies' Scrapbook* focused on the friendship of a gay man with three straight friends since student days at Yale, echoing *The Boys in the Band*. Kramer described the play as being about cowardice and the inability of some men to escape adolescent attitudes and embrace adulthood. It was not successful, but led to *The Big Three at Yalta*, a comic screenplay about two brothers (one straight and one gay) and their love relationships. The film was never produced and although he returned to the theatre, Kramer was—and remains—an ambivalent playwright, ultimately less interested in the medium than in the message. In *The Normal Heart*, the message was inherent in its established time frame; set between July 1981 and May 1984, the play documents the era in which AIDS was first identified as a "gay cancer" and the obstacles faced by those unprepared to face not only the illness itself, but the attendant political, moral, economic, and cultural issues. An ominous tone is established in the play's first line, spoken by a young gay man in a doctor's waiting room: "I know something's wrong" (Kramer, *The Normal Heart* 19). *The Normal Heart* probes experiences of several gay men whose lives are recast by AIDS, but the connecting thread is Ned Weeks, a thinly veiled portrait of Kramer himself. In conversations with Dr. Emma Brookner, a committed health-care professional (a character based on Mathilda Krim), Weeks learns to his horror that she is convinced the mysterious illness of gay men is transmitted sexually. "And you want me to tell every gay man in New York to stop having sex?" (Kramer, *The Normal Heart* 27), the incredulous Weeks asks, and Brookner insists that he must do so: the government and medical establishment are in deep denial, she believes, and vigorous gay activism coupled with abstention from sex may be the only effective responses.

Weeks' temperamental outbursts in dealing with officials and medical authorities, compatriots in his own activist organization, and within his own family steadily isolate him. His lover, Felix, reflecting on the situation tries to be understanding, but tells Weeks' older brother Ben that "there's not a good word to be said for anybody's behavior in this whole mess" (Kramer, *The Normal Heart* 116). Weeks has an uneasy relationship with Ben, a father figure who also serves as society's disapproving voice on the "gay lifestyle," much like Ma in *Torch Song Trilogy*. By the play's end, Ben moves beyond his prejudices toward acceptance of his younger brother, a symbolic image — and an optimistic note — despite the fact that the overall message of *The Normal Heart* is far from optimistic. Some critics and audiences were fiercely resistant to the play during its initial productions in New York and London, and loud disturbances from the audience frequently interrupted performances.

Kramer, never one to shun controversy, previously raised some of the themes in *The Normal Heart* in his novel, *Faggots* (1978), a satirical work about four days in the life of New York's gay community. With its call for monogamous relationships among gays and admonitions against promiscuous sex, Kramer anticipated in *Faggots* the controversial position that would catapult him to the forefront of gay activism over the subsequent three decades. The novel's central focus is Fred Lemish, a thirty-nine-year-old gay man who has built up his physique to perfection and is in search of a lover. Fred's odyssey takes him from the Everhard Baths to the Pines on Fire Island, but he finds only anonymous sex in transitory encounters. Critics debated whether *Faggots* was meant as a realistic portrait of gay life or an attempt to depict reality with a satiric edge. On its most profound level, *Faggots* examines a gay man's longing for connection, commitment, and true love, not unlike Fierstein's Arnold Beckoff's search in *Torch Song Trilogy*. The fact that Fred cannot fulfill his longings in a gay culture focused almost exclusively on secretive and fleeting sexual experiences is depicted as both tragic and comic. At the story's bittersweet conclusion, Fred becomes immersed in this culture and, as he marks his fortieth birthday, finds himself alone: "Happy Birthday Me," is his final sad statement.

Not long after completing *Faggots*, Kramer threw himself into AIDS activism supporting research and treatment, and issuing strident demands for immediate action from a variety of public officials and institutions, as well as for sexual abstinence among gays. Within five weeks of the first *New York Times* report of an unnamed illness found among gay men, "Rare Cancer Found in 41 Homosexuals" (August 11, 1981), Kramer held a fundraiser at his apartment. He decried slow civic response in a series of articles in a gay newspaper called *The New York Native*, in editorials in the *New York Times*, and elsewhere. Along with others, Kramer founded Gay Men's Health Crisis in 1982, the first significant organization focused on confronting the issues surrounding AIDS. His continued impatience led to his disenchantment with the organization, so he withdrew and founded ACT UP, an activist group with a populist bent that lobbied and demonstrated vigorously to prod (or embarrass) government officials and the medical establishment to respond with greater vigor. In his book, *The Art of AIDS*, Rob Baker describes Kramer's "notoriety as the shrill Cassandra of AIDS activism" (Baker 167) and Kramer unashamedly embraced this persona in service of ending the crisis. As recounted in Randy Shilts' seminal history of the first years of the epidemic, *And the Band Played On*, when Kramer suggested that AIDS might be sexually transmitted, he was angrily countered by other gays, some of whom expressed offense at Kramer's prior criticism of gay promiscuity in *Faggots*. Kramer's energies focused on assaulting the conscience of American society in general and the unresponsive administration in Washington in particular. AIDS arose early in the "Republican Revolution" of Ronald Reagan's presidency and, despite considerable pressure, Reagan failed to utter the word AIDS in public through most of his two-term presidency, despite growing media attention and highly publicized AIDS-related deaths of celebrities, including closeted movie star Rock Hudson. Kramer turned to the stage as a powerful platform for raising the visibility of the conflict and when *The Normal Heart* made its debut at the New York Shakespeare Festival Public Theatre on April 21, 1985, the controversy grew. In the process, Kramer proved again the theatre's power to inspire profound cultural dialogue.

Kramer's activist anger infuses *The Normal Heart*. When Weeks, along with a few colleagues, attempts to arrange a meeting with New York's mayor, they are rebuffed by an unctuous assistant. Weeks sarcastically asks, "Have you told the Mayor there's an epidemic going on?" (Kramer, *The Normal Heart* 80), adding that the Centers for Disease Control has proclaimed AIDS a disease of epidemic proportions, but the assistant responds, "Well, you can't expect us to concern ourselves with every little outbreak those boys come up with" (Kramer, *The Normal Heart* 80). As previously noted, Weeks' temperamental outbursts in such situations, and even with those close to him, causes alienation from friends, family, and colleagues. Kramer does not shy away from addressing Weeks' (and his own) failings and isolation, even as the character cannot restrain himself from expressing disenchantment with what he regards as timid "activists" and with gays who refuse to give up sexual promiscuity, which some equate with hard-won sexual freedom. As Weeks stresses in *The Normal Heart*:

> The only way we'll have real pride is when we demand recognition of a culture that isn't just sexual. It's all there — all through history we've been there; but we have to claim it, and identify who was in it, and articulate what's in our minds and hearts and all our creative contributions to this earth [Kramer, *The Normal Heart* 110].

As the play concludes, Weeks is an outcast for his abrasive demands for sexual abstinence and his tactless dealings with government, media, and medical officials. Kramer claimed to be acknowledging his rancorous departure from the GMHC through his depiction of it in *The Normal Heart*, noting that he did not see the character as a hero. In the play, Weeks is dismissed from the organization he has founded. A death-bed marriage to Felix, who can occasionally moderate Weeks' anger, is also a profound atonement for the character. But even as he atones, Kramer allows the dying Felix to insist on the necessity of fierce activism. Through his tears following Felix's death, Weeks laments, "Why didn't I fight harder! Why didn't I picket the White House, all by myself if nobody would come. Or go on a hunger strike" (Kramer, *The Normal Heart* 118), giving voice to the frustration of those sharing his concerns.

Like other AIDS dramas, although *The Normal Heart* is singular among the gay-themed plays of the 1980s, the play focuses on personal lives and ordinary individuals caught up in the crisis. Yet Kramer sets this into an angry frontal assault on the political and social failure of response to the epidemic, which is always his central concern. As he would later write in the introduction to his next play, *Just Say No*, "Ed Koch and Ronald Reagan would have no choice but to pay attention to AIDS after opening night of *The Normal Heart*" (Kramer, *Just Say No* xxi). Facts about the growing crisis are sprinkled throughout the play and give it, at various points, a near-documentary quality. Constructed in Brechtian (or cinematic) episodic style, the play is made up of sixteen scenes expressing Kramer's angry perspective on the catastrophes of the previous five years and, most importantly from Kramer's point of view, continues in the Brechtian tradition of demanding that the audience ponder their present and future response to the disease as a corrective.

Following Hoffman's *As Is* and Fierstein's *Torch Song Trilogy*, and until the appearance of Kushner's *Angels in America* plays, *The Normal Heart* stood as the most controversial and widely discussed gay play to emerge in the era following *The Boys in the Band*. Among its significant legacies is its pivotal position within the history of gay drama and influence on subsequent gay dramatists.

Following *The Normal Heart*, Kramer's next theatrical work was anticipated with considerable interest, but *Just Say No: A Play about a Farce* (1988) proved a critical disappointment. Comically exploring the ways sexual hypocrisy in high places (during the height of the Reagan presidency) permitted AIDS to become a plague, *Just Say No* features a First Lady, her gay son, and the gay mayor of America's largest northeastern city. Nancy Reagan, her son Ron, and New York's Ed Koch were the obvious targets, but Kramer weaves in references to other icons of contemporary American culture. The play's savagely comic thrust is about hypocrisy among the powerful, jabbing at those who vigorously support a social moral contract that they themselves do not live by. The convoluted plot deals with Mrs. Potentate, the First Lady, and the tone of satire is set from the beginning when Eustacia, a black woman, addresses the audience in mock patriotic tones:

> Listen my children, and you shall hear
> How we came to be screwed so drear
> By Mommy and Daddy, who make all the rules,
> And then live by other ones— making us fools.
> Yet some of us have survived the worst.
> We got out alive, although we are cursed
> For letting them flimflam us yet once again,
> And again and again and again and again [Kramer, *Just Say No* 3].

The play also deals with the mayor of Appleburg, who insists that "We don't have any AIDS in Appleburg. We don't have any homos in Appleburg. They all live out of state" (Kramer, *Just Say No* 46). The play is rampant with jokes about the Reagans' Hollywood past, the media, and all aspects of the AIDS crisis. A disclaimer in the program of the original production notes that any resemblance to real people is "in the eye of the beholder." In *Acting Gay: Male Homosexuality in Modern Drama*, John M. Clum writes that Kramer "grew as an essayist [and activist], while his ability to form a coherent drama dwindled" (Clum 80), although this assessment was largely disproved by Kramer's next drama.

In October 1992, seven years after *The Normal Heart*, a sequel, *The Destiny of Me*, premiered at New York's Circle Repertory Company. The central character was again Kramer's alter-ego Ned Weeks, caught up in family issues and the sweep of late twentieth-century American history. AIDS is the catalyst for an exploration of Weeks' life, sexual orientation, and sense of purpose that is seen to stem from his troubled childhood through his own present health crisis. *The Destiny of Me* begins with HIV-infected Weeks entering an experimental treatment program run by a doctor who is the target of Weeks' most militant criticism (a figure inspired by the National Institute of Health's Dr. Anthony Fauci). Fearing what he assumes is his imminent death from AIDS, Weeks struggles to survive and reflects on his personal past within the context of historical events. Kramer allows all this to spin out from Weeks' hospital bed, as he revisits scenes from his childhood, teen years, and adulthood. Weeks arrives at significant revelations about himself and his experiences through the device of viewing his life at various stages. Arguing with his own persona and dissecting the aspects of his personality he has failed to come to terms with serve to reveal the anger and cynical humor central to Weeks' (and by extension, Kramer's) life. Scenes of the past are set against the present in which Weeks vehemently argues with his doctor over the juxtapositions of AIDS, AIDS research, and activism. The play differs from the angry polemics of *The Normal Heart* in its distinctly melancholy tone and in the evolving (and deepening) character of Weeks, who is haunted by the evocative (and pertinent) lyrics of two favorite musical comedy songs from his past, "Make Believe" and "This Nearly Was Mine." Kramer offers a wrenching exploration of Weeks' traumatic sexual awakening and his drive toward activism. Despite its obvious connection to the long tradition of realistic American family-oriented dramas, Kramer makes use of a range of postmodern theatrical devices. Time periods overlap as characters float in and out of the action (both in the present and in the past) presenting key situations in Weeks' life, but as with *The Normal Heart*, the message matters more than the medium.

Kramer tempered his anger with understanding in *The Destiny of Me*, but in the early 1990s Terrence McNally, a prolific dramatist whose plays had been mainstays of Off Broadway theatre since the mid–1960s, shifted away from the grim recriminations of Kramer's work toward the humanistic tolerance pleas Fierstein, and to some extent Crowley, had pioneered.

McNally had his first major success in the 1970s Off Broadway hit *The Ritz*, but he had endured failure in the previous decade. His *And Things That Go Bump in the Night* (1964) dealt with a crazed mother and her sadistic, bisexual son, but critics were not appreciative and it took time before McNally's work won critical and commercial favor. His entire oeuvre is burnished by a late twentieth-century gay sensibility and many of his plays feature openly gay characters and themes, increasingly from the late 1980s. *The Lisbon Traviata* (1985), for example, focuses on Mendy, a fanatical (and obviously gay) opera fan, who begs his friend Stephen to loan him a rare pirated copy of Maria Callas performing *La Traviata* in Lisbon. Their encounter over the recording exposes the profound unhappiness of both men, who define themselves exclusively through the larger-than-life but artificial passions of opera.

McNally later adapted Manuel Puig's novel, *Kiss of the Spider Woman* (1993), an acclaimed film, into a Broadway musical with a score by John Kander and Fred Ebb. McNally focuses Puig's story through the eyes of one of its central characters, Molina, a gay department store window dresser jailed in a Latin American prison, who escapes fear through fantasies of his favorite movie star, known only as The Spider Woman. Valentin, a defiant political prisoner and hyper-masculine male, joins the politically ambivalent Molina in a cell where their initial dislike turns to mutual respect, helping both face their tragic fates. McNally told *New York Times* critic David Richards that what *Kiss of the Spider Woman* "says about a gay man is very important, although he's not just a gay man. He's a small person who says, 'My life is trivial, I'm inconsequential' and who learns he's not, that we all matter" (Richards 1). In this way, McNally's thematic vision is close to that of Fierstein's early work — particularly *Torch Song Trilogy* and *La Cage aux Folles*— with the human politics of finding acceptance as a gay man trumping specific political issues, even as those issues have an impact on the ability of the characters to find the acceptance they seek.

McNally's assimilationist sensibility is also reflected in *Lips Together, Teeth Apart* (1991), a four-character comedy-drama involving Sally, a woman who has recently inherited a Fire Island beach house from her late brother, who died of AIDS. Sally and Sam, her husband, invite Sam's sister Chloe and her husband John for the Fourth of July weekend, during which comic and tragic memories, past relationships, and the unseen presence of their gay neighbors release unspoken feelings. Homophobic John is so fearful of AIDS that he will not swim because so many gay men live nearby, prompting Sally, thinking of her brother, to respond sarcastically, "I think we're very brave to dangle our feet like this. They may fall off" (McNally, *Lips Together, Teeth Apart* 80). Taking it a step further by drinking a handful of water, Sally shouts, "let's all get AIDS and die!" (McNally, *Lips Together, Teeth Apart* 81). Injecting straight characters into a gay environment, as he had similarly done farcically in *The Ritz*, allows McNally to explore current attitudes about homosexuality and AIDS — and to indict the particularly virulent form of homophobia inspired by the appearance of AIDS.

This approach is also central in *Love! Valour! Compassion!* (1994), for which McNally received the Pulitzer Prize. A bittersweet comedy about the close friendships of eight gay New Yorkers who spend holiday weekends together, *Love! Valour! Compassion!* explores diverse gay characters and their relationships set against the background of living with AIDS and homophobia. In essence, it is a retooling of the central conceit of *The Boys in the Band*, providing a sampling of varied gay personas set against the social reality. In the play, Gregory, a celebrated choreographer, and his sweet-natured blind lover Bobby, live in a renovated farmhouse. Their usual guests include Arthur and Perry, who have been a couple for fourteen years; "We're role models. It's very stressful" (McNally, *Love! Valour! Compassion!* 84), quips the acerbic Perry. HIV-positive Buzz Hauser, another guest, a flamboyant musical comedy buff and costumer for Gregory's dance troupe, verbally jousts with viciously sarcastic John, a British rehearsal pianist, who is flooded with jealousy about the professional and personal success of the others. He brings along Ramon, an ambitious young dancer who aspires to eclipse Gregory's achievements, and who also attempts to woo Bobby away from Gregory. John's twin brother James, a gentle man dying of AIDS, joins the group and develops a close relationship with Buzz. The spectre of AIDS hangs heavily over all the characters, and their fears and losses exacerbate their individual longings for love and commitment as the play moves toward an elegiac conclusion. Even John, who is often a pariah among the men, and Ramon, who severely damages Gregory's relationship with Bobby, expose their deepest fears and longings. All remain a part of this tightly knit group recognizing that the painful process of creating a true community may offer a form of redemption, however imperfect.

Love! Valour! Compassion! was well-received, but the mere announcement of McNally's *Corpus Christi* (1998) set off a firestorm of controversy at the time of its premiere at the Manhattan Theatre Club. *Corpus Christi* similarly focuses on a group of gay men, this time in Texas, putting on a passion play about Jesus Christ's life. Prior to its opening, the play was attacked by various groups ostensibly concerned by the connection of contemporary gay lives with Christ's. Bomb threats and pickets accompanied the play's opening, but the publicity only served to attract more interest in *Corpus Christi* than might have otherwise existed. Thirteen actors play various biblical roles in the play, debating diverse beliefs about the lessons of Bible history. The intersection of Biblical figures with the lives of the actors playing them is a device McNally employs to simultaneously reveal the stories of each character/actor and to draw parallels. This wedding of the traditional and the contemporary, the "straight" version of the Bible and the "gay response" to it, is the play's main purpose. In a preface to the published version of *Corpus Christi*, McNally writes that "I'm a playwright, not a theologian," adding that the "level of dislike of gay men and the vehemence of the denial of any claim they might make for spiritual parity with their Christian 'brothers' that *Corpus Christi* revealed was disheartening" (McNally, *Corpus Christi* v). McNally adds that it is a "passion play" beginning with "the familiar dialogue with ourselves: Do I love my neighbor? Am I contributing good to the society in which I operate or nil? Do I, in fact, matter? Nothing more, nothing less. The play is more religious ritual than a play" (McNally, *Corpus Christi* vii) and one that questions not only what was done to Christ, but what "they did one cold October night to a young man in Wyoming as well. Jesus Christ died again when Matthew Shepard did" (McNally, *Corpus Christi* vii). Curiously, only months after the *Corpus Christi* controversy, a similar play, Paul Rudnick's *The Most Fabulous Story Ever Told* (1998), opened at the New York Theatre Workshop to virtually no public outcry. Rudnick had previously written *Jeffrey* (1995), a broadly farcical chronicle of a gay Everyman in contemporary America, and perhaps the play's debut in a small Off Broadway venue kept it out of the media spotlight.

Despite the controversy engendered by *Corpus Christi*, it caused less furor than that which accompanied productions of a previous gay-themed drama, *Angels in America: A Gay Fantasia on National Themes*, an epic work consisting of two long plays, the Pulitzer Prize–winning *Millennium Approaches* (1991) and *Perestroika* (1992). Its author, Tony Kushner, was well established as a director, adaptor, and playwright in regional theatres prior to *Angels*, but he was thrust into the forefront of American drama when *Angels* reached Broadway following critically acclaimed runs at San Francisco's Eureka Theatre, Los Angeles's Mark Taper Forum, and the Royal National Theatre of Great Britain. *Angels* poses complex questions regarding the future of American society in the wake of Reagan's presidency and AIDS, particularly in the areas of morality, politics, and sexuality. In many respects, *Angels* is a massive culmination of ideas flowing through American gay drama after *The Boys in the Band*.

Angels asks no less a question than can a nation — its society and its people — be considered truly moral if it oppresses any portion of its citizenry. *Angels* suggests the inevitability of change and, with a mixture of outrageous humor and heart-rending drama, peers into the unknown future to ponder whether apocalypse is inevitable or a brighter, more progressive tomorrow is possible for American society. As with such prior gay dramas as *The Boys in the Band*, *As Is*, and *Torch Song Trilogy*, Kushner focuses on private lives at moments of profound personal crisis, but in ways significantly different from his predecessors (with the possible exception of Kramer). Kushner emphasizes the impact of the sweep of history, and on the prevailing societal and political conditions. The troubled lives of the characters are the pivot, but *Angels* spins out to tackle a range of issues facing the United States as the third millennium approaches.

Like *The Boys in the Band* (and the later *Love! Valour! Compassion!*), *Angels* features diverse gay characters—some closeted, some not—dealing with the myriad issues of being homosexual in the darkest hours of the AIDS crisis (with the exception of the final scene of *Perestroika*, both *Angels* plays are set in 1985–86) and at the apex of the neo-conservative Reagan revolution. As the plays begin, Reagan has been reelected and the characters face Kushner's notion of the ways unchecked conservatism is changing the country and impacting their lives. In writing *Angels*, Kushner was inspired, in part, by dramatists of the Stonewall generation and after, as well as American poetic realism (as perfected by Tennessee Williams), but unlike most gay American dramatists of his generation and before, Kushner was deeply influenced by European culture, most particularly classical German romanticism, Brecht's epic theatre, and contemporary British political theatre. Like Kramer, Kushner also found inspiration in activist gay organizations, including Kramer's ACT UP and Queer Nation, whose chant, "We're here, we're queer, we're fabulous," provides a foundational attitude for *Angels*. Finding contemporary American society in an age of intellectual and moral stagnation, an era of staggering political and social crisis, Kushner insists in *Angels* that the moral emptiness experienced in postmodern America results from an abandonment of its founding principles of justice, compassion, inclusiveness, and liberty. With such an emphasis, the striving for survival of gays, particularly in the context of the AIDS crisis, becomes a metaphor for a nation's survival.

Kushner begins *Millennium Approaches* with an ending, the funeral of an elderly Jewish woman, Sarah Ironson, described by the presiding rabbi as an exemplar of the Old World values of late nineteenth-century European immigrants. Having established the death of past certitudes that Kushner believes are the foundation of accepted contemporary American values, he sets his characters adrift with only the wreckage of the past and the realities of the present to both guide and burden them. The play focuses on two couples: Joe and Harper Pitt, unhappily married Mormons, and Prior Walter and Louis Ironson (grandson of the deceased Sarah), a gay couple. All are in the throes of harrowing personal crises when their lives intersect with historical figure Roy Cohn, who won fame (or infamy) as primary aide to Senator Joseph McCarthy during the House Un-American Activities Committee anti–Communist "witchhunts" of the 1950s. Early in the play, Cohn, now a prominent New York divorce lawyer, learns he is suffering from full-blown AIDS.

Joe, a conservative lawyer encouraged by Cohn, who hopes to place Joe in a Justice Department job as his man in Washington, is in profound personal struggle with his long-repressed homosexuality. Raised with traditional values to be a family man, devoutly religious, and politically conservative, Joe feels it all slipping away as his true nature surfaces. In an agonized plea to Harper, who finally demands that Joe tell her whether or not he is a homosexual, Joe exclaims: "Does it make any difference? That I might be one thing deep within, no matter how wrong or ugly that thing is, so long as I have fought, with everything I have, to kill it. What do you want from me, Harper? More than that? For God's sake, there's nothing left, I'm a shell. There's nothing left to kill. As long as my behavior is what I know it has to be. Decent. Correct. That alone in the eyes of God" (Kushner 46). When Joe does acknowledge his homosexuality, he telephones his mother, Hannah, in the middle of the night, revealing his secret in a painful scene that mirrors the experiences of many homosexuals— Kushner himself says that this scene is reminiscent of his own "coming out." Joe subsequently meets Louis, at that point in a desperate flight of fear from his long-time lover Prior, who is HIV-positive and becoming seriously ill. Racked with guilt, the liberal Louis reflects on the Reagan era as a metaphor for his own bad faith, while Harper, addicted to Valium, and a delirious Prior meet in a mutual fever dream in which Harper comes to terms with Joe's true sexual nature. Prior seeks to find hope despite his physical ills and emotional despair, employing camp humor to cope, insisting that he is not a "typical homosexual"— he is "stereotypical" (Kushner 231).

Kushner imbues Cohn with a grim humor drawn from his rapacious, almost absurd corruption. Roy's self-loathing is at the heart of the play's most unsettling depiction of homosexuality, manifested in Roy's deep, angry denial: "Like all labels they tell you one thing and one thing only: where does an individual so identified fit in the food chain, in the pecking order? Not ideology, or sexual taste, but something much simpler: clout" (Kushner 51). Suggesting that he could not possibly be considered a homosexual because he is a political force, Cohn sneers, "Homosexuals are not men who sleep with other men. Homosexuals are men who in fifteen years of trying cannot get a pissant antidiscrimination bill through City Council. Homosexuals are men who know nobody and who nobody knows" (Kushner 51). Roy lives in the closet, but a different kind than the one a frightened Joe hides in, but for Kushner, the closet is inevitably the deadest of dead ends. In a neo-conservative age with AIDS costing the lives of hundreds of thousands of gays, life in closet, as Kushner sees it, is a profoundly immoral place to be.

Kushner's scathing view of Roy as an exemplar of the excesses of twentieth-century American conservatism is balanced by a similarly harsh examination of Louis' brand of liberalism, which is shown to be self-righteous and ineffectual. Louis meets his match in Belize, a gay African-American nurse and close friend of Prior, who also becomes Roy's caregiver in *Perestroika*. Angry at the bigotry and homophobia he finds on both sides of what is now described as the red and blue state divide, Belize tells Louis: "I hate this country. It's just big ideas, and stories, and people dying, and people like you. The white cracker who wrote the national anthem knew what he was doing. He set the word 'free' to a note so high nobody can reach it" (Kushner 228). And of Louis specifically, Belize proposes that his liberalism has him "up in the air, just like that angel, too far off the earth to pick out the details" (Kushner 228) or, presumably, to respond to them in any effective way, either personally or politically. Louis' espousals of liberal compassion are unrealized abstractions; in his own life, Louis seems incapable of caring, even for the person he claims to care about above all others.

Prior emerges as Kushner's iconic gay figure, a character grappling with the politics of existence humanely and compassionately, transcending the traditionally adversarial poles of conservatism or liberalism. At the end of *Millennium Approaches*, an angel appears to Prior in his delirium, bringing what he assumes is either death or redemption. Frightened, Prior quells his fears in a speech Kushner intends to counter stereotypes of homosexual weakness expressed by Cohn. "I can handle pressure, I am a gay man and I am used to pressure, to trouble, I am tough and strong" (Kushner 123), Prior insists, and this viewpoint is reiterated in the final scene of *Perestroika*, which is set five years after the rest of *Angels*. Some of the characters meet at the Bethesda fountain in New York's Central Park, with its statue of an angel, a figure commemorating death but suggesting "a world without dying" (Kushner 279). Prior, whose AIDS symptoms have stabilized, points out that the healing waters of the fountain are not presently flowing, but he hopes to be around to see the day when the waters flow again. Speaking not only for himself, but for those gay characters who have come before him — and particularly those suffering in the age of AIDS — Prior says, "This disease will be the end of many of us, but not nearly all, and the dead will be commemorated and will struggle on with the living, and we are not going away." (Kushner 280). In making this statement, Prior breaks the proverbial theatrical fourth wall to speak directly to the play's audience, leaving no doubt that Kushner had firmly moved gay drama from the sorts of tolerance pleas found in *The Boys in the Band*, *Torch Song Trilogy*, and the subsequent *Love! Valour! Compassion!* to demand full acceptance — equal citizenship — in American life. Kushner also took a gay sensibility into all facets of contemporary American life and the country's post–World War II history — issues of religion and spirituality (not to mention morality), politics, social conventions and popular culture, and economics are centrally explored with the result that Kushner nearly completes a "queering" of American life in its entirety. All that remained was to take gay characters into a few rarified corners of contemporary life.

In the aftermath of *Angels*, gay-themed plays (as well as films and television shows) proliferated and gay characters of every stripe found voice, with subsequent playwrights merging elements from earlier gay-themed plays from several generations. One such recent gay dramatist, Richard Greenberg, a prolific writer with many Off Broadway and regional theatre plays to his credit, scored a breakthrough success with the Broadway production of *Take Me Out* (2003), a play unquestionably inspired by the lyric realism of Williams, the humor and humanity of Fierstein, the polemics of Kramer, and the social and historical vision of Kushner. Mixing dramatic and comic elements to imagine the impact of a popular major league baseball player publicly announcing his homosexuality, Greenberg shapes *Take Me Out* around prevailing homophobic attitudes in a changed America; like the acclaimed film, *Brokeback Mountain* (2005), which zeroed in on homosexual love among hyper-masculine cowboys in the closeted 1960s, *Take Me Out* takes homosexuality into one of the last presumably exclusively heterosexual bastions — the national pastime, baseball. It found Broadway success (as *Brokeback Mountain* found cinematic triumph and Academy Awards) in rapidly changing attitudes about gays in the first decade of the twenty-first century. American gay drama had come full circle from stereotypes and pleas for acceptance as an oppressed "other" to equality, visibility, and liberation. The closet door had fallen off with a resounding thud — and in the new millennium, as gay marriage became a central element in national political debate, gays resided on American stages, depicted as full citizens in all walks of American life, just as Prior Walter insisted.

BIBLIOGRAPHY

Baker, Rob. *The Art of AIDS*. New York: Continuum, 1994.
Berkvist, Robert. "Broadway Discovers Tennessee Williams; Tennessee Williams on Broadway." *New York Times*, December 21, 1975.
Blanchard, Bob. "Playwright of Pain and Hope." *Progressive Magazine*, October 1994.
Clum, John M. *Acting Gay: Male Homosexuality in Modern Drama*. New York: Columbia University Press, 1992.
Fierstein, Harvey. *Torch Song Trilogy*. New York: Samuel French, Inc., 1978.
Fisher, James. *The Theater of Tony Kushner: Living Past Hope*. New York: Routledge, 2001.

_____, ed. *Tony Kushner: New Essays on the Art and Politics of the Plays*. Jefferson, NC: McFarland Publishers, Inc., 2006.
_____. *Understanding Tony Kushner*. Columbia, SC: University of South Carolina Press, 2008.
Kazin, Alfred. "The Writer as Sexual Show-Off: Making Press Agents Unnecessary." *New York Magazine*, June 9, 1975.
Kinsley, Michael. "The Quiet Gay Revolution." *Time*, June 25, 2007.
Kramer, Larry. *Just Say No: A Play about a Farce*. New York: St. Martin's Press, 1989.
_____. *The Normal Heart and the Destiny of Me*. New York: Grove Press, 2000.
_____. *Reports from the Holocaust: The Story of an AIDS Activist*. New York: St. Martin's Press, 1994.
Kushner, Tony. *Angels in America*. New York: Theatre Communications Group, 1995.
Mass, Lawrence D., ed. *We Must Love One Another or Die: The Life and Legacies of Larry Kramer*. New York: Palgrave/Macmillan, 1999.
McNally, Terrence. *Corpus Christi*. New York: Grove Press, 1998.
_____. *Lips Together, Teeth Apart*. New York: A Plume Book, 1992.
_____. *Love! Valour! Compassion!* Garden City, NY: Fireside Theatre, 1995.
Richards, David. "Theatre, a Working Playwright Edges into Fame." *New York Times*, August 29, 1993, sec. 2.
Shilts, Randy. *And the Band Played On*. New York: St. Martin's Press, 1987.
Zimna, Silverman. *Terrence McNally: A Casebook*. New York: Garland, 1997.

Mainstream Theatre, Mass Media, and the 1985 Premiere of *The Normal Heart*

Negotiating Forces Between Emergent and Dominant Ideologies

JACOB JUNTUNEN

War during Peacetime

Reviewers of the 1985 Public Theater production of Larry Kramer's *The Normal Heart* could not fathom the death toll that would be caused by HIV/AIDS, and the reviews tend to describe the play as "hysterical" (Rich C17). While discussing the "nearly 5,000" total dead from AIDS (Kroll 87), reviewers do not believe the play's warnings that the disease will only continue to spread if it is not checked by public institutions and activists. Now that 6,000 people die from the disease daily (Gay Men's Health Crisis), 5,000 total deaths seems an unimaginably low number.

Far from inevitable, these deaths from HIV/AIDS were, as many posit, avoidable. In 2007, no one questions that government institutions, the media, and even most activists failed to safeguard the public from the AIDS epidemic in the 1980s. In the end it was not the news media, the President, the Congress, the NIH, or the CDC that brought public attention to AIDS and all the failures in its management. It was a mainstream play: *The Normal Heart*.

Mainstream theatre is a term that needs to be carefully defined. As Lizbeth Goodman points out, mainstream theatre is often classified purely in relation to "alternative" theatre — a form of politically active theatre that emerged out of the social unrest of the 1960s in London and New York (17–18); David Román suggests that mainstream theatre productions are characterized by "opening nights, world premieres, [and] the critical review process that facilitates their official registration into theatre history" (xx). Here, mainstream theatre is defined as any theatrical production with a heterogeneous audience, a high public profile, and that is reviewed in many national periodicals such as the *New York Times*, or the *Wall Street Journal*.

Because of the commodification of art that took place in the West, scholars, particularly those aligned with the Frankfurt School, doubt mainstream theatre's ability to support any but the dominant ideology. For instance, in 1999, noted Professor of Drama Baz Kershaw asserted that modern capitalism bled mainstream theatre of its radical potential by reducing it to a mere commodity (5). While Kershaw argued for the primacy of radical performance, Professor of Film and Drama John Bull implicitly critiqued his colleague's over-determinism by recognizing mainstream theatre's continued centrality to the political process. Bull maintained that while mainstream theatre may not serve as the site where emergent ideologies materialize, it persists as a mediator between the conventional and subversive — the place where the dominant culture has the ability "to take in, to assimilate, and to render more safe, more marketable, the products of any oppositional programme" (134). By combining cultural theory with empirical data, this paper investigates how *The Normal Heart* supported an emergent ideology.

This essay takes up the conversation about politics and theatre by using a methodology proposed by Ric Knowles known as materialist semiotics (15). Materialist semiotics concentrates on three fundamental areas of inquiry: the performance text, the conditions of production, and the conditions of reception. Due to length restrictions, this paper is not a study of all three areas of inquiry. Instead, it highlights the oft-ignored conditions of reception by paying particular attention to the review process, arguing that a review is trying to incorporate a theatrical production's ideology into the worldview of its periodical. The review functions to interpolate the periodical's readers and confirm the periodical's ideology. This argument is supported by the theories of James Carey. In his work on media theory, Carey distinguishes between "transmission" and "ritual" views of communication (17). Basically, the transmission view posits communication as a simple exchange of data: one knows information and conveys it to another. The ritual view of communication is based instead on the creation and maintenance of ideologies. Carey argues that popular media is more inclined toward "ritual" communication. For instance, a subscription to the *Nation* will not only transmit information but will also confirm a liberal ideology; likewise, a subscription to the *Wall Street Journal* will transmit information while confirming a more conservative ideology. However, there are moments when the dominant ideology shifts, and utilizing Carey's ritual view of communication allows one to see how the reviews of *The Normal Heart* transmitted information and also helped challenge the dominant ideology. Thus, this paper argues that the ritual communication taking place in theatre reviews is one of the overlooked elements in the current theories of politics and performance.

Theatre scholar Susan Bennett argues that because reviews, advertisements, and other ideologically coded factors surrounding a production influence a spectator's "selection" process, each ticket bought is comparable to the purchasing of a particular ideology (118). That is: to choose to watch a play is to be ideologically swayed by the advertising and reviews. This paper shows what ideology spectators bought with their tickets to *The Normal Heart* and how the interpellation that occurred in these transactions potentially worked to challenge the dominant ideology. It also demonstrates how the reviews of the production amplified the production's emergent ideology to newspaper readers who never became spectators.

The plot of *The Normal Heart* is well known, so it will only receive a brief treatment here. It follows the story of Ned Weeks, a writer who begins a volunteer organization to combat the spread of a mysterious disease that preys mainly on homosexual men. AIDS and the GMHC are never mentioned, but the accounts are very similar to the disease and real organization. Because of Ned's confrontational style of activism, he is kicked out of the volunteer organization he helped start. Along the way, Ned meets Felix, a gay reporter at the *New York Times*, and they fall in love. When Felix is diagnosed with the disease, Ned cares for him until Felix dies. This love and dedication on Ned's part helps reconcile Ned and his straight brother, Ben, who up until then cannot understand Ned's "gay lifestyle."

The Normal Heart was not the first play to take on the topic of AIDS — there were "such artists, playwrights, and theatre collectives as Robert Chesley, Jeff Hagedorn, Rebecca Ranson, and San Francisco's A.I.D.S. Show Collaborators, among others, whose AIDS performances were produced as early as 1983" (Román xx). One reason these performances before 1985 remained relatively obscure is that they "were simply that, performances without opening nights, world premieres, or the critical review process that facilitates their official registration into theatre history" (Román xxii). However, *The Normal Heart* had another complicating factor: one month before the opening of Kramer's play, another play that dealt with AIDS opened at Circle Repertory Theater. The play, William Hoffman's *As Is*, is the story of two gay lovers who have broken up: one now has AIDS, the other is healthy and returns to take care of his ex-lover "as is." Its focus is much more on the personal aspects of a gay relationship than on the politics of AIDS, and it does not have the critical, angry stance of *The Normal Heart*. (Because *As Is* makes no attempt at activism and it garnered four reviews, it is excluded from serious analysis in this study even though it is contemporaneous.) Even though they were not the first plays to take on the topic of AIDS, they were the first to receive mainstream media attention; they

> generated an avalanche of press in both gay and mainstream publications, including major reviews in the *New York Times*. For the most part mainstream critics lauded the plays for introducing AIDS to the stage, virtually unaware of the various plays and performances already in circulation throughout the early 1980s. Since both plays were produced at major established venues and employed well-known actors, directors, and technical designers, a lack of critical coverage would have actually been more unusual. Indeed, the critical attention directed toward both these plays, but especially *The Normal Heart*, was unprecedented for any cultural text about AIDS at the time [Román 58].

Indeed, beyond the "unprecedented" critical attention given to *The Normal Heart*, it also became the longest-running production in the history of the Public Theater, a title it still holds as of 2007. Because this essay is an examination of the political work of mainstream theatre and not a history of AIDS theatre, it makes sense to focus on *The Normal Heart* rather than the previous AIDS performances. This is not because *The Normal Heart* is more important than the previous performances, but because its position in the mainstream did a kind of political work less mainstream plays could not. In particular, it produced an awareness of AIDS in mainstream theatre audiences and the mainstream media that more obscure, unreviewed performances did not.

David Román credits the success of *The Normal Heart* to "remarkable shifts in both the quantity and nature of depictions of AIDS [that] took place," from "*Life* magazine's notorious July cover story, 'Now No One Is Safe from AIDS,' to Rock Hudson's public announcement and subsequent AIDS death" (Román 60). But the events Román lists happened months after the April 1985 opening of *The Normal Heart*. A more careful analysis of the conditions of reception during the spring of 1985 is necessary to understand its success. Such a methodology, moreover, allows the scholar to investigate how the production and its media coverage contributed to and made possible the subsequent media coverage devoted to AIDS in the summer of 1985.

Spectators of the Public Theater production of *The Normal Heart* would have had varying amounts of knowledge about AIDS as they entered the theatre, ranging from GMHC volunteers who knew tremendous amounts, to people who had never heard of the disease. If it seems unlikely that in April of 1985 there could be people who had still never heard of AIDS, remember that in February 1985 "the official position of New York City was that the AIDS epidemic was not yet a crisis" even though the city's "cases surpassed 3,000" (Shilts 533). And media coverage of New York City's crisis was scarce: "the first series of newspaper articles investigating New York's response to the

AIDS epidemic were published, not in New York, but in the *San Francisco Chronicle*" (Shilts 533–34). Nevertheless, every audience member, regardless of his or her knowledge of the disease, would probably have been affected by the material aspects of the production. The architecture of the Public Theater is somewhat imposing with its red- and brown-bricked Renaissance Revival facade, and its stone steps leading to a large lobby with a vaulted ceiling. It seems especially grand in its East Village location where most of the other buildings are simple shops and walk-up residential buildings.

Once inside the building, audience members would have walked past pamphlets about AIDS from the AIDS Medical Foundation, GMHC, AIDS Resource Center, Health and Human Services, Children and AIDS, and the American Red Cross Home Attendant Program; there was also a study guide prepared by the AIDS Medical Foundation, printed lists of organizations and their addresses where the audience members could send donations, and lists of suggestions about how audience members could get involved in volunteering to help find a cure for AIDS and to care for its victims. All of this was located in a literature rack in the center of the hallway between the two sets of stairs that lead from the lobby to the Anspacher Theatre ("Audience Involvement at Public Production"). There was also a sign-in book for the audience members to leave their names and addresses; this information was given to the various AIDS support groups (mentioned above) for their direct-mail campaigns. The Public Theater also used the list for its own mailings and telephone solicitations. Inside the programs was an insert that read:

What you can do!

1. Go downstairs to our lobby and buy a "Normal Heart" Tee Shirt, button or the actual published script. The proceeds will go to AIDS research and the care of its victims.

2. Get the facts about AIDS by picking up the pamphlets on display. Education and Funding are two of the strongest tools we can use to fight this dreaded disease.

3. Donate money to one or all of the various organizations that are involved in combating AIDS. Pick up a list that we have prepared of organizations that need your financial help.

4. Volunteer your time to one of the organizations now involved in the research of AIDS, the care of its victims, or educating the public through the various AIDS HOTLINES.

5. Tell your friends, family, colleagues, and students to come see "The Normal Heart." There is a 50% DISCOUNT for groups of ten or more. Please contact Clifford Scott in our Group Sales office, (212) 598-7107 ["Audience Involvement at Public Production"].

The insert also stated that money made from the proceeds of the merchandise would go to the AIDS Medical Foundation, GMHC, and the AIDS

Resource Center ("Audience Involvement at Public Production"). Audience members could have looked at this information either before the show, during intermission, or after the show. Regardless of when they looked at it, the information related the facts in the fiction they were viewing to the real world. This gave spectators concrete ways to get involved with the problems the fiction of the play presented to them. Also, and perhaps more importantly, the literature in the lobby "hailed" spectators as people who would *want* to get involved. It assumed a spectator who would be moved into action by seeing the needless deaths of young, gay men. *The Normal Heart* was not the source of this emergent ideology — indeed, the emergent ideology probably originated in the earlier performances of AIDS that Román documents (xx, 64) — but the Public Theater was a site with the ability "to take in, to assimilate, and to render more safe, more marketable, the products of any oppositional programme" (Bull 329). In the process it may have made the emergent ideology less "radical" (in Baz Kershaw's terms), but it also made the ideology more visible, and even without "radical" politics, it still interpellated the spectators as activists.

By using the proceeds of merchandise to fund organizations directly related to the political cause of the performance itself, the production was able to use consumerism to further AIDS activism. This contrasts with Baz Kershaw's negative assessment of consumerism in the theatre; Kershaw criticizes the merchandise that inevitably comes with commercial theatre in the West at the end of the twentieth century by arguing that "the power of performance is sucked dry by the peripherals of theatre as it is transformed into a service industry with subsidiary retail outlets. The commodification of the theatre is achieved by reshaping the patron in the image of the consuming shopper" (47). *The Normal Heart*, however, used the money of the "patron" to further the production's activism and provided spectators with literature that instructed the "patron" on other ways to get involved — from philanthropy to volunteering. In this way, the space around *The Normal Heart* did not reshape "the patron" into "the image of the consuming shopper." Instead, it presented the spectators with a variety of ways to become activists. Though this would not have been possible without the Public Theater and Kramer deciding to donate the profits to activist agencies, the downtown, Village location also contributed to this image as being "activists" rather than "shoppers." Since the Village is generally seen as the location of intellectuals and rebellious artists, the geographic placement of the theatre also contributed to the sense of spectator as activist rather than shopper.

Before any of this could happen, however, spectators had to decide to see *The Normal Heart*, and it is likely that many of them based this decision to some extent on advertising, especially before reviews came out. The main advertising that existed a week before opening was a quarter-page advertisement in the *New York Times* theatre section; the advertisement was mainly white writing against a black background that read, "At least 300,000 Americans have already been infected by the AIDS virus, according to Dr. James Curran who heads the AIDS program at the Centers for Disease Control." Below the large quote was a small logo of "The Normal Heart" which is a valentine-shaped heart with the title written over it. Underneath the play's logo was more text: "A play about the most serious public health crisis of the 20th century" (Public Theater "Pre-Opening *Normal Heart* Advertisement"). This advertisement frames the production as a serious discussion about the AIDS crisis more than as a piece of art. For instance, there is no claim that the play is well written, riveting, or a great piece of theatre. Instead, the advertisement frames the play as educational by using the bulk of its space to quote a doctor from the CDC. Seeing the play as educational rather than artistic is a frame that was rehearsed by the reviewers.

Once the play opened, it received a considerable number of reviews. Using the ritual view of communication espoused by Carey, one can infer that reviewers' reactions are representative of a group of spectators. This paper analyzes reviews to determine how a particular periodical incorporated *The Normal Heart* into its ideology. From this, it is possible to suggest how a member of that periodical's community of readers would likely have been interpellated by that review.

The reviews that came out on April 22, 1985 (the day after opening night) were generally negative about the aesthetic value of the play, but their reactions to the play's politics and message were a mix of agreement and denial. Frank Rich, perhaps the most important critic then at the *New York Times*, wrote a review that included more information about the AIDS crisis than the *New York Times* published in the first years of the epidemic. Rich writes that *The Normal Heart* is "the most outspoken play around" and that its subject "justifies its author's unflagging, at times even hysterical, sense of urgency" (C17). The justification for the "urgency" is the "foot-dragging" of "the Governmental, medical and press establishments.... Mayor Koch, various prominent medical organizations, The New York Times ... [and] most of the leadership of an unnamed organization apparently patterned after the Gay Men's Health Crisis" (C17). Rich's review not only provided information to the readership of the *Times*, but also gave legitimacy to an emergent ideology that saw AIDS as a real threat and condemned official "foot-dragging." While the subject is "urgent," Rich blasts the play's "pamphleteering tone" that "is accentuated by Mr. Kramer's insistence on repetition ... and on regurgitating facts and figures in lengthy tirades" (C17). In the end, Rich does praise this "shrill" play, in part for its set, "a whitewashed box, on which are emblazoned the names and state-by-state death tolls of AIDS victims. While one wishes that the play's outrage had been channeled into drama as fully compelling as its cause, the writing on the theater's walls alone could drive anyone with a normal heart to abandon what Mr. Kramer calls the 'million excuses for not getting involved'" (C17). Just like the literature in the lobby, this review interpellates its readers as people who care about the AIDS crisis; it suggests that the community has "a million excuses for not getting involved," but that this play would convince those excuses to be abandoned.

Next to Rich's review was "a denial of Kramer's accusation that the [*New York*] *Times* had failed to cover AIDS and the defense that the newspaper had sent a member of the science staff to cover the story as soon as it had been informed of the existence of the disease" (Shatzky 133). This play generated a review that put facts about AIDS into the *Times* and even made the paper feel the need to defend itself. It therefore challenged the ideologies of its readers in two important ways: first, it suggested that AIDS was a significant story, and second that the *Times* was at fault in its coverage of the epidemic.

Also on April 22, Douglas Watt of the *Daily News* found "many shortcomings" in the script, but wrote that almost all of them "are swept away by the immediacy and forcefulness of the drama" (38). He compared *The Normal Heart* to a Living Newspaper, and wrote that "you may find a lot to quarrel with in this evening, but there's no denying the factual evidence or Kramer's fervor, and you are bound to come away moved" (38). Here is a newspaper, which theatre scholar Marvin Carlson argues is a voice of "authority" regarding a production's merit (23), that confirmed Kramer's play as "factual evidence." Similarly, on April 22, Howard Kissel wrote in *Women's Wear Daily* that "if the facts were not so outrageous, so troubling, they might seem more suited to a lecture or an editorial" (14). He, too, claimed that Kramer's play was factual; he also mentioned the numbers written on the set and suggested that the acting saved the play from being agitprop. He ended his review by writing, "Over the years I have railed against Joe Papp for having confused kneejerk politics with theater ... the resources of the Shakespeare Festival, often put to trivial use, are here applied to something major" (14). By stating that the play is factual and relevant, these reviews challenged readers' ideologies by chastising the press's general lethargy regarding the AIDS crisis.

The other two reviews from April 22, however, did not agree that *The Normal Heart* was socially important. Allan Wallach of *Newsday* wrote that "Kramer's [play] fails to involve us deeply with its characters; it does not make us feel the loss and terrible waste when young men die of AIDS" (17). He called the play "shrill" and "polemical" and did not find redeeming qualities in it (17). This was nothing compared to Sy Syna's review for the *New*

York City Tribune, which was titled, "*The Normal Heart* Offensive and Boring." Syna wrote,

> There are several infuriating aspects of 'The Normal Heart': its interminable length, author Larry Kramer's need to set each scene up as an opportunity for one character or another to deliver an impassioned lengthy speech, and his demeaning equation of Jews during the Holocaust with homosexuals during the AIDS crisis. The first two merely offend aesthetically. They are examples of poor dramaturgy. His latter analogy, which permeates the entire play, is an ethnic affront [6B].

Instead of addressing Kramer's analogy of AIDS and the Holocaust — which is certainly a debatable analogy — Syna blamed gay men for AIDS by writing, "Now that their 'alternative lifestyle' has developed lethal complications in the form of AIDS, an internal conflict develops within the homosexual activist group which Ned founded" (6B). This review, then, unfortunately echoed an ideology that blamed gay men for AIDS. However, even this negative reaction placed coverage of AIDS into the newspaper, which was one of the goals of *The Normal Heart*.

Alongside these April 22 reviews was press coverage of a surprise announcement by Mayor Koch. As Shilts tells it:

> Just hours before the first preview performance, as photocopied scripts of *The Normal Heart* circulated among the city's news organizations, Mayor Ed Koch hurriedly called a press conference to announce "a comprehensive expansion of city services" for local AIDS patients. Koch shifted responsibility for AIDS from Health Commissioner Sencer to Deputy Mayor Victor Botnick and instituted the plans for coordinated care and long-term facilities that had been proposed years before by AIDS clinicians. Included in the new $6 million program were pledges of expanded home and hospice care, day-care programs for children with AIDS, and funds for ten interdisciplinary patient care teams at hospitals with large AIDS caseloads [556].

These were political events that anticipated the performance of *The Normal Heart* and, according to Shilts, they sought to lessen the impact of its accusations. They were reported in the media on the same day as the first reviews of *The Normal Heart*. This coverage of Koch's announcement also affected reception of the play, lending the production an air of activist journalism rather than theatre, which augmented what reviews were saying about it being factual.

After the opening night reviews came out, the Public Theater put out a new advertisement for the play in the *New York Times* that continued to frame the play as activism more than art. This half-page advertisement included carefully selected quotes from reviews (even some from reviews that disliked the play overall), but across and obscuring all the quotes from reviews was a block of text in a bigger, more dramatic font. This text read, "Once in every ten years or so a play comes along that fulfills my original idea of what role my theater must play in society. 'The Normal Heart' is that play — Joseph Papp" (Public Theater "Post-Opening *Normal Heart* Advertisement"). In this advertisement, the political role of the play literally overshadowed the reviewers' opinions about its artistic merit.

In a number of reviews from April 25 to May 15 — including a second *New York Times* review, this one by Mel Gussow (It is not normal for the *New York Times* to have two reviews of the same play, but this is what happened in the case of *The Normal Heart*) — the dramaturgical shortcomings continue to be noted, but less and less so as the political importance of *The Normal Heart* became the focal point. In Gussow's *New York Times* article, which to some extent revised Rich's earlier review, he compared Kramer's hero Ned Weeks to Ibsen's hero of *An Enemy of the People*, Thomas Stockmann. In Gussow's opinion, "the principal problem in 'The Normal Heart' is not Acquired Immune Deficiency Syndrome (a subject that is not mentioned by name in the course of the play), or even the broader question of a bias against homosexuals. As Ned affirms, 'This is not a civil rights issue. This is a contagion issue.' In common with Stockman [sic], he is trying to staunch an epidemic. He is a whistleblower and he is surrounded by people who are worried about their careers, their images and their sex lives. Life itself is at stake" (B3). Gussow saw this play as less about AIDS than about people's inability to realize when it is necessary to give up petty differences in order to survive. While he criticized Kramer for not having the "irony" of Ibsen, he praised *The Normal Heart*'s "polemic purpose" (B3), and his review again interpellated readers as people who presumably would prefer to remain alive rather than worry "about their careers, their images and their sex lives" (B3).

Michael Feingold, writing for the *Village Voice,* also compared the play to *An Enemy of the People*, and wrote that Ibsen's irony sees "the idealist as both necessary and a problem" (105); he wished Kramer employed similar ironic techniques. Instead, according to Feingold, Kramer used Ned as "strictly an author's mouthpiece" (105). Feingold ended his review by writing that "*The Normal Heart* can't solve the problems of the gay community any more than it can discover a cure for AIDS. What it can do is what any usable piece of political theatre does: nag at the viewers, rouse them to the prospect of accomplishing something. Kramer in person, like his hero, may be part of the problem; his play is at least a tiny part of the solution" (105). *The Normal Heart* was again seen as dramaturgically flawed, but "part of the solution." This production could not only "rouse" viewers, it also presented them with clear actions to take. Instructions were laid out in the lobby displays that connected the play's message to tangible activities spectators could take outside the theatre. This production did more than "nag"; it also provided the means to take action and interpellated spectators as activists.

While an April 25 review in the *Villager* found that Kramer "oversteps himself at times in references to Jewish apathy during World War II," the reviewer ultimately wrote, "'The Normal Heart' is a reminder that no one is innocent and that an age of self absorption, denial, and narcissism may lead to destruction as easily as a nuclear explosion" (Manishchewitz 13). This review was very similar to Gussow's since it takes the theme of the play to be less about AIDS than personal responsibility.

A later *Village Voice* review wrote that *The Normal Heart* "can provide something that's in short supply in modern urban culture, and not often enough perceived as a need in this crisis: a forum for public grieving" (Massa 106). The *Daily News* argued that *The Normal Heart* "tells us things we don't want to hear—for instance, the government spent $20 million investigating the seven Tylenol deaths while it largely ignored AIDS until it was a full-blown health crisis with thousands of dead and dying" (Smith 10). This review interpellated its readers as people who needed "a forum for public grieving" over dead and ill gay men (as opposed to an ideology that thought this disease was deserved because of a "lifestyle" choice); it also put into the public media the difference between the government's spending on the Tylenol scare and AIDS crisis.

While Clive Barnes of the *New York Post* experienced the writing of *The Normal Heart* as "banal" and "more of a tract than a play," he also wrote of its political importance and asked, "How many people of the thousands who will see the play, and be stirred by its sheer intensity and passionate concern, would have read the tract?" (17). Further, would a tract have attracted an equal amount of attention from the *New York Post* and had its message carried vicariously to the readers of the *Post* and every other paper that reviewed the play? Similarly, John Simon, writing for *New York*, argued that "what could have been a mere staged tract — and, in its lesser moments, is just that — transcends often enough into a fleshed-out, generously dramatized struggle, in which warring ideologies do not fail to breathe, sweat, weep, bleed — be human" (92). This review framed the play not just as tract, nor even as simply a moving play, but as a play about gay men with AIDS that are nevertheless "human." In 1985, this was quite a remarkable statement, especially for a mainstream magazine like *New York*, and it would have challenged the ideologies of many mainstream readers. *Variety* also found *The Normal Heart* to be "strong agit-prop theater" and suggested that it was "flawed but socially worthwhile" and that it "merits consideration for production by nonprofit groups who want to hold the mirror up to contemporary American life" (Humm 106).

In May, as the buzz surrounding the play was turning into sold-out crowds and the first extensions of the run, *The Normal Heart* even received some positive reviews regarding its aesthetics from the national magazines *Newsweek* and *Time*. Jack Kroll wrote for *Newsweek* that "Kramer produces not a series of debates but a cross fire of life-and-death energies that illuminate the many issues and create a fierce and moving human drama. It is bracing and exciting to hear so much passionate and intelligent noise on a stage again" (87). This was one of the first reviews that argued that *The Normal Heart* was actually a good play based on its aesthetics instead of its politics, and *Time* seconded that opinion when its review asserted that what made *The Normal Heart* "so deeply affecting is that [it] portrays anguish and doom in individual human terms and enables audiences of every sexual inclination to grasp a common bond of suffering and mortality" (Henry III 85). These positive reviews did not mention its politics as prominently; because of this, they did less to spread the play's messages. However, these reviews did mention the "common bond" between people regardless of "sexual inclination," which no doubt challenged many readers' ideologies. But the work of *The Normal Heart* was less about "normalizing" homosexuality and more about educating the public about AIDS; thus, these positive reviews were less efficacious than negative reviews that nevertheless mentioned the play's politics. The *Christian Science Monitor* review is the most important example of an efficacious negative review.

The small review in the *Christian Science Monitor* found the play to be "one-sided" and argued that "Mr. Kramer attempts unsuccessfully to combine a plea for responsible official awareness and treatment of a tragic health disaster with a propaganda pitch for society's unreserved acceptance of homosexual lifestyles" (Beaufort 2). Given the magazine's religious affiliation, it is no surprise that it was not in favor of "acceptance of homosexual lifestyles," especially in 1985. The magazine's resistance to "acceptance of homosexual lifestyles" followed a conservative Christian ideology that would, presumably, match the ideology of most of its readers. But even the *Christian Science Monitor* author admitted that AIDS is "a tragic health disaster," implying that something ought to at least be done about that. The article explained in its first paragraph what AIDS was ("the medical acronym for 'acquired immune deficiency syndrome'"), which suggests that readers may not be familiar with the epidemic, and, if that was the case, the article probably educated them. In fact, this is the first article found in the *Christian Science Monitor* to use the term "acquired immune deficiency syndrome," which suggests it may have been the first article about AIDS in the publication's history. If this is the case, the reviewer, as much as he disliked the play, added to the readers' knowledge of the world by explaining this new and deadly disease. By calling it a "tragic health disaster," he also implicitly argued for fighting the epidemic. This potential education and the corresponding ideological shift is an important outcome, even if the review did not lead people to see the play.

An article appearing in late May in the "gay" publication the *New York Native* argued that Kramer's "hysteria" might be justified. It is worth quoting at length:

> A few weeks ago [my straight roommate] told me she wanted me to move out because she was afraid I was going to give her AIDS. Understand, now, that my health is perfectly fine, as both my doctor and insurance company will attest. But *her* doctors tell her that while sexual intercourse seems to be how the virus is transmitted, there's no way of knowing the long-term effects of her sharing a bathroom and kitchen with a gay roommate. After all, he may be healthy *now*, her doctors say, but what if something's incubating away in his bloodstream? [Sommers 45].

While other aspects of the article are a more straightforward review of the play—including a description of the set, script, and acting—this anecdote captures the fear and panic surrounding AIDS at the time *The Normal Heart* was produced. It also captures how important it was for newspapers, even if only in reviews of a play, to be calling out governmental agencies on their failure to act, and to be calling AIDS patients "human" in mainstream magazines like *New York* (Simon 92). While no AIDS camps ever came into existence, it is impossible to know how much acceptance of people with the disease came from *The Normal Heart* and its media coverage; perhaps the play and other pieces of art like it prevented outcomes along the lines of Ned Weeks' fears. Importantly, the article also cites *The Normal Heart* as directly related to his own personal experience; this again provided a writer with the opportunity to express an emergent ideology while using the play as an ostensible topic.

On July 25, 1985, over three months after *The Normal Heart* opened at the Public Theater, the famously masculine movie star Rock Hudson announced that he had AIDS. On July 28, 1985 "AIDS was on the front page of virtually every Sunday morning paper in the United States" (Shilts 578). As Dr. Michael Gottlieb, an immunologist at UCLA who worked on AIDS cases from the beginning, wrote, "There was AIDS before Rock Hudson and AIDS after" (Shilts 585); Dr. Gottleib and Shilts argue that Hudson's announcement drastically changed the frequency and quality of AIDS coverage in the media. After Hudson's announcement, the disease was public knowledge and even in the spotlight. This awareness of the disease created a new frame for *The Normal Heart*. As time passed, there was less and less talk of the play's "hysterical" tone in articles about the play. This shift in tone may have occurred because of previous reviews that already framed the play as factual, and perhaps because of the growing death count that affected more and more people personally. One review in October in the liberal *New York Native* optimistically suggested, "Someday [*The Normal Heart*] is going to be a standard script to be read in high schools" (Fettner 40). All these reviews, articles, and contemporaneous events regarding AIDS affected people's desire to see *The Normal Heart* and kept it running longer than any play at the Public Theater before or since.

The writing on the AIDS crisis of the 1980s is filled with war metaphors. Shilts begins the epilogue to his masterful work *And the Band Played On* with an epigraph by Hermann Hesse: "There was no need to think at all of any reader but myself, or at the most, here and there another close war-comrade, and I most certainly never thought then about the survivors, but always about those who fell in the war. While writing it, I was as if delirious or crazy, surrounded by three or four people with mutilated bodies—that was how this book was produced" (583). This epigraph shows how gay men felt like they were at war during the early years of the AIDS epidemic, but the general public was unaware of this war. The emergent ideology held by these gay men that compared their experience to wartime was not yet part of the dominant ideology. *The Normal Heart* helped to change that. Joseph Papp recalled,

> Every night, at the end of *The Normal Heart*, ten, twelve or fifteen young men would sit there and be unable to move, absolutely stunned. Sit in their chairs, not leave. What would happen is, several other people in the audience, mostly men, would go over and sit with that person. Downstairs, another play called *Tracers* was running—a moving portrayal of young men dying in Vietnam. Exactly the same thing. All the Vietnam veterans would come over to a veteran, sit there and put an arm around him. You could have duplicated those two scenes. They both dealt with the same thing—buddies under fire, under threat of death [Papp 266–67].

To those who fought AIDS since the early 1980s, it felt like they fought a war of which most of the country was unaware, a war during peacetime, and *The Normal Heart* was one of the first major acts that helped combat apathy, homophobia, and ignorance. Through information given to audiences both during the performances and through pamphlets in the theatre lobby and reviews describing the play and its subject matter, *The Normal Heart* informed U.S. citizens about the epidemic. Even without examining the performance text and the aftermath of its production, it is possible to say *The Normal Heart* made a difference. The production's reviews "hailed" spectators and readers as people who cared about the AIDS crisis and wanted to do something about it. Though this emergent ideology had been expressed in the alternative, "gay theatre" (Paller 238; Román xx, 64), when it was presented by *The Normal Heart* in a mainstream theatre setting, it was amplified by the national media. This amplification helped integrate the emergent ideology that AIDS was a crisis in need of attention into the dominant ideology. This demonstrates how a mainstream production can successfully be a part of the process of integrating an emergent ideology into the dominant one.

The Writing on the Wall

As already described, spectators of the Public Theater production of *The Normal Heart* walked past pamphlets and mailing lists in the lobby before entering LuEsther Hall, a long performance space with a high ceiling. They sat on two sides of the theatre "basketball-court style" (Feingold 105); in the intimate space, spectators were close to the action on stage, and they could watch audience members across the stage "squirm as some particularly painful moment" was played out (Feingold 105). One reviewer described the sensation of "looking down as in an operating room" (Gussow 2:24). The set design by Eugene Lee and Keith Raywood surrounded the audience "with walls covered with numbers and names, state by state, city by city, of AIDS victims" (Sommers 45). According to Howard Kissel, "these numbers are the real setting against which the action takes place" (Kissel 14). Like a "Brechtian kaleidoscope," these numbers were constantly updated throughout the run of the production (Fettner 40). As literary critic Gregory Gross describes it, "these Brechtian announcements flash numbers all over the stage and audience — numbers about AIDS cases, numbers about AIDS deaths, numbers of news articles printed in major papers, numbers of dollars spent, numbers of various dates and some corresponding and contrasting numbers related to the 1982 Tylenol scare. Along with the numbers, people's names appear in the fashion of the Vietnam Veterans Memorial in Washington, D.C." (64). Combined with the script and the mise-en-scène, these Brechtian elements in the design made spectators aware of the world outside the fiction and prodded them toward taking action after leaving the theatre.

As directed by Michael Lindsey-Hogg at the Public Theater in 1985, the acting and set were based in the traditions of realism, except for the writing on the walls of the theatre surrounding the audience. If there was no "fourth wall" because of the alley configuration, and if simple set-pieces were meant to convey an entire setting (a hospital bed to represent a hospital room, for instance), the idea was not to be symbolic but to suggest a realist set simply. This direction seemed an appropriate choice because the script itself was not often symbolic, preferring instead to chastise real public figures and institutions (Mayor Koch, the *New York Times*, the CDC, etc.). In fact, literary critic Joel Shatzky attributes the production's "electrifying effect" on audiences to the playwright not treating "the AIDS epidemic in symbolic terms" (134). He explains that since the play was produced at a time when the epidemic was so real, symbolism was not necessary and would have only taken away from the strength of the work. Tony Kushner writes that *The Normal Heart* has "precisely one, and only one symbolic, metaphoric moment which gains much of its power from its absolute isolation" (viii). The moment to which Kushner refers is when Ned, frustrated beyond belief with Felix's refusal to eat anything but junk food, throws health food groceries to the floor, one by one, until a carton of milk explodes onstage (Kramer 113). This scene stands out because it is one of the few scenes without statistics, and numbers, and there is a visual, symbolic representation of waste and death that does not exist in any other scene in the play. Many of the reviews and the subsequent literature on *The Normal Heart* address the scene. John Simon, writing for *New York*, wrote that "we can choke back our sobs over a gallant death, but cry rightly over a carton of spilt milk" (92). Likewise, Michael Sommers, in the *New York Native*, wrote that "the impact of a quart of milk splattered all over the place is indescribably shocking" (45). It is perhaps the key moment of the play's emotional resonance.

The power of an exploding carton of milk comes from the scene's deeply emotional content within the context of so many numbers and statistics. Gregory Gross points out that the play moves "from the big to the small, from the abstract to the concrete and from the general to the highly personal" (65), and this is exactly what occurs in the scene with the milk. After nearly two hours of long monologues full of statistics of the dead and dying, tirades about the numbers of newspaper articles or amounts of funding, Ned finally says,

> Felix, I am so sick of statistics, and numbers, and body counts, and how-manys, and Emma [Felix's doctor]; and every day, Felix, there are only more numbers, and fights—I am so sick of fighting, and bragging about fighting, and everybody's stupidity, and blindness, and intransigence, and guilt trips. You can't eat the food? Don't eat the food. Take your poison. I don't care. You can't get up off the floor—fine, stay there. I don't care. Fish—fish is good for you; we don't want any of that, do we? (*Item by item, he throws the food on the floor*) No green salad. No broccoli; we don't want any of that, no sir. No bread with seven grains. Who would ever want any milk? You might get some calcium in your bones (*The carton of milk explodes when it hits the floor.*) You want to die, Felix? Die! ... Felix, please don't leave me [Kramer 113, ellipsis in original].

This scene moves from the utter frustration that his partner will not fight (represented in Ned's line, "Die!") to the equal fear and horror of his partner's death (represented by Ned's line, "Please don't leave me"). After throwing the milk, seeing it explode all over the stage, and shouting, "Die!"

at the cowering Felix, Ned falls to the floor and Felix crawls through the milk and debris to hold him.

This scene is only a few minutes from the end of the play and by this point the audience shares Ned's frustration with the "statistics, and numbers, and body counts" that make up the bulk of the script, and it is at this moment of frustration that the play finally produces a visual representation of the loss of a generation of gay men. What could be a better symbol of waste than spilt milk, the loss of nutrients and the ability to help one grow? Milk is representative of a maternal, caretaking force that these men's lives lack as they attempt to take care of their own ill. It is a food staple of the young; its waste mirrors the waste of a young man dying. Seeing Felix crawl through it is akin to watching him crawl through a representation of all the young men's lives cut short. The fact that the milk and detritus from the rest of the thrown groceries remains onstage throughout the remainder of the play is a constant visual reminder of that waste.

Even if that is the only overtly symbolic moment in the play, realism is itself a symbolic representation of life, and Kramer's particular use of realism made *The Normal Heart* especially appealing to a wide range of spectators. David Bergman detects "at least three major strains" in *The Normal Heart*: "the grating soprano of the enraged child, the wounded contralto of the guilt-inducing mother, and the rasping bass of the humiliating father" (179). Bergman continues, "Because I hear these voices coming not only from Kramer's page but also from my own head, I respond to them with an unusual intensity. Kramer's ability to address the subconscious of gay readers accounts in large part for the power he exerts on and the anger he arouses from [them]" (180). While Kramer's ability to cipher the interior voices of a gay man may account for the play's popularity with gay spectators, John Clum argues that "to the straight audience [Kramer] is the representative gay man, the good fairy who will speak for what being gay should mean" ("Kramer" 202). While Kramer's text may be tapping deep into the subconscious of a gay spectator, that same text may be showing a straight spectator a "good fairy," a positive role-model of a gay man. Nicholas de Jongh points out that "Kramer stresses affinities with heterosexuals rather than differences" (183). This can be seen in Ned's attempts to explain to his straight brother all the things they have in common, and by ultimately finding acceptance from his brother after the non-state-sanctioned death-bed marriage ceremony Ned and Felix undergo (Kramer 117). The reason *The Normal Heart* stressed affinities with heterosexuals rather than differences is explained by Clum's observation that it "came from those moments when [Kramer] felt he lost his gay audience, when he felt separated from or betrayed by the groups he founded: after his 'snub' by the board of Gay Men's Health Crisis, which led to the writing of *The Nor-*

mal Heart" ("Kramer" 204). This might be another reason that Kramer did not seek out a "gay" theatre to produce *The Normal Heart*; he may have wished to reconcile artistically with a "straight" audience after his "snub" by the GMHC. Bergman writes that "placing the gay community within the bosom of the heterosexual family is, I think, one reason why [Kramer's] work speaks so powerfully and uneasily to gay readers, for it suggests a vision of reconciliation that is both keenly desired and frustratingly delayed" (179). Likewise, "placing the gay community within the bosom of the heterosexual family" is surely a reason why *The Normal Heart* could be accepted so readily by so many mainstream, straight spectators. The title itself is a plea for that type of acceptance and it is easy to give when similarities rather than differences between gay and straight communities are being stressed.

While reconciliation between gay and straight cultures might have appealed to some spectators, there were many spectators for whom it did not. Obviously there were straight spectators who, because of homophobia, religious beliefs, or other reasons had no desire to see the gay community reconciled with straight culture. The *New York City Tribune* review that suggests that gay men's "'alternative lifestyle' has developed lethal complications" and suggests that the play is "offensive to anyone except a homosexual who feels that society has an obligation to pick up the tab for the unsavory implications of their 'lifestyle'" clearly does not accept Kramer's plea to be seen as one with a normal heart (Syna 6B). Clum has completely different reasons for being uncomfortable with the reconciliation desired in *The Normal Heart*:

> Through Felix, Ned has found a way to bridge homosexuality and heterosexuality and place his homosexuality within a paradigm that straight Ben understands. He may not support all his brother's political alliances, but he will support his marriage. Herein lies the subtext of *The Normal Heart*: the paradigm of marriage validates homosexuality. However, alas, Ned seems more content with the role of widower than with the role of spouse ["Kramer" 209].

Clum criticizes this model of reconciliation because Ben does not truly support Ned's "political alliances," such as fighting for gay rights. He merely supports Ned's entrance into the "paradigm" of "marriage." Likewise, by stating that Ned is "more content with the role of widower," Clum suggests that Ned is more interested in finding acceptance from his brother than having an active partnership with Felix. De Jongh sums up this argument: "Weeks seems unable to appreciate that if you condemn, stigmatize, penalize and even ostracize an entire sexual subgroup, then once it achieves some liberation from its stigmatists, many in that subgroup will reject the forms and behaviours of those who have oppressed them. The play does not consider such an argument" (183). By stressing affinities between homosexual and heterosexual communities, Kramer overlooks legitimate differences and, while this is pleasing to some members of the gay and straight communities, it offends others.

Perhaps more importantly given this production's role in early AIDS education, Ned's condemnations of promiscuity — such as his statement that "having so much sex makes finding love impossible" (Kramer 51) — do not acknowledge that

> Gay Liberation did not cause AIDS. The dissemination of the HIV virus was assisted by the failure to take seriously the first prognoses of the epidemic's gravity, and by delayed programmes of political education and medical information. And the conception of gay marriages would no more terminate promiscuity than heterosexual marriages necessarily discourage adultery and fornication [de Jongh 183].

While educating the public that promiscuity could potentially lead to AIDS was absolutely essential in the 1980s, blaming AIDS on promiscuity is dangerously similar to the *New York City Tribune*'s review that blamed AIDS on the "gay lifestyle" (Syna). Furthermore, the play claims that "there's absolutely no such thing as safe sex" (Kramer 71). Bergman writes that this line "could be justified in the early stages of the health crisis as a reasonable response to a disease whose cause and mode of transmission were unknown" (178), but in 1985 enough was known about the disease to educate spectators about the effectiveness of condom use. As early as 1982 there was advice about the use of condoms to promote a safer way of having sex; for example, Michael Callen's forty-page pamphlet *How to Have Sex in an Epidemic: One Approach* was published in 1982 and reviewed in the *New York Times Review of Books* (Callen). In *The Normal Heart* "there is no discussion of the role that safer sexual acts may have on gay lives in the midst of the epidemic" (de Jongh 182). The relative lack of discussion about actions sexually active people can take to halt the spread of AIDS also contributes to what David Román sees as one of the "conventional concepts of dramatic tragedy," which presents "AIDS as a totalizing and inescapable condition, a condition with little or no agency to fight the powers contributing to the epidemic and with little or no hope for those affected" (238). While this is a good critique of the script, it ignores some of the material aspects of the Public Theater production, such as the long lists of ways to get involved that greeted spectators both coming and going from the theatre. The script may present AIDS as a totalizing force, but the script's failure to address ways to be sexually active in a less risky way does not mean the production gave actors and spectators no "agency" in this epidemic. The very act of presenting the play, seeing the play, and informing spectators about ways to take action, gave the actors and spectators an "agency to fight the powers contributing to the epidemic" in a way beyond what the script offered (Román 238).

Gross writes that the early plays about AIDS "are history plays performed in the midst of their own history. The players, the spectators and those walking around outside the theatre stand engaged in the same situation" (63). In *The Normal Heart* "what is testimonial and what is fictive ... collide" (Nelson 2), and in that collision — such as the writing on the wall versus the words spoken by the actors—came much of the production's political power. The script itself may have presented AIDS as a totalizing force, but the act of performing the contemporaneous moment was an extremely empowering act.

There is much made of the Brechtian elements of the staging in contemporaneous reviews of and later critical writing on *The Normal Heart*. Almost all these references to Brecht deal with the statistics, names, and facts written on the walls of the set. Clum attributes this mixture of a realistic script with a Brechtian set to "Kramer's political confusion" and sees it as a failure of consistency of form (*Still Acting* 64). There is no need to see this inconsistency as a failure, however. Both the realism and the alienation are necessary to give the spectators a dual awareness of the reality of the fiction and the reality outside the theatre. D. S. Lawson suggests that "Kramer's abandonment of conventional stage realism" isolates

> his characters and their actions from a recognizable landscape [that] both allows a Brechtian distancing, whereby the audience can react critically and objectively to the play and formulate a politically correct response to it, and projects an image of homosexual men as pariahs, outcasts from a world whose ideology is so well perpetuated in literary and dramatic realism [142].

But Kramer does not abandon realism. The script is quite realistic, and in the Public's production the acting and direction are all in the realistic tradition. The only non-realistic aspect of the production is the writing on the walls, and this single element is not enough to separate the characters "from a recognizable landscape." While the numbers may produce an alienating effect, it is also possible to be absorbed by the realist acting of a realist text on the minimalist but ultimately realism-based set. Watching this production, a spectator would move back and forth between alienation and absorption.

This paper argues for a particular definition of Brechtian "alienation" based on the writings of Min Tian, Viktor Shklovsky, Craig Kinzer and Mary Poole. Alienation, here, does not mean that when a spectator experienced "alienation" he or she was somehow emotionally disengaged from the production. Instead, this essay follows Shklovsky who argues that "art exists to help us recover the sensation of life" (qtd in Scholes 48). The idea, then, is not that alienation distances spectators from the production, but that it awakens senses dulled from habit. This essay also asserts, following Kinzer and

Poole, that "alienation" can actually *increase* emotional engagement between spectators and actors. As Kinzer and Poole write, "the experience of actors and spectators implies that the key to Brecht's notion of alienation can be viewed less a question of *increasing* the distance between actor and character as *decreasing* the distance between actor and audience" (82). The decrease in distance between actor and audience is accomplished through reminding the audience of the reality of life outside the reality of the play. There were moments in *The Normal Heart* that made the spectators aware of the contemporaneous events that made up the AIDS crisis. This awareness allowed them to become a community mourning the dead and ill — and performing that mourning — alongside the artists who were performing the same ritual of mourning.

The Normal Heart is set in 1983, two years before its first performance date. That slight difference in time collided fictional time and non-fictional time: "when Joel Grey [the actor playing Ned Weeks] shouted something about there already being 40 deaths in New York City alone, all eyes cut to the number '4280' hanging over center stage. And shuddered" (Fettner 40). The spectators not only had the number "4280" to turn their eyes to, they also had each other; because they were seated in two sections across from each other, spectators were able to watch each other's reactions (Feingold 105). This review reports spectators being psychologically absorbed by the events onstage, then becoming aware of the performance and their present situation (watching theatre).

J. Robert Cox argues that this type of alienation, which becomes a co-performance both by actors and spectators, can produce "remembrance and a refusal of silence" and in the process "re-position 'audience' as this larger community of memory/speech" (386). In the moment where fictional time and non-fictional time collided, a community was formed, not only among spectators, but also with the actors, and the production became a ritual that was about remembering the dead and refusing to be silent about how to save the living. This was, as Joseph Roach puts it, one of those times when a production made "publicly visible through symbolic action both the tangible existence of social boundaries and, at the same time, the contingency of those boundaries, their constructedness, their anxiety-inducing instability" (378). This production showed the horrible consequences of "social boundaries" that allowed a disease to run amok because it at first mainly affected gay men; but the production also showed the "contingency" of those boundaries, and the production and the literature in racks outside the theatre showed how to help change those boundaries and how to help save lives. In this sense, much like the Missouri State production of *The Normal Heart* that Cox and Roach discuss, the Public Theater production challenged the audience's notion of community. By publicly mourning the dead, spectators and performers alike imagined the boundaries of a community that included themselves. As this community was performing mourning, it re-imagined its boundaries outside the theatre to include those who were dead or ill because of AIDS. This re-imagining (caused by alienation) combined with the opportunities to get involved described in the lobby made it possible for *The Normal Heart* to inspire action among its audience members.

If this seems too hypothetical, examine the eyewitness account of the Public's literary manager, Bill Hart: "There was something about this ritual going on downtown night after night after night in the theater. There was a kind of testifying going on, a kind of witnessing" (Papp 266). This "testifying and witnessing" were possible because of the production's juxtaposition of a topical, realistic script and performance style with a set made from contemporaneous facts and figures. This juxtaposition created moments of alienation that allowed the audience to band together as a community, to mourn, and, if so moved, to become activists themselves. The production, the information in the lobby, and the reviews all "hailed" spectators and readers as people who cared about the AIDS crisis and wanted to do something about it. Though this emergent ideology had been expressed in the alternative, "gay theatre" (Paller 238; Román xx, 64), when it was presented by *The Normal Heart* in a mainstream theatre setting, it was amplified by the national media. This amplification helped integrate the emergent ideology that AIDS was a crisis in need of attention into the dominant ideology. Though *The Normal Heart*'s pleas for reconciliation with the straight community seemed inappropriate to some in both the straight and gay communities (Clum "Kramer" 209; Syna 6B), these sentiments were outweighed by articles like Mel Gussow's that reported that the production "could drive anyone with a normal heart to abandon what Mr. Kramer calls the 'million excuses for not getting involved'" and help stem the AIDS epidemic (C17). This representative reporting came in the widely read *New York Times*, and, combined with the analysis of the production itself, this essay reveals how the Public Theater's *The Normal Heart* was a mainstream theatrical production that helped incorporate an emergent ideology into the dominant one.*

Bibliography

"Audience Involvement at Public Production." New York Public Library Archive: Lincoln Center, 1985.

*Dan Smith and Meghann Pytka provided extremely valuable comments on this essay; much credit for whatever insights it offers must go to them.

Barnes, Clive. "Plague, Play and Tract." *New York Post*, May 4, 1985.
Beaufort, John. "Review: *The Normal Heart*." *The Christian Science Monitor*, April 29, 1985.
Bennett, Susan. *Theatre Audiences: A Theory of Production and Reception*. 2nd ed. New York: Routledge, 1997.
Bergman, David. "Larry Kramer and the Rhetoric of AIDS." In *AIDS: The Literary Response*, edited by Emmanuel S. Nelson, 175–86. New York: Twayne Publishers, 1992.
Bull, John. "The Establishment of Mainstream Theatre, 1946–1979." In *Cambridge History of British Theatre*, 326–48. Cambridge: Cambridge Univ. Press, 2004.
Callen, Michael. *Surviving AIDS*. New York: Harper Collins, 1990.
Carey, James W. *Communication as Culture: Essays on Media and Society*. Boston: Unwin Hyman, 1989.
Carlson, Marvin. *Theatre Semiotics: Signs of Life*. Bloomington: Indiana Univ. Press, 1990.
Clum, John M. "Kramer vs. Kramer, Ben and Alexander: Larry Kramer's Voices and His Audiences." In *We Must Love One Another or Die: The Life and Legacies of Larry Kramer*, edited by Lawrence Mass, 200–214. London: Cassell, 1997.
———. *Still Acting Gay: Male Homosexuality in Modern Drama*. New York: St. Martin's Griffin, 1992.
Cox, J. Robert. "Performing Memory/Speech: Aesthetic Boundaries and 'The Other' in *Ghetto* and *The Normal Heart*." *Text and Performance Quarterly* 12.4 (1992): 385–90.
de Jongh, Nicholas. *Not in Front of the Audience: Homosexuality on Stage*. London and New York: Routledge, 1992.
Feingold, Michael. "Part of the Solution." *Village Voice*, April 30, 1985.
Fettner, Ann Giudici. "Heart Minus Snarl." *New York Native*, October 21–27, 1985.
Gay Men's Health Crisis. "Homepage," 2005. Last accessed 10 July 2005. http://www.gmhc.org.
Goodman, Lizbeth. *Contemporary Feminist Theatres: To Each Her Own*. New York: Routledge, 1993.
Gross, Gregory D. "Coming Up for Air: Three AIDS Plays." *Journal of American Culture* 15 (1992): 63–67.
Gussow, Mel. "Confronting a Crisis with Incendiery Passion." *New York Times*, April 28, 1985.
Henry III, William A. "A Common Bond of Suffering: Shows about AIDS Make Good Drama as Well as Propaganda." *Time*, May 13, 1985.
Humm. "Review: *The Normal Heart*." *Variety*, May 15, 1985.
Kershaw, Baz. *The Radical in Performance: Between Brecht and Baudrillard*. London: Routledge, 1999. Kinzer, Craig, and Mary Poole. "Brecht and the Actor." *Communications from the International Brecht Society* 20.1,2 (1991): 79–84.
Kissel, Howard. "Untitled." *Women's Wear Daily*, May 15, 1985.
Knowles, Ric. *Reading the Material Theatre*. London: Cambridge Univ. Press, 2004.
Kramer, Larry. *The Normal Heart and the Destiny of Me*. New York: Grove Press, 2000.
Kroll, Jack. "Going to the Heart of AIDS." *Newsweek*, May 13, 1985.
Kushner, Tony. "Foreword." In *Two Plays: The Normal Heart and the Destiny of Me*, vii–xxv. New York: Grove Press, 2000.
Lawson, D. S. "Rage and Remembrance: The AIDS Plays." In *AIDS: The Literary Response*, edited by Emmanuel S. Nelson, 140–54. New York: Twayne Publishers, 1992.

Manishchewitz, Leora. "'Normal Heart' Takes an Unsparing Look at AIDS." *Villager*, April 25, 1985.
Massa, Robert. "T-Cells and Sympathy: Making Theatre out of AIDS." *The Village Voice*, April 23, 1985.
Nelson, Emmanuel S. "Introduction." In *AIDS: The Literary Response*, edited by Emmanuel S. Nelson, 1–10. New York: Twayne Publishers, 1992.
Paller, Michael. "Larry Kramer and Gay Theater." In *We Must Love One Another or Die: The Life and Legacies of Larry Kramer*, edited by Lawrence Mass, 235–55. London: Cassell, 1997.
Papp, Gail Merrifield, "Larry Kramer and the Public Theatre." *We Must Love One Another or Die: The Life and Legacies of Larry Kramer*, edited by Lawrence Mass, 256–70. London: Cassell, 1997.
Public Theatre. "Post-Opening *Normal Heart* Advertisement." *New York Times*, 1985.
———. "Pre-Opening *Normal Heart* Advertisement." *New York Times*, 1985.
Rich, Frank. "Theatre: '*The Normal Heart*,' by Larry Kramer." *New York Times*, April 23, 1985.
Roach, Joseph. "Normal Heartlands." *Text and Performance Quarterly* 12 (1992): 377–84.
Román, David. *Acts of Intervention: Performance, Gay Culture, and AIDS*. Bloomington: Indiana Univ. Press, 1998.
Scholes, Robert E. *Semiotics and Interpretation*. New Haven: Yale Univ. Press, 1982.
Shatzky, Joel. "AIDS Enters the American Theatre: *As Is* and *The Normal Heart*." In *AIDS: The Literary Response*, edited by Emmanuel S. Nelson, 131–39. New York: Twayne Publishers, 1992.
Shilts, Randy. *And the Band Played On: Politics, People, and the AIDS Epidemic*. New York: St. Martin's Press, 1987.
Simon, John. "Untitled." *New York*, May 15, 1985.
Smith, Liz. "Untitled." *Daily News*, May 1, 1985.
Sommers, Michael. "Casualties." *New York Native*, May 20, 1985.
Syna, Sy. "'The Normal Heart' Offensive and Boring." *New York City Tribune*, April 22, 1985.
Wallach, Allan. "Drama of Official Apathy towards AIDS." *Newsday*, April 22, 1985.
Watt, Douglas. "The Tragedy of AIDS." *Daily News*, April 22, 1985.

"Not Just Any Woman"
Bradford Louryk, a Legacy of Charles Ludlam and the Ridiculous Theatre for the Twenty-First Century

SEAN F. EDGECOMB

"I must say that clothes are simply a side issue—one isn't born to wear clothes, actually. Ah, clothes are a habit that one accumulates."
—Christine Jorgensen

Introduction

Bradford Louryk, actor and self-professed "creator," extends the legacy of the Ridiculous Theatre by reinventing the genre for the twenty-first century. This essay examines how Louryk reimagines the Ridiculous by fusing and subverting the classical theatrical traditions and the pop-cultural pastiche of Charles Ludlam's (1943–1987) Ridiculous Theatrical Company (RTC) with his own creative vision. Additionally, Louryk draws inspiration from "Ethyl" James Eichelberger (1945–1990), the late Ridiculous performer who left Ludlam's troupe and reclaimed the genre in order to appropriate it into his own unique style of solo performance. (Eichelberger also authored and performed in group theatre pieces, though his solo performances are the most characteristic of his unique style of performance.)

Between 1967 and 1987, Ludlam rebelliously changed theatre in America for the next generation. As the founder of the RTC and the author of twenty-nine raucous and highly entertaining plays, Ludlam quite literally became the "belle of the ball" of the West Village counter-cultural theatre scene. (One of Ludlam's most entertaining and critically acclaimed roles was that of Marguerite Gautier, derived from Dumas fils' *La Dame aux Camélias*, which Ludlam metamorphosed into his *Camille* 1973.) Ludlam revealed his personal philosophy and purpose for the Ridiculous in his manifesto: *Ridiculous Theatre, Scourge of Human Folly*,

> This farce is not a Sunday school. Illustrate hedonistic calculus. Test out a dangerous idea, a theme that threatens to destroy one's whole value system. Treat

the material in a mildly farcical manner without losing the seriousness of the theme. Show how paradoxes arrest the mind. Scare yourself a bit along the way [Ludlam].

While Ludlam's description of the Ridiculous may initially invoke the avant-garde creeds of Jarry, Tzara, or Artaud, it succinctly reflects how Ludlam reacted against the corrupt politics and civic inequalities of his time by acting as a mouthpiece for those on the fringes of mainstream society in mid–twentieth century America, using sarcasm, wit, and humor. Theatre critic Gerald Rabkin spoke to this, suggesting,

> Ridiculous theatre, reacting against both the naturalism that has dominated mainstream American theatre for half a century, and the metaphysical abstraction of Absurdism and its heirs, responded to images and imperatives closer to home: a world on the brink of sanity and survival, of speed-freaks, drag queens, and would-be super stars, a parochial world which nonetheless spoke metaphorically to the perilous state of the human condition in the mid twentieth century [Rabkin 41].

In the *New York Times* Ludlam related a simpler intention for his chosen theatre genre, stating, "All I'm doing here is working with a comic tradition using character types that have been around for centuries. I'm just trying to make them live again in a way that's funny and thought-provoking" (Shirawaka H3). In part, this mission is drawn from Aristophanic farce, which had comparably ridiculed the dysfunction of democratic society in ancient Athens. The uniqueness of Ludlam's Ridiculous is in its approach to the political: rather than calling for reform through protest, it instead reflects and satirizes contemporary life through a lens of queer identity, anti-hegemonic possibility, and the embrace of farce, danger, and the imagination.

Because Ludlam was responding to the current events of his time, he drew from and ridiculed the world around him. Of his Ridiculous Theatre, Ludlam insisted, "I am of my time, of the perfect moment" (Samuels 221). Louryk fulfills Ludlam's Ridiculous objective by consciously reacting against key points of Ludlam's manifesto in an effort to maintain a genre that reflects and comments on shifts in contemporary social mores, rather than a museum recreation of the work originated by Ludlam, which took a stance to support homosexuality as a valid lifestyle choice. Ludlam commented,

> My work is very much for people who might not approve of the gayness. I take them over bumps, make them draw certain conclusions about sexism through parody, hold seism up to ridicule. The same techniques that other playwrights use to maneuver their audience into a sexist position can also be used to make them accept something they wouldn't ordinarily accept. In a sense, I think I have a big influence on there being such a thing as gay theatre [Samuels 229].

In a 2006 interview, Louryk referred to Ludlam's mission, stating, "How do you honor someone who is so subversive ... you subvert!" (Edgecomb, Louryk). Whereas Ludlam's camp-infused text and performance style was intended to speak primarily to a gay audience toward social acceptance and community building through coded language, double entendre, and repossessed glamour drag, Louryk simplifies and de-glamorizes drag in an effort to deliver a visceral existentialist experience to a broader "theatre-going" audience, commenting on his disenchantment with the current state of the American theatre and conservative political climate. Kenneth Yates Elliot offers an excellent definition of the Ridiculous Theatre in context to this purpose,

> [The Ridiculous] expos[ed] the ridiculousness of dominant culture. It often did so by parodying high/and or low literary and theatrical forms of the past, especially pop culture. It was a non-illusionistic, self-conscious performance style marked by camp, cheap theatrics, the grotesque, sexual ambiguity and drag performances. Its founders were gay men, and the theatre they created was a direct assault on the mainstream values of the time [Elliot vii–viii].

Although Louryk often plays women in his work, his interpretation of drag is not uniquely dependent on female impersonation [as is more traditional cabaret drag performance]. Louryk's use of drag is closer to Esther Newton's description in her essay "Mother Camp: Female Impersonators in America." Judith Butler reiterates this in her essay "Imitation and Gender Insubordination," writing: "Drag is not an imitation or copy of some prior and true gender; according to Newton, drag enacts the very structure of impersonation by which *any gender* is assumed. Drag is not the outing on of a gender that belongs to some other group, i.e. an act of expropriation or appropriation that assumes gender is the rightful property of sex.... Drag constitutes the mundane way in which genders are appropriated, theatricalized, worn and done; it implies that all gendering is a kind of impersonation and approximation" [Butler 127]. Charles Ludlam wrote, "The Ridiculous is really about rugged individualism. It didn't come out of any communal, left-wing, sentimental, folksy thing" [Samuels 14]. I introduce and define the concept of visceral existentialism in theatre as: a ruggedly individual didactic style that draws from and subverts preexisting Ridiculous conventions and addresses the audience directly. This is in an effort to reassign historical text and context without attempting to invoke radical activism or enlightenment; instead, it attempts to incite an inner dialogue and intellectual narrative with and of the isolated self, promoting communities where individuals maintain their individuality and uniqueness. Louryk achieves this objective in performance using a combination of sound manipulation and enhancement, precision of gesture, complex linguistics, and timing, to create what he refers to as *moments of beauty*. These *moments of beauty* are developed through Louryk's dedication to precision and authenticity in the use of prerecorded sound and the embrace of imperfections on original recordings. This is in an effort to make incarnate environmental sounds, by drawing attention and reassigning imperfections rather than masking them or rendering them inaudible. Of this convention Louryk remarks, "That moment of a sound and the perfection of the moment is in the gesture and the timing and every facet of the execution ... it represents every ideal that I have" (Edgecomb, Louryk). Specific examples of these *moments* shall be examined in the second part of this essay.

I. In Practice

Louryk first became acquainted with the work of Ludlam in high school when his drama director gave him a copy of the anthology, *The Complete Works of Charles Ludlam,* which he professes to have devoured from cover to cover. It was in reading the collection of Ludlam's plays that Louryk garnered an "an appreciation for more traditional theatre" (Edgecomb, Louryk), motivated by Ludlam's tendency unapologetically to collage great literature and high culture with pop-cultural pastiche. After high school Louryk entered the Experimental Theatre program at Vassar in Poughkeepsie, New York. Inspired by the work of one time Vassar professor Hallie Flanagan (who headed the Federal Theatre Project during the Great Depression), the mission of the program is to use the stage as a laboratory, where new ideas can be tested and theories examined through performative experimentation. Gabrielle Cody, Vassar professor of drama and Louryk's undergraduate advisor, describes the pedagogical purpose of the program to "produce [theatre] primarily in order to experiment with a text or genre." She continues, "we are not interested in putting together a season of dutifully canonical plays. We also encourage our students to create their own work beyond simply participating in productions as actor, designer, director, or dramaturge. And some of the most exciting theatre has come out of student-generated works" (Cody). It was the exploratory and vanguard nature of this environment that allowed Louryk to flourish and develop a post–Ludlam Ridiculous style that would come to define his work and eventually become "visceral existentialism." In his freshman year, Louryk directed and acted in an abridged version of Ludlam's epic classic *The Grand Tarot.* Through the process of this initial flirtation with the Ridiculous genre in performance, Louryk forged a professional friendship with fellow Vassar student and budding playwright Rob Grace. Louryk was immediately drawn to Grace's "oddball perspective and wicked sense of humor" (Edgecomb, Louryk), promulgating an artistic relationship in which Louryk "is the devisor of projects" and Grace serves as "playwright—a 'helmsman' of creative projects" (Edgecomb, Grace). The working dynamic behind this partnership brings to mind Ludlam's insistence that "I think of myself as an inventor of plays. The wright as in playwright is worker, maker: one who works in wood such as a shipwright. My plays are wrought as much as written. I work in the theatre as well as the study" (Samuels 3). This approach, which merges the collection of data (in this case a collection of preexisting literature and cultural references) to forge experimentation with the precision and trained skill of craftsmanship, is definitive of the same approach that Louryk and Grace used to collaborate a decade after Ludlam's death. The process began when the two undergraduates began composing "violent and humorous and smart" (Edgecomb, Louryk) plays, and then formed a performance group to give readings. These early works prompted Louryk to introduce Grace to Ludlam's epic style, as Louryk recollects:

> I knew that Rob had a great deal of talent and I knew that sometimes his scope was limited. My perspective was always maximal and epic—like Ludlam's plays. I'm not sure which came first, I've always had a tendency in me to like things that are epic, or if that was informed by Ludlam, I'd have to project backward. I remember having a conversation with somebody on a train coming back from New York and talking about how Rob "needs to stop thinking so small." Trying to get him to create character and situations that are much larger.... I always find that he is most successful, interesting, and truest to himself when his plays are enormous and oddball [Edgecomb, Louryk].

Louryk's influence via Ludlam/Eichelberger within his collaborative partnership with Grace resulted in their first Ridiculous play, *The Tragedy of Hamlet, Prince of Denmark* at Vassar in 1999. The text episodically intersects thirty bizarre characters who are searching for contentment in circumstances that range from priestly molestation and alien invasion to the Judeo-Christian God's secret desire to become a funk singer. The overarching story line involves a family of siblings named after characters from Shakespeare's *Hamlet*; Laertes (played by Louryk in the original production) seeks to lure unsuspecting audience members into his pornographic theatre by titling the unrelated plays after great works of the western canon, hence the title of the play: *The Tragedy of Hamlet, Prince of Denmark*. Louryk's Laertes as theatre producer cum pornographer epitomizes a Ridiculous sensibility drawn from Ludlam's chosen conventions as driven by Louryk's skill and personal taste. For example, in scene IV of the play, Laertes speaks the following monologue that reveals his opinion on the current state of the theatre:

> LAERTES: About ten years ago I was at this production of *Ivanov*. It was very decadent. Very naturalistic and—Well, I was a starving artist at the time, before

I really made it, and seeing this play was a very big deal for me. Imagine the most colorful, imaginative, brilliantly crafted version of *Ivanov* you can possibly imagine. That was what I was watching that night. Chekhov himself rose from the grave to see this production. That's how good it was. The acting was phenomenal. Lebedev, especially — Brilliant. Best performance of that character I've seen to this date. The costumes and set had this emerald green motif — They had these curtains — It was beyond words. And I'm sitting there, completely taken in by the performance and the perfection of it all, and I'm intensely bored. Understand, you couldn't ask for a more talented group of actors and designers. And I'm sitting there completely bored. And boredom can fester and well up inside of you to the point where you just want to stand up and scream or jump up on stage and start beating one of the actors with your shoes. Take Sasha. She was beautiful. That young actress, whoever it was, had this intense presence and charisma. Genuine pure raw talent. And I had to get out of there. My head was about to burst. My mind was pounding at the inside of my skull. My heart rate tripled. I started looking around the rest of the audience frantically, hoping to see someone else that felt the same way. But they were just staring blankly at the stage. They laughed at all the jokes. Clapped at all the scene changes. I put my hands together and prayed to God. And I don't believe in God. "Do something," I told him. "Save me." I looked up, practically on the verge of tears, and I noticed a man three seats down from me sitting there with his penis in his hands, masturbating. Everything in my mind froze. I stared at him. He just kept going and going. All the way through Act I, all the way through Act II. Intermission, he zips up, grabs a bag of Sun Chips, the lights go back down, he unzips and keeps going. Understand, this production was at least two and a half hours long. At least. Then finally, it's the finale. Ivanov is raising the gun to his head, about to commit suicide, and right as he pulls the trigger, the man reaches orgasm. It was literally the climax of the play. It was beautiful. And that's when this revelation hit me. What do people want? When they wake up in the morning. When they're doing their dishes, when they're paying their taxes, what do they really want? Sex. Sex. Let's face it, theater can't compete with television and film anymore. The intimacy of the close-ups, the special effects, the music. At this point in time, the only thing theater can provide that no other medium can is live sex. And that's what people want. They want to see live sex, happening right in front of them, and they want to see it in a socially acceptable fashion. As I was staring at this man, in complete awe, my duty as a writer, a director became clear. To create pornographic theater. I ran home after the show and that very evening I penned my first work, *Rozencranz* [sic] *and Guildenstern Give Head*. At first, of course, nobody understood. People incessantly asked me, how can live sex have dramatic merit. Sex is drama. Drama is sex. They are one and the same. What about that moment when the male reaches orgasm, the woman has not, but the man is too tired and falls asleep? Finally, a medium that can explore moments like these. How the little things get in the way. One of the themes of my play *Clítoris, Clitóris*. Jenkinson here starred in *Pleasure for Pleasure*, my first iambic pentameter work. Since then, he's worked with me on almost every single one of my projects.

This section of text is an example of Louryk and Grace's first original work that is informed by a Ridiculous sensibility, and the closest to Ludlam's, prior to Louryk and Grace's subversion from the Ludlamesque toward their own aesthetic. Nods to Ludlam include the use of high cultural forms (references to Chekhovian plays and characterizations, which also may be read as an homage to one of Ludlam's earliest dada-type plays titled *Southern Fried Chekhov*), puns and double entendre (*Rosencrantz and Guildenstern Give Head*), and the discussion of pornography on the stage — which the conservative press had often accused the RTC of exhibiting due to the use of nudity and seemingly erotic situations in their plays. Ludlam was tolerant toward pornography as a performative medium because; like his work, it was "held in low esteem" (Dasgupta 82), but he also firmly denied that his theatre was pornographic in form or intent. He explicated this opinion in *Confessions of a Farceur* when he wrote, "Pornography is the highest development of naturalism. It was the seriousness of pornography that [the RTC troupe members] were never into. It is not in depicting the sexual act that one becomes a pornographer; it is in demanding to be taken seriously" (Samuels 19). Louryk and Grace also borrowed from this concept — the first scene of *Hamlet* has a priest being fellated onstage from a prepubescent boy named Timothy. This situation is presented as tongue-in-check satire (Timothy is bound by a chain that he drags around the stage with him throughout the play, only to discover that the other end is attached to a young girl who faces the same sticky situation with her own rabbi at the play's conclusion), which is intended to incite humor and stimulate social commentary, not to arouse the audience sexually. This is also a prime example of the "ridiculing" of social occurrences and the resultant discourse (such as the sex scandals that have recently plagued the Roman Catholic Church) within a world that promotes heteronormative morality, and arguably from whence the Ridiculous derived its name.

It was the collaborative process and success of *Hamlet* that led Louryk and Grace to continue their relationship to create Louryk's senior thesis project, which would become the initial version of *Klytaemnestra's Unmentionables* in 2000. This was the first self-devised piece textually constructed with Grace in which Louryk would play all the characters in an evening of solo performance. The origin of this project stemmed from Eichelberger, who stated in *Extreme Exposure: An Anthology of Solo Performance Texts from the Twentieth Century*, "I wanted to play the great roles but who would cast me as Medea?" (Jeffreys, *Extreme Exposure* 72). Louryk responds, "I identified with Eichelberger.... I knew that my thesis would be in drag, but I didn't feel that at that point I could sustain a single character for any lengthy piece" (Edgecomb, Louryk). Eichelberger, a classically trained actor like Ludlam, developed his unique and personal Ridiculous sensibility when he migrated from the RTC in the West Village to the bohemian world of the Lower Eastside in the early 1980s. In turn he became a seminal figure in the post–Stonewall queer theatre movement until he committed suicide in 1990, unable to tolerate the harsh side-effects of the prescribed AIDS medication. This is yet another startling and tragic similarity between Eichelberger and Ludlam, who had died three years earlier from complications due to AIDS-related pneumonia.

Thus, in the Ludlam-Eichelberger tradition, Louryk set out to take on, if not extend, Eichelberger's challenge by portraying several infamous women derived from Greek tragedy in an evening of gender-bending performance. The concept of transforming mythic characters and epic themes was derived from Vassar's 1999–2000 theatrical season, which was dedicated to presenting extant Greek plays, adaptations of Greek plays, and original works inspired by Greek themes. Though the project's theme was conceived by the Theatre Department, the concept was inspired by Louryk's intensive study of art history. The image of Jacques-Louis David's famous painting "Marat Assassinated" (1793) inspired the central element of the set design as well as the climax of the play. The painting depicts the stabbed pallid corpse of the Jacobin revolutionary Jean-Paul Marat submerged in an eighteenth-century bathtub. Drawing upon this, Louryk conceived that all action of the play would take place around a Victorian claw-foot bathtub elevated on a central dais that was filled manually during textual scene transitions. The tub would become a central metaphor and the "site of Klytaemnestra's killing of Agamemnon, Electra's enforced washing of the family's dirty laundry, Medea's infanticide" (Foley 97), culminating at the climax when Louryk-as-Phaedra drowns herself in the now overflowing tub. Furthermore, this convention mirrors Eichelberger's 1990 suicide, in which he slit his wrists in a bathtub, theatrically mimicking the David "Marat" while literally expelling the HIV from his body through the release of his infected blood. Joe E. Jeffreys, the leading Eichelberger scholar, suggests that Eichelberger's AIDS-related suicide may be read as "a call to arms and icon for a revolution," just as David's painting served as a propagandistic device in which "the blood of the martyr is the seed of revolution" (Jeffreys, *An Outre Entrée*).

With these images serving as the inspirational framework, Louryk approached Grace with his ideas for a script. First, Louryk selected the women that he would portray — a diverse group reflecting various ages, types, and personas as filtered through contemporary archetypes of femininity. Foley thoroughly yet succinctly lists the antecedent performances that informed Louryk's selections:

Louryk's portrait of a Klytaemnestra paralysed by fear of retribution was influenced by Greek tragedy, Charles Mee's 1994 *Agamemnon*, and Jean-Paul Sartre's *Les Mouches* [1943] (as Louryk put it in interview, Klytaemnestra's "dead-white look" is borrowed from Sartre's guilt-ridden heroine with her deathly white make-up); his Electra by Aeschylus, Sophocles, and Euripides, *Les Mouches*, and Eichelberger; his Medea by Ludlam, Heiner Müller, Cherubini's Opera *Medea* [1797] as performed by Maria Callas [1953], and the story of Andrea Yates, the troubled Houston housewife who drowned her five children in 2001; his Phaedra by Euripides, Racine, Eichelberger, and Sarah Kane's *Phaedra's Love* [1996].

Additionally, Louryk created the original character of the Fury in order to present a performance drawn specifically from his own set of skills. Foley's research corroborates Louryk's use of Ludlam's original Ridiculous formula in play-making: combining a variety of literary and cultural references as well as current events in a collage that both embraces and rejects influences in order to create new characters that relate to contemporary contexts and issues, (i.e., presenting Medea in the guise of a modern-day Yates).

While Grace's text (divided into sections dedicated to each character) draws from these influences, the text proved problematic for it was a series of disconnected interrelated monologues, lacking a trajectory that brought together the characters and themes. This was remedied through a direct homage to Ludlam and Eichelberger, drawing from their preexisting texts and in turn inserting them as transitions between the episodes of the performance. These transitions took the form of voice-over film footage of Louryk that played as he changed into the costume and makeup of each character at a dressing table before circling the stage to pour water into the bathtub. The transitional text, which presented Louryk discussing his cross-dressing performance, was divided into six sections. The initial projected section opened the play with Louryk mimicking Eichelberger and, after defining his purpose (drawn from Ludlam/Eichelberger), sought to answer the question:

> LOURYK: The characters I play tend to be women who are misunderstood. And given enough distance in time, I can distort who they were for my own "nefarious" ends.
>
> It's all a matter of whom you want to emulate. Whom you play affects your life, so I decided to play the most beautiful, eminent women I could find.
>
> I wanted to play the great roles, but who would cast me as Medea? Who would cast me as Phaedra?

In setting up the performance with his prerecorded naturally masculine voice, deportment and aesthetic, and in reinterpreting celebrated Ludlam/Eichelberger quotations, Louryk makes clear his pursuit of the Ridiculous tradition and sensibility in a performance that, as Ludlam stated of his Camille, "is simultaneously both terribly funny and terribly moving, both ethereally beautiful and grotesque, both real and artificial, both a man and a woman in a dress" (Roemer 101). Louryk completes the introductory monologue with:

> LOURYK: To Frantz [sic] Salieri, transvestitism was a spectacular act with no sexual or erotic meaning. To one interviewer, he explained that he found boys were the most prodigious actors, and when they played women, there was "a double phenomenon of distance between the character and his interpretation."
> I have to convince myself that I am beautiful before I go on. If I believe it.... Belief is the secret to reality.
> I know it's acting. I never think I'm a woman. I am not trying to kid anyone into thinking I am a woman. I am trying to wrench something artistic from the experience.

With Louryk's mission as an actor and artist firmly defined, the play continues with Klytaemnestra's monologue before the second transition that defines the marginal social position of the drag artist-as-performer in American society:

> LOURYK: When his dream of the part calls for playing the opposite sex, the actor must reconcile his sense of truth with his sense of the theatrical. Drag embodies the paradox of acting.
> People are disturbed by female impersonation. They don't realize or understand its inner motive. They see something that is humorous. They don't understand what it means to play a woman. To defiantly do that and say women are worthwhile creatures, and to put my whole soul and being into creating this woman and to give her everything I have, including my emotions (remembering that the greatest taboo is to experience feminine emotions), and to take myself seriously in the face of ridicule was the highest statement. It allows audiences to experience the universality of emotion, rather to believe that women are one species and men another, and that what one feels, the other never does.

Here, Louryk comments on the origin of the Ridiculous sensibility. In taking himself seriously "in the face of ridicule" he stresses the function of the Ridiculous theatre to reflect and mimic hetero-normative and moralistic social judgments, while also subtly invoking the bigotry and intolerance that Ludlam and Eichelberger faced and in turn challenged in their own time for being openly gay. The other transitions that separate the monologues borrowed directly from Ludlam and Eichelberger's essays and performance texts, including Ludlam's essay "Costume Fetishism or Clothes Make the Man," which defines his list of characteristic costume tenets essential to presenting oneself as "butch" or "drag." Louryk's interpretation of Ludlam's list declares:

> LOURYK: Be artificial. Wear as much underwear as possible. Foundation garments, garters and shoes should be tight enough that you are always conscious of them. Suggest a captive in some aspect of your dress. If you are wearing them,

see to it that your heels are too high to walk or run comfortably. Take on yourself the burdens of your womanhood, the seven dolors of the Blessed Virgin Mary. The transvestite "berdache" of the Apache Indians cut themselves on the inside of the thigh and let the blood run down their legs once a month....

Finally, after the Fury's, Medea's, and Phaedra's monologues (interspersed with more Ludlam/Eichelberger-generated wisdom in the transitions), the play closes with a direct homage to Eichelbergerian performance, as a lingerie-clad soaked Louryk (just drowned by suicide as Phaedra) rises from the bathtub to lip-synch Eichelberger's trademark song *Women Who Survive*. The lyrics of the song, which were initially sung by a concertina-wielding Eichelberger at the conclusion of his solo performances of granddames such as *Jocasta, Medea, Nefertiti, Clytemnestra,* and the Obie-award-winning *Lucrezia Borgia*, deliver a survivalist message that speaks beyond gender in order to address any audience member who has fallen victim to discrimination or marginalization within the construct of American society. This final scene, which relies on his self-styled impersonation of Eichelberger, is unique only to *Klytaemnestra*; Louryk avoids such direct impersonations in his more recent work, because he reflects that it held "too much hubris" (Edgecomb, Louryk). Nonetheless, this conclusion becomes the "moment of beauty" in the production. By fusing Eichelberger's song with his own prerecorded voice, for the first time in the performance, Louryk is de-dragged and revealed in person, as he has to this point appeared as himself only in the media-generated transitions. With the layered makeup of the six characters streaking his face, he emerges in a "Botticelliesque" fashion, rising from the water in the claw-foot tub as an actor stripped to a bare minimum: without his voice and only remnants of a now transparent costume, he appears as both himself and the personification of the "other" in one, blending gender lines and aesthetics in an almost shamanistic fashion. Additionally, he serves to represent a rebirth of the Ridiculous spirit, embodying Ludlam's and Eichelberger's texts to cheat death emblematically and return to the living in ritualistic honor of his prematurely deceased Ridiculous forefathers.

The original thesis production of *Klytaemnestra* performed at Vassar in 2000 was met with excitement from both the student body and faculty. Cody commented on this performance, "Louryk reconnected [the Experimental Theatre Program at Vassar] to the essence of what theatre is: a ghosting of truths. It demonstrated both to students and faculty how much bold virtuoso theatricality can accomplish, how much it can help deepen our understanding of theatre as an art form, and to remind us why we need theatre." She goes on to state,

> In many ways, Louryk is bringing back an old fashioned ethic of showmanship. He has a real belief in the power of theatricality, but he also has a postmodern

sensibility. I would call him a Brechtian-Feminist performance artist rather than a female impersonator. Louryk has a lot he wants to say and do through his ability to hear and speak voices that might otherwise remain inaudible in our culture. Louryk's desire and respect for the feminine in a culture that is deeply misogynist is an incredibly important intervention. He is not simply a brilliant performer, he also thinks in very nuanced ways about how we inhabit gender. He is creating work that is as useful as it is marvelous [Cody].

The eager reception, effectiveness, and popularity of *Klytaemnestra* led to its revival performance at New York City's HERE Arts Center running from December 1–17, 2001, centrally if not coincidentally located between the lower Manhattan neighborhoods where Ludlam and Eichelberger had performed twenty years before.

Having achieved success with their first Off Off Broadway production of *Klytaemnestra*, Louryk, with the textual assistance of Grace as playwright, set out to tackle the infamous Lucrezia Borgia, who had inspired a solo performance piece that garnered Eichelberger an Obie award in 1982. It was during the process of constructing a conceptual framework that would examine the conflicting accounts of the Italian Renaissance noblewoman that Louryk found unique inspiration. While browsing in the East Village's Footlight Records, Louryk stumbled upon a 1958 record of Christine Jorgensen. Jorgensen was the ex–Army GI (born George William Jorgensen) who was credited with receiving the first "sex-change" operation to become "Christine" as reported by the *New York Daily News* in 1952. (This claim was untrue. In 1931 pioneering German sex doctor Magnus Hirschfield had performed sexual reassignment surgery on the Danish artist Lili Elbe through his Institute of Sexual Science in Berlin. Jorgensen differed because her reassignment process included the prescription of artificial hormones.) Louryk bought the record because he thought that it might yield some material to be used in the third act of the new *Lucrezia Borgia* script, borrowing from the lipsynch conventions that he had developed for *Klytaemnestra*. Louryk was initially drawn to the cover, featuring a smartly dressed attractive blond woman surrounded by salacious questions such as "Is she a woman? Can she have children? What about her love life?" and finally, "The answers to all of these questions with the world's most sensational celebrity!" After taking the record home and listening to it repeatedly, Louryk "fell in love with the text of [the recording] and Christine. What I could hear clearly was some of the most exciting, stunning, articulate perspectives on identity, on personhood, on gender, on sexuality, on many topics that people have a hard time being articulate about today" (Wallenberg). The potential for theatre to be derived from the recording seemed manifest, and Louryk began to consider how best to approach the piece in a form that would stay true to Jorgensen's experience while also speaking with a contemporary nonmoralistic intention.

With the script of *Lucrezia Borgia* in its eleventh draft and in need of more attention, Louryk and Grace temporarily abandoned the project and separated briefly to work on several independent theatre projects dissociated with a Ridiculous Sensibility. It was then that Louryk realized the unique opportunity that the Jorgensen recording could offer. He was driven to create a piece of theatre from the original recording because, as he explained in a 2006 interview,

> As both an audience member and as a person who makes theatre, I often feel that [most plays] are not theatrical enough for me. I always want something to be as grand and as operatic in its scope and its scale as possible. I want to be blown away by whatever it is that I see onstage. I don't want to go to a play and see something that I could sit in my living room and get the same thing out of. This interview and [Jorgensen's] story just felt very theatrical [Wallenberg].

The passion behind this sentiment is inspired by Ludlam's maxim, "I hate minimal art. I hate conceptual art. I am for *execution*. I am for *maximal* art" (Samuels 221).

It was in the winter of 2004/2005 that Louryk and Grace reconnected to discuss their next collaborative work. They decided to temporarily shelf the *Lucrezia* script and concentrate instead on the recording of Christine's 1958 interview with comedian Nipsy Russell. (Though Russell was also a pioneer of sorts as a pre–civil rights African American actor, his race is not mentioned in *Christine Jorgensen Reveals*.) This would also provide the opportunity for Louryk and Grace to act together for the first time. (Louryk and Grace appeared briefly in a production of *First Year Born*, sharing only half a scene and exchanging one line of dialogue.) Though the two had known each other since 1996, they had been given little opportunity to appear on the stage jointly, as Grace had primarily served the role of playwright in the artistic partnership. It would also continue their pursuit of using lip-synch as their signature post–Ludlam Ridiculous theatrical device. The decision to use Jorgensen's original voice rather than his own stemmed from the desire to share "this sociological, historical document with other people" and because Louryk was charmed by Jorgensen's voice, "which is just so extraordinary" (Wallenberg). Louryk would appear in drag to interpret Christine and Grace would portray the role of the male interviewer, Russell. Due to the fact that Grace had relocated to Los Angeles to pursue another career path, it was determined that in order to remedy his absence, he would be filmed to appear as Russell on a period television set, lending another layer to the performative detachment and then repossession of voice and sound. Because the performance was dependent on the original recording, the first step was to have the record digitally remastered and enhanced. In the meantime, Grace attempted to edit and rework the recording in an effort to create a more theatrical structure with an engaging arc, but in the end only two words were lost. Because the recording was nearly fifty years old, even in its restored state, one section was marked by a series of scratches that could not be erased. It was the decision to embrace this imperfection that led to the most poignant "moment of beauty" in the performance. Louryk originated the idea to reclaim and even highlight the scratching sounds when Jorgensen loses composure as Russell grills her with the question,

> MR. RUSSELL: Christine — do you think the time will ever come when your complete past, or at least this episode in your life, will disappear? When people will think of you as Christine Jorgensen — photographer, or Christine Jorgensen — actress, or whatever your pursuits might be at that time? And not as Christine Jorgensen, woman-formerly-man?

Clearly straining to stay composed, Christine responds with dignity,

> CHRISTINE: No, Mr. Russell, I don't think the time will ever really come when the past — as you say — Christine Jorgensen, formerly a man, will ever be forgotten, should any event come up in my life such as my marriage, or, even, my death, the newspapers would have a Roman holiday and rehash the whole past, but the strange part of it is, is that the people who know me — know me a very short time, and they forget about the past.

It is in the midst of this tense exchange that the record is marked by the aforementioned scratches. In an effort to stay true to the emotion and intention in this brief dialogical exchange, Louryk as Jorgensen brushes her taffeta skirt, so that the scratches become a nervous physical manifestation, in reaction to Russell's condescending query. This technique behind "the moment of beauty" borrows from Brecht's *gestus*, which is dependent on the "subtle use of rhythm pause, parallelism, and counterpointing" in order to express "basic human attitudes — not merely 'gesture' but all signs of social relations; deportment, intonation, facial expression" (*http://www.universalteacher*). It is this gestic moment of beauty that Louryk says "represents every ideal that I have" (Edgecomb, Louryk).

With the recording and text prepared, Louryk contacted producers in New York and London who were immediately interested in staging the new play, which was titled *Christine Jorgensen Reveals*. The original production, directed by Josh Hecht, opened at the Manhattan venue 59E59 on July 12, 2005. The play was part of the "East to Edinburgh" series, featuring plays that would travel to be part of the Scottish capital's Fringe Festival the following month. With a run of three weeks and six total performances, by the closing performance, the production had been critically praised. The first review, which appeared on theatremania.com read:

Louryk is so natural in his performance that the result is something completely unexpected. Rather than a camp send-up of unenlightened people dealing with what they considered a "freak," the show quickly settles into a genuine appreciation of Jorgensen as a pioneer. She was a remarkably poised and articulate woman who was able to deal with the world in her own terms, looking back at Christine Jorgensen, one can't help but be impressed with her courage and fortitude. The play is a fascinating testament to an amazing human being [Siegel].

This review is accurate in its recognition that the production and Louryk-as-Jorgensen subvert the common formula of camp and drag, in favor of a restrained and *gestic* characterization that results in a visceral existentialist experience.

Furthermore, this original production of *Christine* attracted a celebrity (and even cultish) audience including: photographer David LaChapelle, transgender icon Amanda Lepore, and fashion bad-boy Richie Rich (half of the Heatherette duo) — all three of whom project and credit an aesthetic borrowed from the Ridiculous in their own diverse bodies of work.

Next, Louryk traveled to Edinburgh where *Christine* was featured as part of the Fringe beginning on August 6, 2005. The Scottish press also praised the performance, including one review that celebrated it as "an extraordinary homage to Jorgensen's assurance and intelligence," adding, "Louryk's performance is beautifully poised" (Burnet). After returning to the United States, *Christine* was then revived at Manhattan's Dodger Stages before moving to the state-of-the-art Off Broadway facility at New World Stages from December 2005 to April 2006. The same month, after closing in New York, Louryk and the production traveled to Boston where he appeared April 6–29 at the Boston Center for the Arts in conjunction with the gay/lesbian-oriented Theatre Offensive, in the same city from which Jorgensen had been banned fifty-four years earlier.

The last production of *Christine* took place as part of the 2006 Dublin Gay Theatre Festival May 8–13, 2006. While the critical reception of the play continued to be positive, Louryk received some initial criticism from the contingent of local Irish drag queens, who saw his nontraditional lip-synch performance as verging a bit too close on their own creative territory, but once they saw the performance, they too were won over by the spirit of the play and, according to Louryk, became one of his most effective non–media-generated advertisements for the Dublin production.

Nominations for various 2006 awards began to accumulate for *Christine* after the play had been performed for nearly a year. Louryk was nominated for the Media GLAAD award, was a finalist for the first annual Ethyl Eichelberger Award sponsored by PS 122, received a nomination for the Dublin Gay Theatre Festival's Micheal MacLiammoir Award for best actor, and finally, he won the Drama Desk Award for "Most Unique Theatrical Experience."

Louryk's use of lip-synch in performance is also inspired by performer Lypsinka, a drag persona first created by John Epperson in 1987. Epperson, who gained fame when working with fellow Ridiculous performer Charles Busch in the mid-eighties bohemian East Village, uses female impersonation in an effort to fight clichéd misogynistic drag humor. Adelina Anthony refers to Lypsinka as "a master of mad elegance, hilarious timing, and perfect physical expression. [Lypsinka's] gender-bending show is also a refreshing delight in the way he explores the dilemma of being pigeon-holed, stereotyped, and feared. His work is very pro-woman, pro-individual, and pro-dignity, without the political preaching" (Rapp). Best known for his solo cabaret act, Lypsinka crafts performances by meticulously combing recordings of music and spoken word, which are lip-synched and in turn interpreted with choreographed gesture, expression, and emotion. Though Louryk's use of lip-synch in his work to date differs with the use of his own voice (*Klytaemnestra*) or the historiographic retention of complete extant recordings (*Christine*), the precision required to lip-synch effectively and believably is inspired by Lypsinka's work. Furthermore, Lipsynka stresses the Ludlamesque Ridiculous sentiment of individualism and gay social acceptance without assimilation. In an interview he said, "When I see gay people who want to be assimilated into the mainstream, I can only say that if Tennessee Williams had wanted to be assimilated into the mainstream, he would never have written *Streetcar*. Being an outsider made him who he was" (Rapp). Although Louryk's message is intended to be more universal rather than specifically gay, it speaks to the same sentiment.

Currently, Louryk and Grace are reworking the *Lucrezia Borgia* script for performance. Louryk comments on the challenge of piece,

> *Lucrezia Borgia* is more difficult to talk about than anything else, because the underpinnings are so diverse. It's ostensibly about, simultaneously about, exploring the ideas of communication and technology — the technology of communication, and exploring this character. Each of the streams informs the other. It's about, for example, Lucrezia had an epistolary romance with a poet and the letters were collected, we use these letters at text for parts of the play. We're also looking at what letter writing does to thought and communication, what the telephone does to thought, the speed of the communication, the philology, it's about premeditation of thought vs. speaking extemporaneously on a subject. Writing a letter — the parchment was expensive, the ink was expensive, you had to send it by a message on horseback to some destination. You have to be careful of executing the thing so that it can be done in a timely manner, get where it's going to go vs. a phone call vs. an email. The character informs the modes of communication, and the modes of communication informs the way we constructed the

character of Lucrezia Borgia. Also, we're looking at how history is made — by people who are on payroll for, or enemies of the nobility. So you have different interpretations of the same people, depending on who is writing the account. In a way we present many perspectives of Lucrezia Borgia chronically throughout her life, in an attempt to come away knowing more about Lucrezia Borgia [Edgecomb, Louryk].

In its current draft, *Lucrezia* is the next step of Louryk's performative work, merging the use of lip-synch with his own voice as well as a series of unexpected sound bites drawn from a huge variety of sources akin to Ludlam's early epic plays, such as *Big Hotel* (1966). The rapid nature of this section most closely resembles Lypsinka's manic style, which mimics her mental state "as she works her way through the existential crises of her life" (Rapp). In its present form, Grace's script draws directly from the films *The Talented Mr. Ripley, Sugar and Spice,* John Water's *Female Trouble, The Thin Blue Line, Grey Gardens, All About Eve, Waking Life,* Hugo's *Lucrezia Borgia* and the recordings *Knockers Up, Judy Speaks, The Sensuous Woman, Phyllis Diller Laughs, Christin Jorgensen Revealed,* and *Joan Crawford Live at Town Hall.* In July 2007 *Lucrezia Borgia* was work-shopped by Louryk and Grace at the Sundance Theatre Laboratory in Salt Lake City, Utah, where recent Broadway successes and Tony award winners such as *I Am My Own Wife* (2004) and *Grey Gardens* (2006) were originated.

II. In Theory

Ludlam stressed that his Ridiculous "[was] the only avant-garde movement that is not academic" (Dasgupta 79). Other avant-garde artistic/theatrical movements such as Tsara's Dada or Artaud's Theatre of Cruelty were promulgated by manifestos that proclaimed the mission behind the movement as well as providing a set of guidelines that the resultant art strictly adhered to. Unlike his predecessors, the genesis of Ludlam's Ridiculous theatre did not grow from a manifesto; instead, he composed his manifesto a decade after the performances of the RTC. This document was based on pragmatic performance experience rather than precursory theoretical intentions. Because Louryk is a lineage of the original Ridiculous movement and to some degree is informed by Ludlam's mid-career manifesto, his work has become more academic as scholars have embraced the Ridiculous theatre and its theories. Though Louryk's work remains a lineage of the Ridiculous, it has metamorphosed in order not to be neutralized as the academy has subsumed it. Therefore, Louryk's Ridiculous is not Ludlam's. Because the relationship of gay culture with mainstream American society had changed rapidly in the past thirty years, Louryk's theatre is responding to new advancements in civil rights as well as previously unconsidered obstacles that challenge marginalized Americans. Within a society of change that appropriates and even celebrates gay taste and style in popular culture, the contagion of the contemporary Ridiculous audience has shifted. Nuances and subtextual references that would have been largely accessible to only a gay urban audience in Ludlam's lifetime are more universal and poignant to theatregoers whose political and personal views are embracing of a normative homosexuality. With their unique theatrical work, Louryk and Grace seek to create new and innovative theatre drawn from Kierkegaard's ideal that "the thing is to find a truth which is true for me, to find the idea for which I can live and die." Therefore, this Ridiculous is more about exploring individual experience and identity, rather than attempting to speak to gay culture as a homogenized singular whole. Because Louryk's theatre is one of elitist language and obscure intellectual references, it is geared toward a highly educated audience, and is groundbreaking for its unapologetic reinvention of female impersonation and drag, introducing the form to audience members far from the drag bars of Chelsea and Hell's Kitchen. Thus, Louryk's plays are more mid-town than lower Manhattan, suggesting that he can find a new home within the world of commercial theatre without forgetting his roots.

To achieve this, instead of applying camp as his modus operandi like Ludlam, Louryk favors declamatory acting, lip-synch, and mimetic ventriloquism to deliver his message and Ridiculous sensibility. This mimetic ventriloquism, which demands a precision of every bodily function down to the last breath, is the ideal example of Louryk's subversion of one of Ludlam's Ridiculous performance theories. Although Ludlam was self-trained as a master ventriloquist, which skills he exhibited in his production of *The Ventriloquist's Wife* (1978), he was averse to more traditional drag performance dependent on lip-synching in which "performers were their own dummies" (Samuels 68). Ludlam insisted that his live, in-your-face, liberated approach to drag, sans lip-synch, was an effort to give an "honest, bona fide account of [the actors] as characters in a play," not the mimesis of a singer whose recorded voice controlled the live drag artist into giving a projected (and often campy) interpretation informed by the original performance. Louryk combats this idea by reincorporating the conventions of lip-synch/ventriloquism as a post–Ludlam Ridiculous convention. Louryk's lip-synch performances take on different forms, depending on the intention of the project. Of his lip-synching in *Klytaemnestra's Unmentionables* Helena Foley remarks:

> Louryk adopts the lip-synching of drag performance but performs to his own voice, thus opening the possibility for tensions between voice and body move-

ment and creating the effect of a ventriloquism in which the performer becomes his own dummy and as well the victim of the larger narrative in which s/he is embedded [Foley 96].

When lip-synching to his own voice, Louryk performs in an almost shamanistic fashion, disembodying his voice and reclaiming it in order to speak through himself to portray the "other" as himself and finally being transformed into what Senelick refers to as "a heightened self or total identification with what lies opposite" (Senelick). Cody compares Louryk's work to that of the Kabuki *onnagata*, delivering a heightened performative effeminacy that is channeled beyond his masculine physical self-embodiment. Louryk is not attempting to fool his audience, but rather to engage them to a point of committed belief that what they are watching unfold before them is genuine. This technique is drawn in part from Ludlam and his drag performances of characters such as Marguerite Gautier. Ludlam explained how he reinvented the tragic story by using his acting talent and charisma paired with cross-dressing in order to "lure [the audience] gradually into forgetting, to make it more amazing later on" (Roemer 101). The movement used in *Klytaemnestra's Unmentionables* strays from naturalism, instead relying on a magnitude of presence that is closer to the declamatory style of the eighteenth and nineteenth centuries. Thus, each of the five characters presented in the play (Klytaemnestra, Electra, Fury, Medea, Phaedra) takes on a unique voice and movement style, all bound by the fact that Louryk has recorded and crafted them to create conflicting presentations of both harmony and chaos; for example, the Fury's violent physicality seems disconnected and out of place with her calm and soothing voice. This juxtaposition serves to inspire the audience to raise questions about surface appearances, first impressions, and presuppositions. Although Louryk's transformations appear magical in performance, it is essential to note that he sees his success as derived from years of acting training, academic study, and exhaustive physical and mental preparation for each role that he crafts. Ludlam studied theatre extensively at Hofstra; Louryk graduated from the Experimental Theatre Program at Vassar, where the stage-as-laboratory theory is put to use as "an experimental space in which to test ideas and theories" (Cody). Whereas Ludlam's time at Hofstra heightened his knowledge of theatre history, he in turn rebelled against the strict traditionalism of the Stanislavsky-rooted curriculum in order to "create a new theatre" (Samuels 11). Louryk, however found that the support in the academic/experimental environment of Vassar was essential to the development of his work.

In the program notes to the 2002 production of *Klytaemnestra's Unmentionables* at HERE, Louryk stresses that he is not giving a "drag performance. It is an exhibition of both the complexity and subtlety of the female body, the female voice" (Foley 96). He uses lip-synch as a subversive medium, because his predecessors (Ludlam and Eichelberger) were so against it. In a 2006 interview in *The Boston Globe,* Louryk referred to this, responding:

> Ludlam [compares] drag queens who lip-synch to ventriloquism — that they're both the ventriloquist and the dummy simultaneously. He had a low opinion of them. And I thought: Well, here's this man who is so irreverent in everything he does, it seems that the best way to honor him would be to slap him in the face, to thumb my nose at whatever he thinks and do the opposite — to subvert that paradigm. And hopefully by doing that, you come out with something new at the end. So I started recording myself and then lip-synching to the recording — basically taking away one of the tools that an actor has, voice and body, so that I only had one left and was at the mercy of the other. I wanted to challenge myself as an actor to overcome this hurdle, so that hopefully the audience will see the story more clearly. Which is kind of how we get to Christine Jorgensen. I'm at the mercy of that recording. I can't stop. I can't breathe at the wrong moment. I can't sneeze. I can't cough [Wallenberg].

Louryk is referring to his interpretation of Christine Jorgensen. In the play he reinterprets lip-synching by reviving it in its original form: by acting as ventriloquist dummy to a preexisting recording by another individual, in this case, a 1958 interview between Nipsy Russell and Jorgensen that was released on record. This is turned on its head not by technical convention, but rather through Louryk's deportment and body language, complimented by restrained sartorial and performative aesthetics. Whereas male-to-female drag lip-synch traditionally presents the male performer as a larger-than-life fictional character embodying if not hyperbolizing a glamorous woman, Louryk presents a restrained interpretive homage to Jorgensen's character as a pioneer for the repressed 1950s (wo)man. This is the approach of a classically trained actor, not an amateur drag queen. Herein, Louryk reinvents a sociological and historical document with grand theatricality that uses the universality of the past to speak to the present. Louryk says,

> People think drag is some tacky, fat guy in a bad wig and loud clothes and awful makeup. They don't know about Lypsinka, Charles Ludlam, Charles Busch — people who have elevated drag to an art form. I never think that I am a woman. I'm trying to wrench something artistic from the experience [Wallenberg].

With this statement Louryk succinctly states his intentions to use his acting training in order to channel the essence of Jorgensen theatrically, not to imitate her as a traditional drag queen might. Ironically, the article where this quotation originally appeared opens with: "Bradford Louryk might be wearing a shiny-form fitting dress, high heels, and a platinum blond Marilyn Monroe-style wig while lip synching to the voice of a famous woman from the

1950s, but he wants people to know that *Christine Jorgensen Reveals* is no campy drag act" (Wallenberg). Christopher Wallenberg, the journalist, implies that though Louryk uses traditional drag conventions such as the "Marilyn Monroe-style wig," in his performance he is striving to present something that subverts the given aesthetic. Wallenberg errs in his description of Louryk as Jorgensen, relying on clichéd description in an effort to paint him as a cheap drag queen who might appear in any local gay bar. As the creative visionary of the entire project, Louryk is extremely selective about his hair, makeup and wardrobe in an attempt to make himself appear as genuine as possible. Inspired by the original album photograph of Jorgensen in a smart green 1950s dress and tasteful period costume jewelry, Louryk's Jorgensen wears an understated custom-tailored green taffeta suit over "three layers of panty-hose and a corset" (Horwitz). Although Wallenberg plays up the "shininess" of the dress and the "high heeled shoes," Louryk's appearance is closer to that of a mid–twentieth-century society matron, rather than a sequin-bedecked femme fatale. In fact, it is Louryk's conservative restraint in appearance that marks his subversive intention to commit fully to the presentation of Jorgensen as a character, not a female impersonation. The combination of design elements with Louryk's attention to articulation and the precision of every breath with resulting movement (as controlled by the original recording) is in an effort for Louryk to "convince the audience that [he's] not a 5-foot-11 man weighing 155 pounds, but 5-foot-6½ inches tall, weighing 120 pounds" (Horwitz).

In this vein, like Ludlam, Louryk's drag aesthetic strays from the sequins and feather boa formula that defined the female impersonation for most of the twentieth century. Ludlam became famous for a gender-fuck aesthetic that manipulated the sartorially feminine by exposing masculine characteristics rather than trying to minimize them. The most infamous example of this was his reinterpretation of Marguerite Gautier in *Camille* in which his hirsute chest (the epitome of physical masculinity and the height of gay fashion in the 1970s) was exposed and framed by lace trim to reveal his heaving décolletage. In *Klytaemnestra's Unmentionables*, Louryk borrows this convention, exposing his sideburns, which reveal a male persona beneath a corset and panties. These feminine undergarments act as the base on which all the female costumes and in turn characterizations are built on character by character.

The use of gender-fuck and solo performance by Louryk also draws inspiration from Eichelberger. Eichelberger became famous for displaying a full back tattoo of himself as a cross-dressed angel ascending to heaven while he performed in drag. In displaying this body art, he offered a radical edge to his transgendered performance, while also providing a constant visual reminder that he was a man dedicated to using drag in an effort to attack the repression of women, gay men, and drag queens in American society. For example, in his *Medea* Eichelberger used the character to speak to the issue of identity and marginalization: Medea says, "People will strike at one who glitters; I'm an exotic — we're popular this year" (Foley 95). Additionally, Eichelberger's tattoo literally branded him as a bohemian outsider — an East Village pioneer, in an age when tattoos had not yet been appropriated in mainstream youth culture.

Louryk's post–Ludlam take on the Ridiculous theatre results in a dialogical exchange between the audience and the performer, providing a visceral existentialist experience — that is, an experience both approachable and tactile while also prompting the individual to ask larger theoretical questions promulgated by his ability to relate to and personalize the identities and experiences presented. Just as Ludlam and Eichelberger were responding to the contemporary state of American society, Louryk (with the textual collaboration of Rob Grace) is driven to create new works that speak to a current theatregoing audience; he relates, "There's so much discussion about sexuality and identity now, particularly in the wake of the wave of moral righteousness that has swept the country after George W. Bush was elected. Everything in the States is so Right right now" www.bradford.com. Louryk's self-conscious take on iconic women is unique from his Ridiculous predecessors because of his use of lip-synch to channel femininity and womanhood while still retaining the masculine essence of his natural voice, creating a performance that blurs gender lines and challenges preconceived social norms for the twenty-first century and ushers in a new relevancy for the Ridiculous tradition.

Bibliography

Burnet, Andrew. *The Scotsman*, 22 (August 2005).
Butler, Judith. *The Judith Butler Reader*, edited by Sarah Salih with Judith Butler. Malden, MA:
Blackwell Publishing, 2004.
Cody, Gabrielle. E-mail message to Sean F. Edgecomb, October 18, 2007.
Dasgupta, Gautum, and Bonnie Marranca, eds. *Theatre of the Ridiculous*. Baltimore, MD: Johns Hopkins University Press, 1997.
Edgecomb, Sean F. Interview with Bradford Louryk, February 22, 2006.
_____. Interview with Rob Grace, September 14, 2007.
Elliott, Kenneth Yates. "Beyond the Ridiculous: The Commercialization of an Alternative Theatre Movement from Jack Smith to Hairspray." PhD diss., University of California, 2004.
Foley, Helene. "Bad Women: Gender Politics in Late Twentieth-Century Performances and Revision of Greek Tragedy" In *Dionysus Since 69: Greek Tragedy at the Dawn*

of the Third Millennium, edited by Edith Hall, Fiona Macintosh, and Amanda Wrigley. Oxford: Oxford University Press, 2004.

Horowitz, Simi. "Self-Starter: Bradford Louryk." *Backstage*, February 10, 2006. http://www.backstage.com/bso/news_reviews/features/feature_display.jsp?vnu_content_id=1001995486.

Jeffreys, Joe E. *An Outre Entrée into the Para-Ridiculous Histrionics of Drag Diva Ethyl Eichelberger: A True Story (Female Impersonators, Comedy)*. PhD diss., New York University, 1996.

———. "Ethyl Eichelberger." In *Extreme Exposure: An Anthology of Solo Performance Texts from the Twentieth Century*, edited by Jo Bonney. New York: Theatre Communications Group, 2000.

Jorgensen, Christine. *Christine Jorgensen Reveals*. J Records-J1 LP, 1958.

Ludlam, Charles. "Manifesto: Ridiculous Theatre, Scourge of Human Folly." In *The Complete Plays of Charles Ludlam*. New York: Harper & Row, 1989.

McGlone, Jackie. "From GI to Glamour Girl." http://brad-ford.com/pop/scotsman_cjr_feature.html.

Rabkin, Gerald. "An Introduction." *Performing Arts Journal* Spring/Summer (1978).

Rapp, Linda. "Epperson, John." In *GLBTQ: An Encyclopedia of Gay, Lesbian, Bisexual, Transgender, & Queer Culture*. http://www.glbtq.com/arts/epperson_j.2.html (accessed November 20, 2007).

Roemer, Rick. *Charles Ludlam and the Ridiculous Theatre Company: Critical Analyses of 29 Plays*. Jefferson, NC: McFarland & Co., Inc., 1998.

Samuels, Steven, ed. *Ridiculous Theatre: Scourge of Human Folly: The Essays and Opinions of Charles Ludlam*. New York: Theatre Communications Group, 1992.

Senelick, Laurence. *The Changing Room*. New York: Routledge, 2000.

Shirawaka, Sam H. "The Eccentric World of Charles Ludlam." *New York Times*, July 3, 1983.

Siegel, Barbara, and Scott Siegel. "Read Her Lips." http://brad-ford.com/pop/theatermania_cjr_feature.html (accessed November 3, 2007).

Wallenberg, Christopher. "A Man Playing a Woman Who Used to Be a Man: Actor Channels Sex-Change Pioneer on Stage." *The Boston Globe*, April 2, 2006. http://brad-ford.com/pop/bostonglobe_cjr_feature.html.

Mamet, Homophobia, and Chicago Politics

Charles Eliot Mehler

On the Broadway stage and the commercial American stage in general, it is rare that a year passes in recent years during which the subject of homosexuality does not come up in a significant production. For example, in the 2003 season, *Take Me Out*, the story of a homosexual baseball player who faces hostility among his teammates, took home the Tony Award for best play. (In a manner similar to that used by queer theorists, this author has chosen to reclaim the word *homosexual* as direct and to the point concerning people involved in same-sex relations. Words like *gay* and *lesbian* will be used when colloquially appropriate.) Film and television have followed suit, with such efforts as *Brokeback Mountain*, *The Hours*, *Far from Heaven*, *Queer as Folk*, *The L-Word*, and *Six Feet Under*. All these efforts have something in common with the works of dramatist David Mamet. They all deal with homosexuals as people who must live their lives in a poisoned environment. Specifically in the works of David Mamet, the playwright creates much of the grand ethos of plays like *American Buffalo* and *Glengarry, Glen Ross* based on this idea. Hatred and fear of homosexuals is a given response among the presumably heterosexual male characters in the cutthroat worlds of these plays. Furthermore, this hatred and fear of homosexuals often become the weapons of choice among Mamet's cutthroats, especially at critical moments.

Yet the world changes and becomes more accommodating. In Mamet's native Chicago, the regular Democratic Party political machine, once a bastion of these homophobic values, has become quite the opposite. Sensing a change in attitude with respect to popular views on homosexuality, this machine now actively encourages participation from homosexuals. In fact, the subject has touched the personal lives of any number of these centrist, if not slightly right-wing, politicians. Hence, the critical reader needs to be concerned with what happens to the works of David Mamet once this central tenet — that homosexuality is something to be hated, feared and used as a weapon — becomes obsolete.

This essay looks at the works of David Mamet in light of the perhaps-not-central yet pervasive homophobia presented in two works in particular, *American Buffalo* and *Glengarry, Glen Ross*. It examines critical reaction to these works, as well as the political environment of the modern Chicago Democratic Party machine with respect to treatment of homosexuals. In light of these aspects, it then examines alternatives to the interpretation of David Mamet in a changing world.

In "Phallus in Wonderland: Machismo and Business in David Mamet's *American Buffalo* and *Glengarry, Glen Ross*," Hersh Zeifman quotes David Mamet as saying, "[P]etty crime goes unpunished; major crimes go unpunished" (Zeifman 123). One crime with which Mamet's characters may be indicted is that of homophobia. Zeifman first focuses on the proposition that these plays, *Buffalo* and *Glengarry*, are populated exclusively by males. Such a world, according to critic Michelene Wandor (as quoted by Zeifman), "provide[s] an imaginative opportunity to explore the gendered perspective ... without the complexities of the 'mixed' play" (Zeifman 124). For our purposes, this skewed, single-gendered world provides us a social-science laboratory in which homophobia among presumably heterosexual males may be explored.

Qualities often associated with male homosexuality exist at the sidelines of the worlds of these plays. "[T]he exclusion of women from these plays," says Zeifman, "implies that the values the male characters traditionally associate with the 'feminine'—compassion, tenderness, empathy, spirituality—are seen as ... weakness" (Zeifman 125). In contrast to such perceived weakness, there exist the worlds of *Buffalo* and *Glengarry*, in which these qualities are both feared and avoided. The world of Teach and Bobby, of Ricky Roma and Shelly "The Machine" Levene, are not places in which one lets one's guard down to show any sign of traditional femininity if one wishes to survive.

This begs the question of what one must guard against, what Mamet's men must hide. Zeifman quotes Mamet again. "Men get together," says Mamet, "to do business.... Men also get together to bitch. We say, 'What does she want?' ... [And the] [brackets *sic*] final way in which men get together is for That Fun Which Dare Not Speak Its Name, and which has been given the unhappy tag, 'male bonding'" (Zeifman 125). It is hard not to notice the implied homophobia of this reference. The quip being paraphrased dates back to an 1894 poem by Lord Alfred "Bosie" Douglas, *Two Loves*, in which the male partner/paramour of Oscar Wilde invokes reference to "the love that dare not speak its name" (Martin). In his well-publicized trials, Wilde would deny that this was a reference to homosexuality. Nevertheless, as in the aforementioned Zeifman commentary on Mamet, if it looks like a duck, it probably is a duck. Clearly, Mamet and "Oscar and Bosie" are talking about homosexuality.

The male bonding that reveals both homophobia and homophilia among segregated men serves as a threatening motif in both these plays. In *American Buffalo*, Don's junk shop serves as a place where such male-bonding activity goes on regularly. Even the lesbian presence of Ruth and Grace, a presence that exists below the radar screen of the on-stage action of this play, is presented in the context of an arena of male bonding — the poker game. And in *Glengarry, Glen Ross*, the attempted bilking of Roma's client Lingk is presented in a context of conspiracy against the foreign female element: Lingk's wife, who wants to "queer" the whole land deal.

That Mamet describes such interactions as "unhappy" begs another question: Why should such otherwise pleasant (in the case of *Buffalo*) or emboldening (in the case of *Glengarry*) interactions be seen as "unhappy?" Zeifman begins to unravel this conundrum by borrowing a term from Eve Sedgwick, *homosocial*.

> "Homosocial" is a word occasionally used in history and the social sciences where it describes social bonds between persons of the same sex; it is a neologism, obviously formed by analogy with "homosexual," and just as obviously meant to be distinguished from "homosexual." In fact, it is applied to such activities as "male bonding," which may, in our society, be characterized by intense homophobia [Zeifman 125].

Zeifman equates this seemingly contradictory homophobia in Mamet's business plays with misogyny. "A woman," says Zeifman, "by macho definition, is not a 'man'; neither is a homosexual" (Zeifman 127).

If homophobia is not the point of either *American Buffalo* or *Glengarry, Glen Ross*, then it is certainly a motif. Zeifman points to Teach's description of lesbian Ruth as a "dyke cocksucker." "Never mind," says Zeifman, "that the phrase is oxymoronic; for the moronic Teach it makes perfect emotional sense. The patently illogical has been transformed into the patently tautological: in Teach's pantheon of abuse 'dyke' and 'cocksucker' are simple equivalencies" (Zeifman 127). More to the point, that homophobia is a constant, underlying motif in Mamet's business plays, is the moment when salesman Ricky Roma takes office manager Williamson to task. Throughout the play, the salesmen lament the descent of their real estate business into "a world of clock watchers, bureaucrats, officeholders" (Mamet 105), perhaps giving their Machiavellian quest a twisted sense of honor. But when matters come to a head, and Roma perceives Williamson as having made a critical mistake in the handling of the Lingk sale, Roma lets his homophobia shine to the fore. Roma rants at Williamson as Roma realizes that he has lost the prized Cadillac, as well as perhaps his job.

You stupid fucking cunt. Whoever told you you could work with *men*? .... I'm going to have your *job*, shithead.... I don't care *whose* nephew you are, who you know, whose dick you're sucking on.... What you're hired for is to *help* us—does that seem clear to you? To *help* us. Not to fuck us up ... to help men who are going *out* there to try to earn a *living*. You *fairy*. You company man [Mamet 105].

In *Glengarry*'s ultimately illuminating moment of truth, Roma quite clearly reveals that the wallpaper of the real estate office on the northwest side of Chicago is not decorated with misogyny only. It is resplendent in shades of homophobia as well. For not only is the sub-human Williamson a "woman," he's a "fairy" as well. Also interesting to note is the equivalency Roma makes between being a "fairy" and a "company man." The clock watcher, the office holder, the bureaucrat is also a faggot.

In concert with the homophobia behind the behavior of our salesmen in *Glengarry, Glen Ross*, Zeifman stresses the importance of "partnership" in the sales experience. "A businessman," says Zeifman, "is constantly putting his life on the line—like a soldier, like a cop. 'You can't learn [what it takes] [brackets *sic*] in an office...,' Levene instructs the desk-bound Williamson. 'You have to learn it in the streets.... 'Cause your partner *depends* on it.... Your partner ... a man who's your 'partner' depends on you ... you have to go *with* him and *for* him'" (Zeifman 131).

In the mind's eye, one can imagine the plight of the homosexual who must work in this environment. With specific respect to *Glengarry, Glen Ross*, it is not beyond the realm of statistical probability that one of the five men (Levene, Williamson, Moss, Aronow and Roma) is in fact a closeted homosexual. By this, we mean to say that this man has not merely encountered the "Christ, was I drunk last night syndrome" (Crowley 28) as described in Mart Crowley's *The Boys in the Band*, and has experimented with men. It is no stretch of the imagination to conceive of men like Teach or Roma engaging in homosexual activity after having become seriously inebriated. To imagine them involved in anything remotely resembling a "gay lifestyle" would be more difficult yet nevertheless possible. Here, we are talking about someone whose primary attraction is to men, and who cannot discuss this for fear of losing his tenuous livelihood.

For the sake of argument, let us take Shelly "The Machine" Levene, perhaps the most persecuted of the *Glengarry* lot, as our candidate for homosexuality. In this context, one imagines this Shelly as a man who hangs on for dear life to a long-term, otherwise stable marriage to a woman, but who frequents places and people of ill repute on the side. In 1970, sociologist Laud Humphreys described this phenomenon as "tearoom trade," in reference to otherwise heterosexually involved men who frequent public restrooms (and in Shelly's case, perhaps other seedy venues) to find sexual encounters with other men (Sieber). This is the kind of "action" our Shelly Levene might seek. Our enhanced Shelly would never use the words "gay" or "homosexual" to describe his feelings, even if that was the preponderance. He probably even would have trouble with the word "bisexual." After all, Shelly is "The Machine," the macho-man who taught everyone else how to survive in *Glengarry*-dom. What would our closeted-homosexual Shelly do the night after the action in *Glengarry* transpires? Assuming he's been arrested, surely his wife would arrange bail. In either event, it is reasonable to assume that Shelly would head for his favorite place of ill repute for some sexual relief. This scenario provides an interesting subtext for any actor attempting the role of Shelly Levene.

It is easy to establish that the people who populate David Mamet's white ethnic northwest side of Chicago come from a background of entrenched homophobia, as Mamet has succeeded in doing effectively. It is even less of a stretch to further establish that the electoral and political patterns and opinions reflect this homophobia. (From this point forward, owing to my experience as a political reporter for the weekly Chicago newspaper *GayLife* in the 1970s and as former president of Chicago Log Cabin Republicans in the late 1990s, I act as my own journalist.) If Teach, Donny, Shelly "The Machine" Levene and Ricky Roma lived in the real world, these would be the members of the very core group of people upon whom the Chicago Democratic Party machine relies to maintain its power base. In the early 1980s, the time period of the plays in question, the assumption of rampant homophobia among these regular Democrats might be accurate. These assumptions are no longer as true.

In the time period before this play takes place in stage time, one must concede that the attitudes towards homosexuals presented by Mamet reflected an accurate reading of the political climate. Before the late 1970s, it was rare that a regular, non-reform Democrat would venture into what was considered the wide, weird world of gay civil rights. (There was one notable exception. Clifford Kelley, a black regular Democratic alderman from the south side, was the chief sponsor of the homosexual rights bill that languished in the Chicago City Council from the early 1970s until just before the election of Richard Michael Daley in 1987.) Bar raids were frequent, as were arrests of homosexual men in the cruising areas in Lincoln Park. A great deal of protection money paid by businesses catering to homosexuals to local police and ward bosses changed hands.

In 1979, a shift in culture occurred. Chicago police, in what had been accepted as typical form, raided Carol's Speakeasy, a homosexual bar in Chicago's Old Town neighborhood, a short walk from Second City at the corner of North and Wells. In the not-too-distant past of this raid, most bar patrons would have accepted these raids as normal and expected. This time, at Carol's in 1979, such acquiescence would not happen. For the first time in Chicago political history, thousands of homosexuals descended on City Hall to protest the raid. Michael Bilandic, a former southwest-side alderman, had been installed as caretaker mayor after the death of Richard Joseph "Dick" Daley in the mid–1970s. (This happened about a decade before the mayor's son, Richard Michael "Richie" Daley, would become mayor.) A member in good standing of Chicago's Democratic Party political machine, Bilandic paid little attention to this protest.

Bilandic also paid little attention to a devastating snowstorm that hit Chicago in early 1979. Jane Byrne, the late Mayor Dick Daley's commissioner of consumer affairs, parlayed her personal flair (Bilandic had earned the nickname "Mayor Bland," and worse), the snowstorm, and her feminist appeal into a victory against Bilandic in the March 1979 Democratic primary election. Ultimately, Byrne would become Chicago's first (and at this writing only) woman mayor. Though she was a product of the regular Democratic machine herself, Byrne campaigned heavily among homosexual constituencies along the lakefront. In winning, Jane Byrne opened the door to homosexual participation in machine Democrat politics.

In the next decade, Byrne would lose reelection as a result of (then Cook County State's Attorney) Richie Daley splitting the white vote with her in the 1983 Democratic primary election. Thus, in 1983, Harold Washington became Chicago's first black mayor. Washington's victory ushered in a period of racially charged "council wars," led by Alderman Ed Vrdolyak. Besides his difficulties with Chicago's first black mayor, Vrdolyak was noted for his virulent homophobia. (Vrdolyak has since changed his party registration to Republican, and is now considered something of a pariah among regular Democrats.) Thus, the advances made by Jane Byrne in favor of homosexual participation in machine politics suffered a setback in the Washington era. Washington, a reformer, was very popular among homosexual voters.

After Washington's sudden death in 1987, Richie Daley ran against southside Alderman Eugene Sawyer, a black regular Democrat who served as a compromise candidate among members of the City Council to serve as caretaker mayor until a special election could be held. Richie Daley won the special election. As mayor, Daley started out on rocky footing with homosexual voters. After becoming mayor, Daley had a number of troublesome encounters with Chicago's homosexual community. First, he appointed Sister Sheila Lyne as health commissioner. While this Catholic nun was otherwise perfectly qualified for the position, AIDS activists confronted Daley on his choice, fearful that Catholic dogma might prevent Sister Lyne from dispensing condoms to prevent infection. According to Warren Silver, a former high-level administrator for the Chicago Transit Authority, Richie Daley left the town meeting with AIDS activists when the activists accused Daley of not understanding what it is to lose a loved one early in life. (Silver and I have been friends since our undergraduate days in the late 1970s at Northwestern. In fairness to Warren, when I spoke to him about this essay, he restated his claim that there was really no such thing as a "Democratic machine" anymore. As evidence, he pointed to the fact that since the 1995 election, Richie Daley has gotten over 80 percent of the vote city-wide, even in reform wards. I would counter that a machine-style alderman like Richard Mell could never get elected as alderman along the lakefront, as a reform alderman like 49th Ward alderman Joseph Moore could not get elected in Mell's ward. The divide, at least to some extent, still exists, as evidenced by *Chicago Tribune* commentator John Kass' observations on the ascent of Rod Blagojevich as machine Democrat governor of Illinois.) In fact, Daley and his wife Maggie had lost a child to leukemia a number of years before. Daley took personal offense at the accusation, and stormed uncharacteristically out of the meeting.

The difficulty with Sister Lyne happened at the approximate time of the city's annual Gay Pride Parade. Like many local politicians, while serving as State's Attorney before becoming mayor, Daley always took part in the parade. In fact, Daley usually waved at crowds from the back seat of a vintage turquoise Ford Thunderbird. Nevertheless, after the incident with the AIDS activists, Daley announced that his wife insisted that Sundays be spent with his family, and that no political activity would take place on that day. That the first event to be cancelled under this new policy was Daley's appearance in the Gay Pride Parade struck many observers as no mere coincidence. As a result of these difficulties, the new Mayor Daley had left the homosexual community with a sense that they were dealing with a typical socially conservative machine politician who was weak on homosexual issues.

In the years that would follow, relations improved between Mayor Daley and the homosexual community. Mayor Daley was responsible for the creation of a Chicago Gay and Lesbian Hall of Fame. In 2006, Daley keynoted the opening ceremonies at the international Gay Games that had come to Chicago. He and his political machine supported the successful election of two openly homosexual office holders, State Representative Larry McKeon and Alderman Tom Tunney, as well as two local circuit court judges, Tom Chiola and Sebastian Pati. It is interesting to note that the anti-machine Independent Voters of Illinois/Independent Precinct Organization had been trying to achieve this exact goal for years, with no success. What we see here is the *Glengarry*-like muscle of the Daley political machine being used to advance the cause of homosexual rights.

In 2003, the issue of same-sex marriage reared its controversial head in the political media. Both the mayor *and* regular Democrat Alderman Richard Mell (father-in-law of Illinois Governor Rod Blagojevich) reacted in ways that might not have been expected from a machine Democrat in the era of *Buffalo* or *Glengarry*. When the Massachusetts Supreme Judicial Court issued its decision effectively legalizing same-sex marriage, Richie Daley made national headlines by announcing his support for the issue. A story on the legalization of same-sex marriage in Massachusetts in *USA Today* had the following lead:

> Mayor Richard ["Richie"] Daley said he would have "no problem" with Cook County issuing marriage licenses to gay couples in Chicago, the nation's third largest city.
>
> Entering a national debate over gay marriage, Daley urged sympathy for same-sex couples because "they love each other just as much as anyone else."
>
> Daley also dismissed a suggestion Wednesday that marriage between gay couples would undermine the institution.
>
> "Marriage has been undermined by divorce, so don't tell me about marriage," he said. "Don't blame the gay and lesbian, transgender and transsexual community" [Associated Press].

The reader especially should note the politically correct usage by Richie Daley of the phrase "gay and lesbian, transgender and transsexual" as evidence of his comfort, or at least his savvy, with the issue.

More important is the reaction of the Mell/Blagojevich family circle to the issue of same-sex marriage. In March, 2003, demonstrators converged on the Cook County building in downtown Chicago to protest, insisting the county clerk issue marriage licenses to same-sex couples. Demonstrators took their case to David Orr, the reform (non-machine) Democrat who was Cook County Clerk, and protested against Orr personally. One of the demonstrators was Deborah Mell, lesbian daughter of the alderman and sister-in-law of Governor Blagojevich. Deborah Mell, who claimed not to be accustomed to such behavior, got caught up in the heat of the moment and threw herself into the street, only to get arrested by police who were trying to break up the demonstration.

The cliché surrounding the old-style Democratic machine is that membership requires an aversion to social protest. This cliché probably owes itself to the image of Mayor Dick Daley ordering police to beat protestors at the 1968 Chicago Democratic Convention. Nothing could be further from the truth than this cliché image of the Democratic machine when seen in the light of the events surrounding Deborah Mell's arrest. Not only was Alderman Richard Mell proud of his daughter for standing up for her beliefs, he came out strongly in favor of fair and equal treatment of homosexuals. In fact, he told the media that any parent that can't handle a child's homosexuality doesn't deserve to be a parent. In the *Chicago Tribune* story that followed his daughter's arrest, Alderman Mell demonstrated his open-mindedness on homosexual issues.

> After being told of his daughter's arrest, [Alderman] Mell came down to the protest and said he supported his daughter and her sexual orientation.
> "Fifty years ago, people would be standing here because of a constitutional amendment against interracial marriage," Mell said. "Fifty years from now, people are going to be wondering what this was all about" [Kim].

The non–Chicago-based reader needs to be reminded that we are not talking about the far-left-leaning Democratic Party of Ralph Nader or Jesse Jackson (who has come out against same-sex marriage) or Dennis Kucinich here. These politicians, Richie Daley and Richard Mell, are the direct political and social descendants of Richard Joseph ("Dick") Daley and the socially regressive Democratic machine of the 1960s and 1970s. This brings us back to the issue of homophobia among David Mamet's northwest-siders. Had these plays, *American Buffalo* and *Glengarry, Glen Ross*, been written today, the incidents of verbal gay bashing would not have made as much sense. After all, the mayor *and* the alderman, virtual spiritual leaders among their flock of petit-bourgeois bungalow owners and six-flat dwellers, have passed the most stringent of litmus tests in support of homosexual rights. They both strongly support same-sex marriage.

The issue then becomes, what is one to make of the endemic homophobia in Mamet's plays in this brave new world of machine political support for same-sex marriage, once considered the most outlandish piece of the homosexual-rights agenda? In this light, we have three options to consider with respect to Mamet's plays:

a) reject Mamet's homophobic motif as outmoded, and therefore consider the plays outmoded,
b) accept Mamet's works as reflective of the period, much like we consider the works of Mark Twain in light of race or Shakespeare's *The Merchant of Venice* in light of anti–Semitism, or
c) consider what *Glengarry*-dom might look like without the endemic homophobia.

Let us look at these three alternatives.

First, because Mamet's works fail to deal with the real-world change in attitude on homosexual issues, these plays become obsolete in themselves. In a work like John O'Hara's *The Last Hurrah,* the author acknowledges a similar change for his character. Frank Skeffington, O'Hara's old-style machine politician, fails to see that his style of politics will work in a modern, media-driven world of politics. Yet, in *American Buffalo* and *Glengarry, Glen Ross*, the essential homophobia is never questioned and is, in fact, treated as if it were a part of the wallpaper of these people's lives. As a counter-example, a work like Rodgers and Hammerstein's *Flower Drum Song* comes to mind. In a recent Broadway revival, the producers considered the story extremely dated and obsolete in its quaint view of Chinese immigrants in San Francisco in the 1950s. The producers brought in playwright David Henry Hwang, of *M. Butterfly* renown, to completely renovate the book for contemporary audiences. The question becomes whether *Glengarry* or *Buffalo* could withstand a change similar to *Flower Drum Song*. In light of Zeifman's commentary, the misogyny and homophobia in these plays would seem to be essential to the drama. Therefore, obsolescence is not an unreasonable future for these plays, especially as rank homophobia becomes more offensive to contemporary audiences in the way that the racial stereotypes of the old *Amos and Andy* radio and television performances have become.

In the second model, in direct contrast to the first, one might view *Buffalo* and *Glengarry* the way one views works like *Gentlemen's Agreement*, with respect to Jews, or *Showboat*, with respect to African Americans. *Gentleman's Agreement,* for example, deals with the treatment of American Jews before the great gains in both economics and stature of the 1950s. And *Showboat*— in particular, the 1936 film version — presents black people as "smiling darkies," shuffling servants to the white majority. These works may reflect social attitudes preserved as if in aspic in a time and place. That these attitudes are no longer relevant does not necessarily detract from the dramatic and literary value of these works. In this light, the same might be said for *American Buffalo* and *Glengarry, Glen Ross* with respect to homosexuality.

Finally, we consider how well these pieces would work if homophobia were to be taken out of the literary equation. Is it possible for Mamet-world to exist without this seemingly essential homophobia? Contemporary presentation of homosexuals in the performing arts lies at a crossroads. This presentation lies somewhere between the extreme of the nearly flawless Sidney Poitier character in *Guess Who's Coming to Dinner* and James Earl Jones's performance as the flawed Troy in August Wilson's *Fences*. American audiences have proceeded to the point where a black actor can be cast in a non-racially specific role — witness the performance, now of greater than twenty years vintage, of Louis Gossett, Jr., in *An Officer and a Gentleman*. This has not yet happened for homosexuals. Homosexuality is still the issue. Homosexuals no longer need to be as flawless as Poitier's doctor. The "Brian" character on *Queer as Folk* has flaws, much like a more comic take on August Wilson's Troy. Nevertheless, the flaws of Brian and other multi-dimensional homosexual characters are still presented in a "how to deal with gay issues" context. It may take another generation to bring homosexual characters to the level of Louis Gossett, Jr., in which the character's suspect class is not the issue.

What happens when this homophobia fails to exist anymore, the third alternative? What happens when it becomes ridiculous for Teach to call Ruth a "dyke cocksucker" or for Roma to call Williamson a "fairy?" Are we then to have a Mamet-world occupied by Von Trapp family singers and the Care Bears? Does the absence of homophobia, and perhaps even misogyny, neutralize the cruelty of Mamet-world? And most importantly to the work of any good playwright, do we lose the dramatic tension that once existed and, in its time and place, made sense to exist?

This is perhaps the challenge awaiting David Mamet in the new millennium. As he continues to write, we continue to hunger for the tension and cruelty evident in his portrayals of capitalism gone haywire. Homosexuals (and, in Mamet's all-male world, homosexual men in particular) are not immune to this tension and cruelty. Mamet has an obligation to both maintain the tension and cruelty, and to portray the emerging role of homosexuals in this larger world.

One could never accuse Mamet of portraying homosexuals, much less anything else, as "quaint." Thus the first option, rendering Mamet's works obsolete, seems overblown. As Mamet remains a vital force in the performing arts, it is therefore reasonable to expect that we will see a combination of the second and third options. *American Buffalo* and *Glengarry, Glen Ross* will continue to receive much deserved praise for the tautness of the writing, and will be revived regularly. The anti-homosexual moments in these plays will be seen in the same light as *Gentlemen's Agreement* and *Showboat*. One would hope however, in future plays, that Mamet will consider the option of presenting homosexuals as a real part of his cutthroat world as he continues writing.

BIBLIOGRAPHY

"Chicago's Daley: 'No Problem' with Gay Marriage Licenses." *USA Today*, February 19, 2004. http://www.usatoday.com/news/nation/2004-02-19-daley-marriage_x.htm (accessed June 26, 2007).
Crowley, Mart. *The Band Plays*. Los Angeles, CA: Alyson Publications, 2003.
Kim, Gina (and wire services). "Gay Protesters Take to the Street." *Chicago Tribune*, March 5, 2004.
Mamet, David. *Glengarry, Glen Ross*. New York: Grove Press, 1982.
Martin, Gary. "The love that dare not speak its name," 1996–2007. Phrase Finder. <http://www.phrases.org.uk/meanings/364900.html> (accessed June 26, 2007).
Sieber, Joan. "Laud Humphries and the Tearoom Sex Study." University of Missouri <http://www.missouri.edu/~philwb/Laud.html> (accessed June 26, 2007).
Zeifman, Hersh. "Phallus in Wonderland: Machismo and Business in David Mamet's *American Buffalo* and *Glengarry, Glen Ross*." In *David Mamet: A Casebook*, edited by Leslie Kane, 123–25. New York: Garland, 1992.

No Tragedy
Queer Evil in the Metaphysical Comedies of Nicky Silver

Jordan Schildcrout

In the homophobic imagination, queer people do not engage in a lifestyle, but rather a "death style," one that chooses degeneracy over reproduction, and decadence over regeneration. Queerness is a "dead end" that threatens to destroy individuals, relationships, families, and societies. Thus, the figure of the queer murderer, who embodies the conflation of nonnormative sexuality and death, appears in cultural narratives with surprising frequency. Take, for example, the figure of Andrew Cunanan, a gay man who, over a three-month period in 1997, murdered five people, including fashion mogul Gianni Versace, before killing himself. To borrow the semiotic terms of C.S. Pierce (Eagleton 100), homophobes read the media image of Cunanan as not just *iconic* (representing Cunanan himself) but also *indexical* (indicating homosexuals as a group) and *symbolic* (representing concepts such as "murderousness" and death). Indeed, the fight against homophobia often takes the form of a fight against such over-interpretations.

Yet in the unruly realm of theatrical art, we welcome dramatic characters who are open to complex meanings and who are "more than just themselves." Here a murderous queer character can both participate in and subvert the homophobic paradigm that denounces all queer people as dangerous and deadly, and few gay playwrights have wrestled with this dynamic more successfully than Nicky Silver. Of all his plays, Silver's highly acclaimed and often-produced *Pterodactyls* (1993), a dark comedy about a gay man who destroys his family, most astutely combines conventions of realism with nonrealistic theatricality, along with intimations of the metaphysical, thus encouraging the audience to interpret the drama both literally and symbolically at the same time. In doing so, the play boldly challenges the symbolic order that positions the queer as evil.

Queer Evil and the Destruction of the Good

Since evil is an abstract concept that has been described and applied in so many ways, it may be helpful to elucidate my working definition of the term, and then to examine some of the various ways that public discourse frames queer people as evil. At its most quotidian, "evil" can simply mean "morally reprehensible" or "causing harm." Many contemporary theorists of evil approach the subject from a psychoanalytic perspective. C. Fred Alford, author of *What Evil Means to Us*, bases his philosophy of evil on his experience interviewing people who have caused terrible harm — incarcerated murderers, rapists, etc. For Alford, evil is not an aberration, but an impulse experienced by all humans, since we are all mortal and experience dread, i.e., the feeling of being "vulnerable, alone in the universe, and doomed to die." Alford explains:

> Evil is an experience of dread. *Doing evil* is an attempt to evacuate this experience by inflicting it on others, making them feel dreadful by hurting them. Doing evil is an attempt to transform the terrible passivity and helplessness of suffering into activity [3].

Evil, then, is enacting the opposite of the Golden Rule, which requires that we treat others as we ourselves would like to be treated. Evil consists of treating others in precisely the way we do *not* want to be treated, thrusting our suffering and pain onto the other in the hope of avoiding it ourselves. Alford goes on to describe some of the qualities of evil:

> Evil inflicts pain, abandonment, and helplessness on others, so that the evildoer does not have to experience them himself.... It is why torture is the paradigm of evil, master of all three terrors at once.... Hence, all evil has the quality of sadism, defined ... as the joy of having taken control of an experience of victimhood by inflicting it on another [52].

Here Alford hints at the idea that evil is not just about displacing dread, but about controlling it. The sadist's joy comes not just from seeing someone else suffer, but from feeling that he or she is in control of suffering, commanding and redirecting the force that threatens us with doom.

Alford offers a convincing thesis on the psychology of human cruelty and suffering, but another layer of meaning is necessary in order to understand how evil functions symbolically. Alford comes close to this layer when he refers to Melanie Klein, who focuses on *envy* as "the root of all evil, the desire to destroy what is good because one cannot have or be it" (70). Such envy is operating in Nietzsche's notion of *ressentiment*, in which weak people fabricate a system of "slave morality" that falsely characterizes the aristocratic man's will to power as "evil" (Nietzsche 33–36). But envy is also, not coincidentally, one of the Seven Deadly Sins, and Alford touches upon a crucial aspect of evil when he explores religious (and thus, metaphysical) concepts, such as St. Augustine's definition of evil as "the willful depletion of good" (71).

The greatest Willful Depleter of the Good is, of course, Satan. In Judeo-Christian cosmology, Satan, rejected by God and banished from Heaven, is filled with envy, vowing to destroy all that is Good by corrupting God's creations. Satan's dramatic objective is concisely stated by the anonymous author of the medieval *Chester Mystery Plays*:

> LUCIFER: And therefore I shall for His sake
> Show mankind great envy
> As soon as He can him make
> I shall him at once destroy [9].

In this religious worldview, everything has metaphysical significance, because everything in the human sphere plays a symbolic role in the battle between the Holy and the Unholy, the Good and the Bad. Even our modern, supposedly secular understanding of evil exists in the realm of the symbolic. More than ordinary violence or destruction, evil has symbolic value (i.e., is more than just itself) because evil has an *agenda*: to destroy Goodness. To participate in this agenda is to be part of a Force of Evil that is larger than a single individual dealing with his or her psychological dilemma of dread. To call something Evil is to assign metaphysical meaning to it. Evil is larger than the act of a single "bad" or "cruel" person. It is a manifestation of That Which Destroys The Good.

Evil, with all its symbolic connotations, is applied to real people and actions in contemporary discourse. In *At Stake: Monsters and the Rhetoric of Fear in Public Culture*, Edward J. Ingebretsen explains that the label "monster" (i.e., the embodiment of evil) functions as a "metaphysical signifier" and "a perennially useful social tool" that teaches people what is "properly human" by separating and demonizing the "inhuman" (9). Ingebretsen acknowledges that monsters make for compelling narratives *because* they appeal to a metaphysical understanding of reality, and, unsurprisingly, both killers and queers appear regularly in the role of evil monster.

> Like the homosexual, and often in the same terms and for many of the same political reasons, the killer is construed as a larger-than-life force, one who threatens not only private domesticity, but the entire fabric of national civility as well [75].

In other words, the queer and the killer are monstrous because they are not "just themselves"; they are demonized as representatives of a Force of Evil whose goal is to destroy The Good (private domesticity, national civility, etc.). This may seem like a great deal of symbolic weight to put on the shoulders of your average queer person, or, for that matter, even a violent murderer. But when we make the queer and the killer into monsters, they take up residence in the realm of the symbolic, where they are endowed with extraordinary powers.

So how, exactly, are queer people (and queer characters) symbolically configured as evil? The religious right's response to the 9/11 terrorist attacks provides a telling instance. *The Washington Post*'s John F. Harris reported that within 48 hours of the attacks, Jerry Falwell blamed homosexuals *as a group* (along with pagans, abortionists, feminists, and the ACLU) for the death and destruction. Falwell was not claiming that homosexuals actually carried out the attack, but rather that the mere presence of homosexuals in America creates an evil society that will not be protected by God. The underlying argument is that homosexuals must be removed from society, and Michael Bronski rightly points out the similarities between contemporary homophobic rhetoric and medieval anti–Semitic rhetoric, which successfully led to the expulsion of Jews from some European countries:

> Homosexuality functions on a primeval level as the great signifier of evil. Homosexuals have become to the modern world what the Jews were to the medieval world — they corrupt children, they spread disease, they stand outside the sanctified, secure boundaries of nationalism, and they seek the destruction of the state.

The rhetoric of queer evil is based in a belief that queer people are detrimental to 1) the psychological and physical health of themselves and others; 2) family, and the heterosexual monogamy and production of children; 3) community, and the civic and religious systems that organize it; and 4) nation, and the political and military strength that defends it. Examples in each of these categories are numerous, but I will detail a few to elucidate the point.

AIDS has been used as a means to inscribe queer people as dangerous to physical health. As Susan Sontag acknowledged in *AIDS and Its Metaphors*, the disease is more than "just itself" and takes on symbolic meanings, including "pollution" and "punishment." Moreover, AIDS has fostered a culture in which "illicit" sex is the equivalent of death, and the person who has sex is considered a murderer (72). Since, despite so much evidence to the contrary, many people consider AIDS to be a "gay disease," homosexuality is symbolically the equivalent of murder. In 2003, Elisabeth Bumiller of *The New York Times* reported that Jerry Thacker, a nominee to George W. Bush's Presidential Advisory Council on HIV and AIDS, called AIDS "the gay plague" and referred to homosexuality as a "death style" (as opposed to a "life style"). More than 25 years after the emergence of AIDS, a global phenomenon affecting millions of people of various societies and sexualities, some people still insist on using the disease as "proof" of the symbolic link between homosexuality and death.

In his book *No Future: Queer Theory and the Death Drive*, Lee Edelman explains how those whose sexuality exists outside the heteronormative reproductive family are constructed as inherently dangerous to the Child and the futurity that children represent within our society. If procreation is the key to the future, then "the death drive names what the queer, in the order of the social, is called forth to figure: the negativity opposed to every form of social viability" (9). In reality, queer people might produce and raise or otherwise nurture children, but symbolically, queerness signifies a threat to children, most often realized in the imagined conflation of homosexuality and pedophilia. Although Edelman warns queer people against participating in "the familiar familial narrativity of reproductive futurism" (17), one of the social goals of legal battles over adoption and parental rights, as well as of groups such as PFLAG, is to reclaim LGBT people as members of families rather than as threats to them.

Leo Bersani, in writing about "The Gay Outlaw," offers insight into how homosexuality is understood as an "anti-communitarian" threat to the social order. Symbolically, homosexuality has been constructed as infecundity, waste, and sameness (i.e., narcissism), and therefore it does not enact any "real" connection between people. Bersani looks to the French literary *enfant terrible* Jean Genet as the key example of the homosexual-criminal whose "demand that others find him hateful and unworthy of human society stands in sharp contrast to the tame demand for recognition on the part of our own gay community" (161). Indeed, while the current gay rights movement focuses on marriage as part of the battle for political (and, in many cases, religious) legitimization of same-sex relationships in the eyes of society, Bersani argues that Genet wants to be outside society because only then can he be truly free from society. Bersani's argument relies not so much on an understanding of the different ways homosexuality is *actually* experienced in our culture, which can, in fact, be quite communitarian, but on a *symbolic* concept of homosexuality as anti-communitarian. Whether viewed positively by Bersani or negatively by homophobes, homosexuality is symbolically understood to represent a criminal act that destroys the bonds of community upon which our law-abiding society is based.

Along with individual health, family, and community, queer people are imagined to be detrimental to the nation as a whole. Those who fuelled the Red Scare of the McCarthy era expertly exploited the symbolic as they linked queers and communist subversives. In his book on sexual psychopath laws in the 1950s, Neil Miller quotes a *New York Post* interview with Nebraska senator Kenneth Wherry.

> You can hardly separate homosexuals from subversives. Mind you, I don't say every homosexual is a subversive, and I don't say every subversive is a homosexual. But a man of low morality is a menace to the government, wherever he is, and they are all tied together [106].

Decades later, Wherry's symbolic rhetoric is still potent. In 2003, *Village Voice* columnist Richard Goldstein reported that Jay S. Bybee, a George W. Bush appointment to the Ninth Circuit Court of Appeals,

> argued for a Defense Department program that screened "all known or suspected" homosexuals seeking top-secret clearance. People who perform "acts of sexual misconduct or perversion," Bybee told the court, are guilty of "moral turpitude, poor judgment, or lack of regard for the laws of society."

The important point here is not just that homosexuality is immoral. The point is that homosexuality is an *indicator* of "low morality" that can be detrimental to the national well-being.

It is no wonder that the battles of the gay rights movement over the past two decades have focused on AIDS, marriage and adoption, inclusion in schools and churches, and military service. All these battles have symbolic value in overturning the conception of queer people as detrimental to health, family, community, and nation. But I'd like to join the critics who ask whether the goal of a queer movement is to change the position of queer people within the symbolic order, or is the goal to change the order itself? If Evil is a metaphysical force whose goal is to destroy The Good, who gets to decide what constitutes The Good? Whose lives, whose loves, and whose values are allowed to occupy the charmed realm of The Good, and who, then, must be relegated to the abject status of Evil?

The theatre is a forum in which artists and audiences can confront and challenge the symbolic order. Theatre can create its own world in which the values of Good and Evil are questioned, challenged, or wholly reinvented. Being well versed in the power of the symbolic, theatre artists can challenge the popular discourse with new symbolic meanings and significance. A play like Nicky Silver's *Pterodactyls* enacts the very evil of which queer people are often accused in homophobic discourse. But the play does more than reiterate homophobic rhetoric through camp or irony. It wrestles with the status of queer people by asking the questions that every queer person existing within a homophobic society must, at some time or another, ask him or herself: *Am* I evil? How evil am I?

Killer Queers in the Comedies of Nicky Silver

Nicky Silver began his career in the 1980s as a wildly prolific, self-produced playwright at the Vortex, a small gay theatre on the fringes of New York's Chelsea neighborhood. By the mid–1990s, he had become one of the most widely produced American playwrights, regularly premiering his plays at more mainstream artistic homes such as the Woolly Mammoth Theatre in Washington, DC, and the Vineyard Theatre in New York. Silver's work is notable for its combination of a wide variety of influences, from Greek tragedies to television sitcoms. David Savran locates Silver in the "black farceur" tradition of gay playwrights such as Oscar Wilde, Joe Orton, and Christopher Durang (213). I would add that Silver has built his reputation largely on exploring the absurd nightmare of the dysfunctional American family, perhaps linking him most directly with Edward Albee. Like Albee, Silver is often concerned with the intertwining of sexual desire and death, and how these elements play out in the Freudian family romance. Many of Silver's plays feature a prodigal gay son who returns home, bringing with him some shameful crime (incest, murder, pedophilia), and this transgression creates a rupture in the facade of familial stability and happiness. The queer criminal son forces a confrontation with the long-avoided truth, often involving sexuality, violence, addiction, the dissolution of the family, or, in *Pterodactyls*, the mortality of the entire human race.

Many of Silver's plays before *Pterodactyls* depict this disruptive queer son as a murderer. His early hit, *Fat Men in Skirts* (1988), centers on Bishop, a young man who is straight but "coded" as gay — he not only obsesses about an old movie queen (Katharine Hepburn), but he fears and feels the rejection of his family and then of society because of his "sexual difference." In this play, the difference is not gayness, but an incestuous relationship, usually described in animalistic terms, with his mother. Bishop acts out the Oedipal fantasy and then some, killing his father, his father's mistress, and finally his mother (*Etiquette* 217–300). In *Free Will & Wonton Lust* (1991), Philip is another young man who is sexually confused rather than actually gay — e.g., when he loses his fiancée, he finds sexual solace in the embrace of his sister. But the climactic revelation of his Act Two soliloquy centers on same-sex attraction and murder. Philip reveals that, although he "wasn't gay," he was obsessed with a handsome young Englishman. When the object of his desire kindly refused him, Philip threw a brick at the Englishman's head, knocking him out, and most likely killing him, although Philip did not stick around to find out. Homosexual desire and the rejection of that desire both create a panicked rage that leads Philip to murder (*Etiquette* 151–216).

The murderous queer son takes on greater symbolic significance in *Ptero-*

dactyls (*Etiquette* 69–150). Todd returns home to his upper-class Philadelphia family because he has AIDS and needs a place to live. His return interrupts the festive marriage arrangements of his sister, and knocks down the tower of denial constructed by his alcoholic socialite mother and his distant fantasizing father. Todd refuses the melodramatic role of sympathetic AIDS victim as he confesses that he knowingly had unsafe sex, casually reminds other characters that they are going to die, and denies the existence of God. He seduces his sister's fiancé, which enacts one of the "evils" of which gay men are often accused: corrupting straight men and ruining the bonds of heterosexual marriage. His macabre statements and this sexual seduction, however, are just the quotidian tip of a much more metaphysical iceberg. Todd finds large dinosaur bones in the family yard and spends the remainder of the play constructing the skeleton of a giant tyrannosaurus in the living room. Between scenes, Todd directly addresses the audience, giving somewhat twisted lectures on the deaths of species and civilizations, focusing particularly on the ice age killing off the dinosaurs, and the ten plagues destroying the Egyptians in Exodus. The improbable existence of dinosaur bones in the front yard and these mini-lectures place the play's action within a historical field that covers millennia, as well as within a supernatural realm that includes divine retribution and plagues from God. Todd also creates a link between these awesome destructions and the destruction of the humble family: he reminds us that dinosaurs "lived as families, traveling in packs" (110) and announces that his "favorite" plague is the slaying of the first born of the family.

Todd shows his true dimensions at the end of Act One. Responding to his father, who insists on calling him "Buzz," the name of some fictional, ideal son, Todd "*explodes in a rage which shocks the others*," repeatedly shouting "MY NAME IS TODD!!" His sister helpfully points out to the audience that Todd's name "means 'death' in German." If this weren't enough to establish Todd as something other than "just himself," he responds to his mother's wail, "MY SON IS DYING!!" with the following proclamation:

> I AM NOT DYING!! ... I WILL NOT DIE! I WILL NOT! I WILL BE HERE FOREVER! WHEN YOU ARE DUST I WILL BE HERE! I WILL OUTLIVE THE TREES AND THE STARS AND THE SEAS AND THE PLANET! [114].

Todd *is* Death, an immortal force that visits all living things but will itself never die. Throughout the play, Todd is associated with darkness and coldness, but he brings Act One to a fiery close with this awesome and terrifying pronouncement. He is the demiurge declaring his own magnificence and revealing himself in all his sublime horror. Furthermore, Todd will now play an active role in bringing death to almost all the play's characters. The play begins as a family comedy, in the summer with the planning of a wedding. The second half of the play slides into autumn and finally winter, the wedding replaced by funerals, family reunions replaced by abandonment and solitude, and sex replaced by death.

In Act Two, death permeates the play. The sister's wedding seems absurdly doomed, as "all the rabbits had cervical cancer and the pâté is contaminated" (118) and the "violinist was killed this morning by a stray bullet during a bank holdup" (123). Todd's wedding present to his sister is a loaded gun, which she will use on herself (and her unborn child) once she learns that her fiancé will not marry her because he claims to be in love with Todd. The fiancé's confession of love for Todd is combined with the revelation that he, too, is now HIV positive. In the final scene, the fiancé's AIDS-ravaged corpse lies in the yard, frozen and unburied. The sister appears as a ghost, having found some peace and wisdom in death, and thankful to Todd for providing her with the gun. The play reaches a chilling conclusion as the lights grow dim and Todd pours more and more alcohol into his mother's glass, until she finally dies. The final images of the play are Todd embracing his sister's ghost, and the lights on the dinosaur skeleton growing brighter and brighter.

So by the final curtain, Todd has been the source or provider of death for his sister (the gun), her fiancé (HIV), and his mother (alcohol). Meanwhile, Todd shows no symptoms or manifestations of AIDS, and, true to his proclamation at the end of Act One, he remains after everyone else has died. In analyzing the desire to do evil, Alford writes, "When we are faced with intolerable, uncontainable dread, the natural tendency is to identify with the persecutor, becoming the agent of doom, as the only way of controlling it" (Alford 58). Todd avoids death by *becoming* Death. In this fantasy of empowerment, Todd takes control of the force that would destroy him and uses it to destroy others. In doing so, he enacts in real terms the evil of which gay men are often accused in symbolic terms: he literally destroys the family, ruins heterosexual marriage, spreads a fatal disease, and even kills the unborn. But Todd is not evil. The sister, fiancé, and mother each play a role in his or her own demise. They are not "innocent victims" of a sinister villain, as Silver successfully complicates such melodramatic categories. Furthermore, Silver repeatedly reminds the audience that death is part of a natural order, one that has no apparent cause or reason. The tyrannosaurus skeleton that dominates the stage is a "monument to the transience of everything" (116), and Todd's final speech reminds us that no one really knows how or why the dinosaurs died out.

> Some people think there was a meteor. Perhaps volcanic ash altered the atmosphere. Some think they overpopulated and the shell of their eggs became too thin. Or they just ran their course, and their end was the order of things. And no tragedy. Or disease. Or God [150].

Todd is Death, but he is not malicious or vindictive. Death simply *is*, an amoral natural force that takes individual lives and will one day take the entire human race.

In creating an amoral comedy of death, Silver accomplishes some interesting work within the symbolic order. His play dramatizes, even exaggerates, a homophobic fantasy of queer villainy, which can also be read as a dramatization of the homosexual's internalized homophobia and guilt. Homophobic discourse accuses queer people of the crimes that Todd performs, and queer people have been taught to feel guilty for those same crimes, whether they have performed them or not. Silver presents a literal enactment of the gay man as symbol of Death and Destruction — and then, shockingly, radically declares that death and destruction are *not* evil, just natural, perhaps even a comforting release from the neuroses and suffering of human existence. The play confronts the homophobic symbolic order head on and asks the question: What if gay men *were* to bring about the death of humanity? Silver invokes the transhistorical view (it's happened to other species before) and the philosophical view (death comes for us all eventually). Silver seems to argue that even if gay men were the walking embodiments of death and destruction, that would not mean that they were evil. Silver lifts the symbolic weight heaped upon queerness and AIDS by the homophobic imagination, and reminds us that all living things are, ultimately, engaged in a "death style," and our deaths are part of the natural order. This is the truth that homophobes would deny by displacing their dread on to the queer, but Todd is here to remind us that mortality is the universal condition.

Nevertheless, *Pterodactyls* is undeniably a morbid play, one that embraces death and, disturbingly, finds more comfort there than in any human lover. Rather than refuting accusations of immorality with depictions of morality, it takes a chilly stance of amorality. As such, the play hardly qualifies as an example of "gay pride." But Silver has done something remarkably brave, actually confronting the symbolic power of the homophobia that most queer people try to avoid or deny in their daily lives. For the relatively brief period of time the audience spends in the theatre, the terrifying vision is given the spotlight, and we are asked to consider it for what it is and what it might mean. Taking on the role of Death, the gay man is empowered, taking control of forces that normally control him. He enacts a revenge against the family and the social order that ignore or reject him. His suffering is dramatized as the suffering of all creatures over the history of existence, and his death is dramatized as part of the cosmic and the awesomely inevitable. Thus, Todd's supposedly imminent death from AIDS does not mark him as monstrous, but brings him into the circle of a frail, mortal humanity. The play bravely wrestles with queer fear and guilt created by the homophobic symbolic order, and it achieves a victory of sorts. For those who can find comfort in realizing that death does not discriminate and that we are all equal and united in mortality, *Pterodactyls* is a cleansing ritual that exorcizes fears and anxieties over the queer's symbolic status as "bringer of death."

Pterodactyls is one of Silver's most acclaimed plays dealing with a queer murderer, but not his last. In *Raised in Captivity* (1995), Silver changes focus to the masochistic "victim" of queer killers. Sebastian refuses to believe that anyone is truly bad or evil. He writes love letters to a convicted murderer, begs for the return of a hustler who has just cut and robbed him, and longs for his dead lover Simon, whom Sebastian believes "willfully" infected other people with HIV. The play asks the question, "Are the men we love murderers?" In the end, Sebastian withdraws from sexual relationships and embraces his nurturing side, choosing to care for his sister's newborn baby, whom he names after his dead lover. The final note is both mournful and hopeful, with Sebastian perhaps being released from his romantic obsession with pain and death, and finding comfort in his love for an innocent child. In *Beautiful Child* (2004), the story of a gay man's love for an innocent child takes a sinister turn, but here Silver focuses on the guilt-ridden parents of the disruptive queer son. Isaac returns home, confessing his crime of pedophilia with an eight-year-old boy. Isaac's mother imagines that one of her son's previous victims has committed suicide, making her son guilty of murder. In the end, the family is reunited, but only in guilt and shame. The parents agree to protect Isaac, but they punish him by blinding him and imprisoning him in their home. The parents condemn Isaac as a criminal, but they also reclaim him as *their* criminal.

In December 2006, Silver himself appeared on stage in a workshop production of his play *The Agony and the Agony* at the Vineyard Theatre. Playing a mediocre middle-aged playwright named Richard who is writing a play about a mediocre middle-aged playwright, Silver presented his most self-reflexive work to date. Appearing on stage as the playwright's conscience and confidant is real-life killer Nathan Leopold, Jr., who with Richard Loeb famously murdered Bobby Franks in 1924. The Leopold and Loeb crime has been reimagined frequently in plays and films, and Silver reiterates a popular interpretation of the case, positioning Leopold as a sympathetic gay man who participated in the killing in order to win the affections of the brutal sociopath Loeb. Through a farcical series of events, Richard has trapped in his apartment the theatrical producer whom he blames for ruining his career. As he contemplates killing the producer, Leopold serves as the voice of reason and morality, convincing Richard that if a villainous murderer like himself can turn over a new leaf and contribute to the good of society, then Richard's career is not hopeless, and murder is not a solution to his problems. Functioning as a Ghost of Gay Murderers Past, Leopold haunts the conscience of the playwright, even becoming his friend, and ultimately inspiring him to turn away from his own murderousness. By forming a bond with the gay murderer, the gay playwright avoids becoming a murderer himself.

Although these later plays do not have the same metaphysical dimensions as *Pterodactyls*, Silver is still appealing to the realm of the symbolic, with characters named after signifying figures: the homoerotic Christian martyr Sebastian, the Old Testament sacrificial son Isaac, and the archetypical and oft-represented queer killer Nathan Leopold. In each play, queer villainy in the form of the queer killer is confronted and psychically released (*Captivity*), pardoned (*Agony*), condemned (*Beautiful Child*) or proclaimed innocent (*Pterodactyls*). In all of them, the guilt and stigma of the criminal is inseparable from the guilt and stigma of the queer, struggling with shame, familial rejection, the loss of love, etc. Silver's plays often seem informed by a Freudian perspective, with Oedipal family romances, neuroses created by trauma, and symbolic dreams. A guiding principle behind Silver's dramaturgy is that the repressed will, inevitably, return. Much of the comedy in these plays comes from the farcical lengths to which neurotic characters will go to maintain a state of denial. Rather than pretending that the homophobic assertion of queer villainy does not exist or has no power, Silver confronts it head on. He does so in a dark comic universe that may be grotesque but is ultimately a realm in which the fear of queer evil can be fully, awfully realized and perhaps exorcized. As every Greek tragedian and Freudian therapist knows, the nightmare must be confronted if we are to be free of it.

Just as "doing evil" may be a method of taking control of terrifying forces, perhaps enacting queer evil on the stage is a method of controlling homophobia, accusations of villainy, and the fear of death faced by queer people in a homophobic society. Within the artful realm of the theatre, *Pterodactyls* and Silver's other black comedies simultaneously liberate the nightmare and control it, setting it free but also making it perform in ways not normally realized in mainstream discourse. By wresting queer evil out of the hands of the homophobes and giving it a new script, these plays allow for the possible creation of new meanings and understandings of the queer and the evil. Given the continuing use of homophobic rhetoric in cultural and political discourse, which positions queer people as monstrous threats to The Good, the need to understand and to challenge the symbolic uses of "queer evil" is perhaps more urgent than ever.*

---

*The author wishes to thank David Savran, Judith Milhous, and Alisa Solomon for their insightful feedback on previous versions of this essay. He is also indebted to Sara Warner, Constance Zaytoun, Nick Salvato, and the LGBT Theatre Focus Group of ATHE.

Bibliography

Alford, C. Fred. *What Evil Means to Us*. Ithaca, NY: Cornell University Press, 1997.
Bersani, Leo. *Homos*. Cambridge, MA: Harvard University Press, 1995.
Bronski, Michael. "Closet Drama." *Boston Phoenix*, Nov. 15, 2001. www.bostonphoenix.com/pages/boston/2001new1115.asp
Bumiller, Elisabeth. "Under Pressure, Conservative Withdraws from AIDS Panel." *New York Times*, January 24, 2003. <http://query.nytimes.com/gst/fullpage.html?res=9A06EEDB1639F937A15752C0A9659C8B63>
Eagleton, Terry. *Literary Theory: An Introduction*. Minneapolis, MN: University of Minnesota Press, 1983.
Edelman, Lee. *No Future: Queer Theory and the Death Drive*. Durham, NC: Duke University Press, 2004.
Goldstein, Richard. "What Gay Friendly Republicans?" *Village Voice*, June 4, 2003. <http://www.villagevoice.com/news/0323,goldstein,44586,1.html>
Harris, John F. "God Gave U.S. 'What We Deserve,' Falwell Says." *Washington Post*, September 14, 2001. <http://www.washingtonpost.com/wp-dyn/articles/A28620200lSep14.html>
Hussey, Maurice, ed. *The Chester Mystery Plays*. New York: Theatre Arts Books, 1957.
Ingebretsen, Edward J. *At Stake: Monsters and the Rhetoric of Fear in Public Culture*. Chicago: University of Chicago Press, 2001.
Miller, Neil. *Sex-Crime Panic: A Journey to the Paranoid Heart of the 1950s*. Los Angeles: Alyson Books, 2002.
Nietzsche, Frederick. *On the Genealogy of Morals*. Translated by W. Kaufmann and R. J. Hollingdale. New York: Vintage, 1969.
Savran, David. *The Playwright's Voice: American Dramatists on Memory, Writing and the Politics of Culture*. New York: Theatre Communications Group, 1999.
Silver, Nicky. *The Agony and the Agony*. Directed by Terry Kinney. Vineyard Theatre, New York, December 9, 2006.
_____. *Beautiful Child*. Directed by Terry Kinney. Vineyard Theatre, New York, February 21, 2004.
_____. *Etiquette and Vitriol: The Food Chain and Other Plays*. New York: Theatre Communications Group, 1996.
_____. *Raised in Captivity*. New York: Dramatists Play Service, 1995.
Sontag, Susan. *AIDS and Its Metaphors*. New York: Farrar, Straus, and Giroux, 1989.

Gay and Lesbian Theatre for Young People or the Representation of "Troubled Youth"

MANON VAN DE WATER
and ANNIE GIANNINI

Gay and lesbian theatre proliferated in the nineteen nineties, leading David Savran to declare, "the U.S. theater is now *out* in a way it has never been before, populated by writers and artists who are now joyously, proudly, — and matter-of-factly — queer" (153). Theatre with and for young people has largely been unaffected by this phenomenon. Plays for young people with gay and lesbian characters or any mention of homosexuality are rare, reflecting the degree to which heteronormativity dominates the field. When homosexuality is represented in theatre for young audiences, it is treated as a calamity, discreetly packaged in plays intended to teach lessons about tolerance. In the last decade, a small body of drama for young people has emerged that includes gay and lesbian characters. By and large, however, these characters are contained by a discourse of "troubled gay youth," which limits representation to those who are victimized because of their sexuality.

Censorship and the Discourse of "Troubled Gay Youth"

Plays with gay and lesbian characters or anything hinting at homosexuality are generally prohibited from being performed at schools or from being watched in a children's theatre. This has lead to a (self) censorship that has severely impacted the field and its audience. Jennifer Chapman, in her dissertation on heteronormativity in high school theatre, the most significant study in the field, discusses the rule in high school theatre that "plays should not be overtly sexual or have non-heterosexual characters (unless for the purpose of a joke)" (2). Chapman argues that "[b]y resisting and refusing to acknowledge non-heterosexual individuals in play choices, textbooks and scene study, high school theatre teaches students to actively ignore those identity positions in their world view" (201). Plays that hinge on "gay rumor," on the other hand, such as *The Children's Hour* and *Tea and Sympathy*, are allowed to be produced in high school theatre, as well as, albeit much less frequently and despite protests of parents and community groups, *The Laramie Project*. Each of these plays seems to demonstrate the taboo on homosexuality rather than challenge these taboos and they are clearly devoid of overt homosexual relationships, no less "healthy and happy" homosexual relationships. In general, those who produce theatre for young people that include gay and lesbian characters or relationships, whether in schools or professional theatres, work under a looming threat of censorship.

In 1999, seventeen-year-old Samantha Gellar won a young playwrights festival award from the Children's Theatre of Charlotte and Charlotte-Mecklenburg Schools for her play "Life Versus the Paperback Novel." The festival, however, refused to produce the play because it involved two lesbian characters, who fall in love (Associated Press A10). The organizers of the festival argued that the play was inappropriate for young people, and eventually agreed to stage it for an older audience. The controversy around the incident drew the attention of prominent artists in New York, including Holly Hughes, who organized a staged reading of the play with Lisa Kron and Mary-Louise Parker as part of a benefit for gay and lesbian youth organizations (McKinley E3).

In 2002, parents in Novato, California sued their school district for having their elementary school aged children watch a performance of *Cootie Shots: Theatrical Inoculations Against Bigotry for Kids, Parents, and Teachers* (Drukman 15), which has been the most widely produced drama written for elementary school aged children that includes gay and lesbian characters. Norma Bowles and Mark E. Rosenthal of Fringe Benefits, an educational Theatre company in Los Angeles, compiled the collection of skits, poems, and songs devised by young people and adults, as well as donated works from well-known artists such as Luis Alfaro and Tony Kushner. As the title of the collection suggests, the production aims to educate its audience about tolerance of differences in age, race, gender, sexuality, and class. Each piece only lasts long enough to inject its message, providing simple displays of "differences" and two obscure allegories that attempt to bring up issues regarding gay and lesbian rights. The lawsuit against the school district in Novato was eventually dropped (Futcher). *Cootie Shots* led to controversy again in 2005, when a school district in Morris, Minnesota, prevented its elementary school students from attending a performance by the University of Minnesota (Levy 2B).

While specific research within the field of theatre for young audience falls woefully behind, gender theory, in particular Judith Butler, gives insights in notions of gender as "constructed," opposing ontological reflections. In her seminal theory of performativity, Butler states, "There is neither an 'essence' that gender expresses or externalizes nor an objective ideal to which gender aspires, and because gender is not a fact, the various acts of gender create the idea of gender, and without those acts, there would be no gender at all" (*Gender Trouble* 190). The notions of coherent gender and sexual orientation have been established over time through practices that produce the illusion of stable identities. However, sexual identity categories are inherently suspect, because, as Butler contends, "identity categories tend to be instruments of regulatory regimes, whether as the normalizing categories of oppressive structures or as the rallying points for a liberatory contestation of that very oppression" (Butler, "Imitation" 121). Discourses regarding gay and lesbian young people contribute to the formulation of all young people's, not just "gay" young people's, subjectivities. As Butler asserts, "crafting a sexual position or reciting a sexual position, always involves becoming haunted by what's excluded" ("Extracts"). If we want to seriously confront homophobia, rather than perpetuate the notion that "gay" equals "trouble," we have to recognize that *all* young people must negotiate representations of "gay youth," whether they position themselves inside or outside that category.

Recent research in the social sciences, young adult literature, and television has called attention to how gay and lesbian young people have been represented, showing how the discourse of "troubled gay youth" perpetuates a stereotype. The male gendered word "gay" is used purposefully throughout this essay to reflect the disproportionate amount of research regarding gay men as opposed to lesbians. In doing so we acknowledge that the "troubled gay youth" image emerged out of a male-centric context and its prevalence continues to eclipse lesbian experiences. Other methodological factors contributing to the "troubled gay youth" image include the separate study of gay youth from heterosexual youth, which obscures similarity between the two groups, not looking for same-sex attraction within "heterosexual" groups, and inadequate examination of circumstances that lead to problems besides "sexual minority status" (Diamond 492–93). Ritch C. Savin-Williams notes a "narrow focus of research on the dramatic" and a "concentration on what goes wrong in the lives of gay youth" (61). Social science researchers have traditionally ignored same-sex attracted young people who are not victimized because of their sexuality or do not feel compelled to take on a sexual identity label.

Young people are generally constructed as "troubled" (Filax 37–38; Lesko 1–2), but gay youth are often marked as particularly distressed. The "gay youth" entry in the encyclopedia of *Youth, Education, and Sexualities*, for example, asserts that research has consistently found that gay youth are at greater risk than their heterosexual counterparts for: alcoholism, drug use, and substance abuse; mental health problems such as lower self-esteem and poor body image; eating disorders, particularly anorexia. In turn, eating disorders in males are associated with childhood gender nonconformity, which generally results in bullying and harassment — and a tendency to attempt suicide [Sears 348].

While these findings cannot be contested, the discourse of troubled gay youth perpetuates the notion that "being gay" puts you inherently at risk for a plethora of problems: gay young people will either become victims of their own self-hatred, or victims of the hatred of others.

Part of what gave rise to the image of gay young people as particularly troubled in comparison to their "heterosexual" peers are serious methodological flaws in the social sciences, as pointed out by Lisa Diamond and Ritch C. Savin-Williams. The fundamental methodological flaw, according to Diamond and Savin-Williams, lies in how researchers have defined "gay youth," because sexual orientation (defined by attraction), sexual identity (sense of identity), and sexual behavior (practice) frequently do not align. Diamond observes, "[O]ne need not possess a same-sex orientation to seek, experience, and enjoy same-sex sexuality, and correspondingly one need not possess a heterosexual orientation to seek, experience, and enjoy other-sex sexuality" (491). Savin-Williams echoes Diamond's findings: "[S]elf-identified heterosexuals engage in same-sex behavior and have same-sex attractions, and most same-sex oriented adolescents have a heterosexual sexual history and identity" (37). Given the slipperiness between sexual orientation, identity, and behavior, this research calls into question what defines a "gay" young person, remarkably similar to the questions Judith Butler raises. Other methodological factors contributing to the "troubled gay youth" image include the separate study of gay youth from heterosexual youth, which obscures similarity between the two groups, not looking for same-sex attraction within "heterosexual" groups, and inadequate examination of circumstances that lead to problems besides "sexual minority status" (Diamond 492–93). Savin-Williams notes a "narrow focus of research on the dramatic" and a "concentration on what goes wrong in the lives of gay youth" (61). Social science researchers have traditionally ignored same-sex attracted young people who are not victimized because of their sexuality or do not feel compelled to take on a sexual identity label.

The discourse of "troubled gay youth" has also been observed in young adult literature and television. Michael A. Cart and Christine A. Jenkins note that the main problems of gay young people are "discovering one's sexual identity, agonizing over whether or not to come out and suffering the slings and arrows of outrageous homophobia" (134). Rarely are they portrayed in the presence of a supportive gay young adult community (109–12). The same focus on coming out and isolation are the main problems of gay young characters in television (Davis 131; 138–39).

Certainly, those who call attention to the perils of gay young people have benevolent intentions of helping them out. However, Butler asks us to keep in mind "which version of lesbian or gay ought to be rendered visible, and which internal exclusions will that rendering visible institute" (Butler, "Imitation" 126). A particular version of gay youth has been put forth, while other versions have been ignored. What if same-sex attracted young people are no more troubled than other young people? What about the gay young people who enjoy opposite-sex encounters or the "heterosexual" young people who enjoy same-sex encounters? What about the young people who make the political choice to eschew sexual identity labels? How does the construction of "troubled gay youth" as perpetuated through the media, arts, and educational institutions, to name a few, contribute to the perpetuation of gay and lesbians as victims of society? In the following we will look at how compulsory heterosexuality in educational theatre and professional Theatre for Young Audiences is reinforced or contested by analyzing five plays geared toward youth with gay and lesbian characters. (We uncovered a both telling and appalling total of seventeen plays with gay and lesbian characters. These include plays created by young people and older plays not specifically for young audiences such as *The Children's Hour* and *Tea and Sympathy*—see Appendix.)

Homophobia, Rumors, and the Gay Victim

The Wrestling Season and *The Other Side of the Closet* (*The Other Side of the Closet*) originated in Toronto in 1997 [Roy 8]; however it was produced by the New Conservatory Theatre in San Francisco in 2000 [Denizet-Lewis 33; Rowland H9] and the company produced it again in 2007 ["New Conservatory"]) are one-act plays, produced most frequently for young people through touring to schools or inviting school audiences. They generally include post-show discussions or workshops. *A Service for Jeremy Wong* is a documentary play that begins after Jeremy Wong has been killed. All three plays focus on the negative effects of homophobia, but the reductive construction of young people in the plays precludes complex portrayals of young people's sexuality, and the discourses of "troubled gay youth," "coming out/outing" and "homophobia" work to reinscribe heteronormativity in each of the plays.

Various scholars (e.g., Felix; Griffin; Furstenberg; Lesko) have problematized the construction of adolescence as an ahistorical and transcultural developmental phase, challenging the notion of adolescence as a period of biologically determined instability. Nancy Lesko argues against what she calls "confident characterizations," that is, assumptions about adolescents that they "'come of age' into adulthood; they are controlled by raging hormones; they are peer-oriented; and they are represented by age" (2). These characterizations position adolescents in binary relation to presumably stable adults. In other words, it is assumed that teenagers cannot help their behavior because their bodies are out of control. All three plays discussed below clearly limit young people to "confident characterizations," essentializing both heterosexual and gay youth to stereotypical representations of adolescence. In accordance with the "raging hormone" label, the primary objective of several characters is to engage in heterosexual sex, or to create an image for themselves of one who does so. The majority of characters in each play — with the exception of one or two who represent moral consciousness — would instantly betray their long-term friends to save themselves from their surrounding oppressive peer group, taking the "peer oriented" stereotype to the extreme. According to these plays, young people are fundamentally naive, only caring about what other people think, albeit unfortunately.

The Wrestling Season centers on the lives of eight high school students, four of whom are young men in the midst of heavy competition over the wrestling season, with Luke and Matt rivaling Willy and Jolt. The four young women in the play have varying relationships to each other and the young men. Heather, Nicole, and Melanie are friends, while Kori is the outcast who befriends Matt and Luke. Homophobia emerges as a dominant problem of the play when a rumor spreads that the two main characters, Matt and Luke, are gay. No one in the play identifies as gay, although the play implies that Luke questions his sexuality throughout. Luke's questioning of his sexuality receives minimal attention because the play focuses on the dramas of the heterosexual social world. Nevertheless, the play recognizably perpetuates discourses of "homophobia," "outing/coming out" and "troubled gay youth."

The majority of characters are homophobic, except for the school outcast, Kori. At the beginning of the play, Willy witnesses Matt comforting his best friend Luke. Willy spreads the rumor to his friend Jolt that Matt and Luke are gay, calling them "perverts" and "disgusting" (Brooks 17). Jolt believes the rumor and shares it with his girlfriend Heather who happily consumes and passes along the latest juicy gossip (18–20). When the word "faggot" appears written on his locker, Luke decides to avoid Matt (21). Not only is the group of main characters generally homophobic, but so is the larger high school community. Matt complains to Kori:

MATT: They stare at me like I'm some kind of freak.
KORI: Who?
MATT: Everyone. They stare at me and then look away real fast when I see them. Like they're waiting for me to do something [23)].

Members of the high school community gawk and gape at anyone they think might be gay. Luke and Matt immediately take action to shake the dreaded "gay" label, Luke by continuing to avoid Matt, and Matt by dating Melanie, who is considered the school slut (26). It turns out that Luke may have been "outed" because the gay rumor causes him to doubt his heterosexuality, leading him to hint at "coming out" twice. Alienated from Matt, Luke turns to Kori for friendship and tries to communicate his doubts:

LUKE: Sometimes I do think about ... I don't know. Don't tell Matt.
KORI: I won't.
LUKE: I don't know if ... I don't know what it means [44].

Although he never directly states what "it" is, the implication is that he is doubtful of his heterosexuality. In a later scene, after two unknown assailants beat Luke in an ambiguously implied hate crime, he has another vague "coming out" moment:

LUKE: Don't you know why? They got me pegged. Pinned. Figured out. I'm a freak. And everybody knows it.
MATT: You're not a freak. They don't even know you.
LUKE: Maybe they do. Maybe they know something I don't.
MATT: They don't know anything.
LUKE: What if it's true about me? Have you ever thought about that?
MATT: No, I haven't.
LUKE: Well, maybe you should [51].

Through its focus on the perils of falling victim to the "gay rumor," the play contributes to the discourse of "troubled gay youth." Regardless of Luke's attractions or sense of sexual identity, several calamities befall him because of the gay label. He becomes a victim of verbal and physical harassment, suffers isolation from his friends and peers, spirals into self-doubt, and stops caring about himself. In addition to calling himself a "freak," Luke advises Matt he would be "better off" leaving him in the freezing garage (51).

Luke's victimization at the hands of his overwhelmingly homophobic peers reinforces heteronormativity by presenting a binary between the presumably heterosexual majority and those who question their heterosexuality. Further, Luke's inability to articulate the specifics of his inner confusion indicates that he finds the possibility of same-sex attraction too abhorrent to utter, aligning him, ideologically at least, with his homophobic peers. In this context, heterosexuality is not only the norm, but also homophobia. Interestingly, Brooks chose not to write Luke as a "gay" character "because sexuality is not as clearly defined as we all would like it to be. It's very difficult to put labels on anybody" ("Wrestling with Taboos" 46). Brooks may have intended to locate Luke's sexuality outside the terms of the gay/straight/bisexual system of compulsory identification that dominates contemporary society. However, Luke's inability to utter does more than position him outside the labeling system, or imply that he questions his sexuality; it also implies he is horrified by the possibility of same-sex attraction. In contrast, the majority of other characters in the play have no qualms about discussing and demonstrating heterosexual desires.

Although an ethos of "challenging taboos" surrounds productions of *The Wrestling Season*, the play does little more than reinscribe heteronormativity. As mentioned earlier, the reduction of young adults to stereotypes precludes complex portrayals of their sexuality. Reviewers have described the characters as "all-too-familiar teen stereotypes" (Liner), and "attractive, recognizable types, who might have stepped out of 'Dawson's Creek' or other teen TV series" (Berson E3). At one point or another, the objective of most characters, Jolt, Willy, Matt, Melanie, and Heather, is to maintain their reputations as popular heterosexuals. While the play attempts to problematize such objectives by didactically showing the cruel consequences, it simultaneously normalizes them by conveying the idea that most young people play heterosexual charades at all hours of the day.

Statements about productions of the play are quick to disclaim its "homosexual" subject matter, assuring that *The Wrestling Season* will not challenge the dominance of heteronormativity. In an outright bigoted statement, the Children's Theatre of Maine claimed,

"We want to make sure we're not promoting any sort of lifestyle. It's more about peer pressure in general and establishing an identity in general, and (homosexuality) just happens to be a component in that." (qtd. in Staff 7E). The Seattle Children's Theatre assured, "It's more about rumors and people accusing people of being a certain way. It's not saying anything's OK; it's saying you don't push people into corners." (qtd. in Armstrong 12). Indeed, the public need not fear the play will communicate the acceptability of gay sexuality or same-sex attraction, rather it will convey a safer, generalized, moralistic message about "rumors."

Like *The Wrestling Season*, *The Other Side of the Closet* focuses on the perils of being labeled "gay" in a homophobic high school context in which everyone seems obsessed with heterosexual sex. However, the homophobia in the play is taken to extreme proportions. The play opens with Carl, the gay main character, and a group of male friends beating up a man while screaming anti-gay epithets (Roy 10). Anti-gay slurs and statements appear on most pages of the play. Every main character hates gay and lesbian people, save one, Paulette, who regularly disparages the attitudes of her peers on behalf of her gay uncle (13–14).

Carl's story epitomizes "troubled gay youth." When his gay-hating friends, guided by their ringleader, Rick, drive past the local gay bars and spot Carl entering one of them, they unleash their hatred toward gays on him and "out" him, setting off a chain of unfortunate events. Miscellaneous students in the hallway gossip about Carl, surrounding him in a cacophony of hate speech:

> SECOND MALE STUDENT: I hope Rick kicks the crap out of him, because if he doesn't, I will.
> FIRST FEMALE STUDENT: Think he'll show up for the fight?
> SECOND FEMALE STUDENT: If he doesn't we'll just go and find him.
> FIRST MALE STUDENT: Faggot.
> SECOND FEMALE STUDENT: Homo.
> SECOND MALE STUDENT: Fairy.
> FIRST FEMALE STUDENT: Queer.
> ALL: Fag, homo, fairy, queer! Fag, homo, fairy, queer! *Fag, homo, fairy, queer! Fag, homo, fairy, queer!!* Fight!! Fight!! Fight!! [27–28].

Eventually, Rick physically beats Carl, but the harassment continues at home through phone calls that his parents intercept. When Carl comes out to his parents, they have homophobic reactions as well. Carl's mortified mother laments the thought of him "getting that disease" (39) and his father stops speaking to him (40).

Life at school gets progressively worse for Carl until he exiles himself to an alternative school program for gay and lesbian students. However, once he is there, he still cannot escape his own homophobic attitudes. Carl complains to Paulette about an argument with another student in the program:

> CARL: He acts real faggy. And after we saw a documentary how the Nazis persecuted gays in the concentration camps the class had a discussion and I said ...
> PAULETTE: What?
> CARL: That maybe the Nazis would've left gays alone if the more, you know, queeny ones could've acted normal [44–45].

Just as Carl begins to warm up to his new environment, Rick hunts him down for another confrontation. The truth comes out that Rick is really persecuting Carl because he feels ashamed about some sexual contact they shared as twelve-year-olds. Carl beats Rick severely and subsequently commits suicide, quintessentially fulfilling his "troubled gay youth" destiny. Carl and Rick both suffer because of their same-sex interaction. Rick may not be attracted to other men anymore, but he certainly suffers for his previous same-sex encounters.

Similar to *The Wrestling Season*, the play reinforces heteronormativity by conveying the idea that most young people are homophobes obsessed with heterosexual sex. Moreover, nearly all the adults mentioned in the play, Carl's parents, his friend's parents, and the school principal, carry anti-gay and lesbian attitudes, except for Paulette's gay uncle, who never appears onstage. The only place Carl finds acceptance is while he is in exile from his high school and friends. There is a clear binary between the heterosexual and homophobic majority, and the gay and lesbian minority. The play communicates the lesson: "Homophobia is bad," with the corresponding message that same-sex attracted young people are doomed to a life of exile characterized by hatred, violence, and isolation.

Reviewers attack the stereotypical binaries in the play, deeming it "a portrait of a bigoted society in stark shades of black and white" (Coulbourn 42) and "a black-and-white mortality play" (Wagner). While the focus is on homophobia, previews of the productions carry disclaimers, assuring it will not convey the idea that it is okay to be gay. Just as *The Wrestling Season* is about how bad it is to spread rumors, *The Other of Side of the Closet* is posited as being about the idea that hatred is bad in general. A preview of the initial production in Toronto assures, "Instead of attempting to explore and justify the gay lifestyle, Roy ... concentrates on the morality of a society that allows unreasoning hatred to thrive, regardless of the subject of that hatred" (Coulbourn 42). A preview from California notes, "The secret in the play ... is being gay. But organizers said it could just as well be any other issue that involves discrimination" (Rowland H9). The play is not actually affirming gay or lesbian people, it simply warns against hating anyone, attempting to criticize homophobia while simultaneously preserving heteronormativity.

A Service for Jeremy Wong by Daniel Kehde is the most extreme in terms of its emphasis on the discourses of "homophobia," "troubled gay youth," and "tolerance." However, the play is different from the others in that its primary focus is on the reaction of a small rural high school in West Virginia to the fatal beating of Jeremy Wong, an "out" gay student. In this instance, Jeremy's "trouble" comes solely from those who persecute him to death, rather than a combination of self-hatred and anti-gay harassment. The documentary style play begins post-mortem and explores the issue of whether the students will hold a memorial service.

The majority of young people in the play are racist and homophobic and they speak in a stereotypically teenaged manner. The play begins with a high school student, Debbie, disclosing the central dilemma of the play in a confessional style:

> What am I supposed to do, you know? I mean, I know I'm president of the student council. I know that I'm supposed to lead the school. But ... I mean, I didn't

know him. Most of us didn't know him. Those of us who did didn't like him....
I know it's all wrong to think this but ... I mean, this is West Virginia, you know?
It doesn't get anymore redneck than this. And Jeremy Wong was gay. And not a
closet case either. But right out there, in-your-face gay. And I know this is wrong
but ... it was only a matter of time, wasn't it? I know I'm supposed to be outraged
at what Butch and the Clam did, you know?.... I mean ... it's Jeremy Wong, you
know? This would be a whole lot easier if he'd been a football player [Kehde 5].

All the young people in the play use a "teenaged" language that is composed of so many "I mean," "I know," "you know" phrases that they emanate immaturity, in contrast to the adults who speak concisely and clearly. In addition, several young characters make racist statements (6, 19, 24, 51). From the beginning, the play presents a group of close-minded students who need a lesson about "tolerance."

The overwhelmingly homophobic high school community is initially stratified between those who relentlessly persecute gay people, the few who have sympathy for Jeremy in death, but condoned his persecution when he was alive, and the Christians whose beliefs prohibit them from mourning for Jeremy. Butch and Clam, Jeremy's heartless murderers, lead the gay-haters. Butch has no idea he did anything wrong, and Clam at least acknowledges that they committed a crime:

BUTCH: I can't believe they're doing this.
CLAM: Shut up.
BUTCH: He's just a little faggot.
CLAM: Yeah, well he's a dead little faggot now.
BUTCH: Dad says he is going to get us out on bail. We won't have to spend the
    night again.
CLAM: Wrong. You don't get it, do you?
BUTCH: What?
CLAM: We killed him, Butch. That makes us murderers.
BUTCH: We were just fooling around [8].

Similarly cold-hearted students come to Butch and Clam's defense and discourage other students from mourning. For example, Samantha argues with a classmate who is crying over Jeremy's death, asking, "Is this someone who deserves to be treated like a martyr?" (10). In Butch and Clam's absence, another student, Greg, leads a posse that continues to persecute the gay students at the school and intimidate anyone who shows support for Jeremy. They succeed by deterring students from attending a candlelight vigil for Jeremy (33), and they break a student's arm for wearing an armband in Jeremy's honor (58). In order to counter Jeremy's memorial service, Greg campaigns for a "decency rally" (58) to protest Jeremy's sexuality based on their "right to hate" (65).

Almost as despicable as the villainous gay-hating students are the Christians whose religious upbringing somehow prevents them from mourning Jeremy's death. Mary, the president of the school bible club, expresses this viewpoint:

> A bunch of us have been raised Christian ... well we have. Donnie, you and I've been going since we were born it seems like, and we've been told — and Cynthia and Tiff and Maryellen — I mean really told over and over again about how being, you know, the way Jeremy was, you know, how that was totally wrong. No, now listen. I've got to tell you, I'm not sure I feel comfortable making all the kids come to the service like that. I mean, there's an awful lot of us who thought he was really disgusting and I mean, I don't mean to talk ill of dead, but, I, I'm sorry, I ... I really can't feel that sorry for him. And I feel guilty about feeling that way, I guess, but I know I'm not alone here. And I don't think we'd better make anyone come to this service who doesn't want to. I mean, I wouldn't go. Never in a thousand years [12].

Homophobia is taken to an extreme because students and parents use Jeremy's death as an opportunity to reiterate their moral convictions against gay people (11, 54). One step above these students are those who mourn Jeremy's loss, but condoned Jeremy's harassment while he was alive.

Only two students were actually friends with Jeremy: Timmy, a fellow victimized gay student, and Veronica. Their perspectives receive minimal attention throughout the play. A few other students in the school are implicated as victims of harassment but they never appear and no one discusses them in depth (45, 66).

As the play progresses, the students change their minds and the majority of the school decides to attend Jeremy's service. When Greg crashes the service, preaching hatred, a reformed Clam intervenes on Jeremy's behalf, publicly describing Jeremy's gruesome death and expressing remorse over what he has done (66–67). In the aftermath, the students at the school learn to embrace "tolerance." Debbie narrates this shift:

> A month after Jeremy was killed, the student council passed a resolution stating that this school,
> "Shall always strive to be free of all intolerance
> Be it based on intelligence, socio-economics,
> Age, race, gender, or sexual orientation."
> It's on a plaque by the office when you first come into the school. But a lot of us are wondering, you know, I mean, shouldn't it have always been that way? [68].

In the conclusion, the play elides its own focus on homophobia in favor of a generalized moralistic message about tolerating differences, and this is perpetuated in public statements about the play: a Minnesota high school drama coach, who quit her job after the school board would not allow her to direct the play, claims that the play is more about "intolerance of difference than specifically prejudice against gays" (Ford 1S).

Confronting homophobia, as any phobia, however, goes far beyond "tolerance," a stance that is corroborated by scholars in the field of education. In the most general sense, Noddings posits that understanding diversity is paramount to any movement toward constructing a global identity: "Where people not only claim difference but also celebrate it, global citizens cannot pretend that differences are unimportant. Diversity becomes essential to all policymaking conversations because we must hear the voice of the other" (14). A focus on diversity and understanding differences in relationships, rather than as categories by themselves, also underlies queer pedagogy.

Queering the Subject

Queering the curriculum as a means of de-essentializing notions of sexuality and identity, destabilizing and changing normative narratives, and disrupting binary discourses that privilege heterosexual behavior and marginalize the "other" has slowly gained support over the past decade, as it challenges the prevailing images of queer youth as victimized by society. Susan Talburt, among others, maintains that "[i]n decentering the homosexual/heterosexual binary, queer curriculum focuses on understanding differences within and among persons rather than differences in categories of persons" (69). Queer can be as much an identification as a challenge to the very notion of identity. Rather than being concerned with identities in and of themselves, it focuses on "what gets represented through certain identities, and what do these same identities veil, obscure, or ignore? ... the shift from identity to identification is a shift from an assimilationist politics to a politics of difference" (Letts 328).

Within the small body of plays we could uncover that include gay and lesbian characters or subject material, only two defy the homosexual/heterosexual binary, "queering" the subject, and in doing so avoiding the perpetuated notions of "troubled youth."

The Geography Club (2003), Brent Hartinger's two-act stage adaptation of his young adult novel of the same name, openly challenges dominant heteronormativity and, as such, has yet to be produced in a theatre for young audiences. The play follows a group of gay, bisexual, lesbian, and straight students who form an alliance. Like the anti-gay bashing plays, the play is situated in a homophobic high school context in which students face pressure to have heterosexual sex. As such, *The Geography Club* contributes to the discourses of "homophobia," "outing/coming out," and "troubled gay youth"; however, these elements do not subdue homosexuality. Instead, the play breaks away from the restrictive modes of representation in the other plays by presenting both gay and lesbian relationships, and showing young people coping healthfully and collectively with the hostile aspects of their environment, thus presenting a world that allows for the possibility of finding enjoyment rather than misery in homosexuality.

At the beginning of the play, Russel narrates his desire for the "hunky baseball player" (1), Kevin, another student in the men's locker room:

> RUSSEL: Okay, so maybe there is a short answer to that question about why I felt so out-of-place in the locker room. I like guys. Seeing them naked, I mean. But this was something that Jared and Nate, and especially Kevin Land there, would never understand [4].

Although Russel feels isolated because he is the only gay person in a homophobic context, he articulates his desire throughout the play. His openness moves the play beyond the muted homosexuality of the anti-gay bashing plays, which exclude direct discussions of same-sex attraction.

Russel soon discovers that he is not the only person with same-sex desire in his high school when he and Kevin nervously come out to each other through coded language about how they are both "[t]oo busy to have a girlfriend" (13). While the elusiveness of their language can be viewed as a response to their homophobic environment, it is also indicative of their mutual desire; they are afraid of being rejected by each other. Russel and Kevin do not find the possibility of same-sex attraction abhorrent, but they do recognize the risks involved in disclosing their sexualities. Following this disclosure, Russel comes out to his best friend Min who responds:

> MIN: Um, Russel. You know Terese Buckman?
> RUSSEL: The soccer-player? Yeah.
> MIN: She's a lesbian.
> RUSSEL: Oh.
> MIN: She's also my girlfriend.
> RUSSEL: Yeah? Cool. Anyway, so you're okay with my being —?
> MIN: No, Russel. I mean she's my *girlfriend*.
> RUSSEL: What are you saying? That you're gay too?
> MIN: Actually, I think bisexual is probably more accurate [17–18].

In contrast to the heterosexual/homosexual binary mode of representation in which a lone gay male comes out to "heterosexual" people who respond with hatred and disgust, *The Geography Club* portrays gay, bisexual, and lesbian young people coming out to each other and finding solidarity.

Russel and Min decide to gather everyone for a meeting, which is awkward at first as Russel comments, "Just because we were all gay, that didn't mean we had anything in common!" (21). The students initially commiserate about their difficult lives, but not without humor. Hartinger mocks the "troubled gay youth" stereotype:

> MIN: We're all alone.
> TERESE: Man, is that true.
> KEVIN: Sure can't tell your family. My dad would go feral if he knew I was gay or whatever.
> IKE: Can't tell your friends either. It's one thing when they're talking about some cause. It's another thing when they're talking about you.
> MIN: Actually, I meant we're all alone in the restaurant. But hey, whatever gets the conversation rolling! [22].

The meeting results in the formation of "The Geography Club," the most boring guise they could think of and a code for a gay, lesbian, and bisexual student organization. Further distancing the gay characters from the gay victim versus homophobic mob model is that not all heterosexual students want to bash gay people: three heterosexual identified students respond supportively when members of the group come out to them. For example, when Belinda, a straight identified student shows up at the club meeting, hoping to study geography, and finds out it is a gay student group she decides to join anyway, enthusiastically exclaiming, "Damn! I'm the token straight!" (62).

At the end of the first act, Russel and Kevin explore their desire for each other in the ultimate taboo breaking scene, in which Kevin admits his feelings for Russel and they kiss each other (50–53). However, their relationship and the entire club begin to deteriorate when the school newspaper announces that an anonymous student spoke to a teacher about starting a group for gay students. In the aftermath, Kevin chooses popularity over Russel and the club, which ends their relationship. The group itself, though, reconfigures to form an open — as opposed to secretive — gay-straight-bisexual alliance (117–18).

It is rather telling that the only play for teenagers that openly defies the homosexual/heterosexual binary — by including not only gay, lesbian, and bisexual characters, but complicating these identity locations by incorporating race, class and other identifiers that shift the focus from identity to identification — has not been produced to date by any professional theatre company. (In an e-mail to the authors Hartinger writes: "There have been three or four 'readings' at theaters, and the first production was ... a week ago, I think. Another is scheduled for February. But it's too 'controversial' for most high schools and children's theaters [so says my agent], so most of the productions are either private companies or GSA programs." [Re: Geography Club"]) In a 2003 interview Hartinger admits that the original novel was initially rejected by seventeen publishers because "there was no market for a book like this" and that the agent "wast[ed] her time on a gay teen book" (Warn 2).

Speech and Debate by Stephen Karam (2007), on the other hand, was the inaugural production of the Off Broadway Roundabout Underground Theatre, which promotes emerging playwrights. The production played to rave reviews and was so successful that the run was extended until December 30, 2007. *Speech and Debate* hinges on rumors, but contrary to the plays discussed earlier, its queer teen characters are the fundamental agents of the play: Howie, a gay transfer student who has been "out" since he was ten; Diwata, the rockstar wanna-be who podcasts her personal diary; and Solomon, the eager reporter who is obsessed with exposing gay men having under-age sex. United by Diwata's podcast, they form an alliance to partake in the speech and debate club and expose the drama teacher. The play is inspired by a transcript of an on-line chat between the former mayor of Spokane, Washington, and an 18-year-old male:

> DANNYBOY: what do you like about youth?
> THERIGHTBI-GUY: energy,
> THERIGHTBI-GUY: wonder,
> DANNYBOY: personally i like the tight ass
> DANNYBOY: lol
> DANNYBOY: but thats just me
> DANNYBOY: lol
> THERIGHTBI-GUY: their hopes for the future. and their whole life in front of them
> DANNYBOY: so their innocence?
> THERIGHTBI-GUY: no, i don't think. i didn't think of you as an innocent
> DANNYBOY: thats good ... cuz i'm not [Karam 2].

Analogous, the play starts out with an on-line chat between Howie and someone who turns out to be the drama teacher of the school. Howie is new in town and recognizes the e-mail address from the syllabus. Hearing Diwata's podcast, in which she publicly debunks the teacher for not casting her in the school musical, hinting that she knows his secret, Howie sends her a message, "have my own dirt on Healy. yur right.... Call me" (23). Howie's message is picked up by Solomon, who decides to interview both for his article, and the three meet in a common quest. However, the play is less about exposing the drama teacher or about, in Solomon's words, "the phenomenon of *Republican conservatives,* politicians who spend their careers championing morality, American values, *the sanctity of marriage*" (12), but more about the characters' own confrontations with their sexuality, religion, parents, and the adult attempts to keep them "innocent," which is epitomized by the statement of the Department of Public Safety to which the school adheres:

> Children should not be asked to keep special secrets from their parents, and, of course, children should not be asked to touch anyone in the bathing suit areas of their body or allow anyone to touch them in those areas [Karam 2].

The metaphorical framework of the play is the speech and debate club, which Diwata uses to show off her self-perceived talents, Howie as a vehicle to start a Gay-Straight Alliance, and Solomon as a medium to get his story out. The plot gets messy when personal secrets are revealed, childhood stories inserted in the "collaborative speech" project, and when a reporter uses their story as a vehicle to promote her book, a somewhat dangling twist. The messiness has a "queering" effect though, exposing taboos and the myth of childhood innocence and painting a far more complex picture of (sexual) relationships, identification, and performativity through the characters. The play lacks a clear ending: as Solomon has decided to talk to his parent that he doesn't want to go to Exodus camp to be "cured," his first blog gets answered by Biguy, the drama teacher.

The website of Roundabout Theatre doesn't indicate whether this production is trying to reach a young, no less school, audience in specific. But in an e-mail to the authors, Roundabout's education department stated that they did have an all-student matinee, and that with the extended run specific educational material may be developed (Figley).

Preliminary Conclusion

In its present state, the field of theatre with and for youth remains for the most part an unexamined vehicle for reiterating heteronormative (mis)conceptions of young people. We have attempted to bring attention to the gap between theatre for young people and the broader realm of gay, lesbian, and queer theatre in the United States. Clearly, there are no easy solutions for diminishing this gap, especially considering that theatre for young people has evaded the call for gay and lesbian visibility of decades past. Nevertheless, theatre for young people is in dire need of a "queering," that is, an understanding of its limitations and a deliberate subversion of those limitations, and this approach need not be relegated to sexuality, although that has been our focus. Several reviews of the plays discussed in this article indicate that young people are eager for a public space in which to acknowledge the diversity of their sexualities. Can theatre for young audiences become a site for such acknowledgment? Or will it continue to assuage adult anxiety regarding young sexuality? Who benefits from packaging homosexuality in didactic narratives of "troubled gay youth"? Through posing these questions, we hope to foster further exploration of how young people can be represented outside the dominant restrictive models so that they, too, may become citizens.

Bibliography

Anderson, Robert. *Tea and Sympathy*. New York: Samuel French, 1953.

Armstrong, Doree. "Rules of Wrestling Set the Stage for Emotional Issues of Teens." PrevIEW of *The Wrestling Season*, Seattle Children's Theatre. *Seattle Post Intelligencer*, Jan. 11, 2002. < http://web.lexis-nexis.com/> (accessed Oct. 11, 2007).

Associated Press. "Festival Bans Play with Lesbian Characters." *New York Times*, February 20, 1999.

Berson, Misha. "'The Wrestling Season' Explores Teen Troubles." *Seattle Times*, January 18, 2002.

Bowles, Norma, and Mark E. Rosenthal, eds. *Cootie Shots: Theatrical Inoculations against Bigotry for Kids, Parents and Teachers*. New York: Theatre Communications Group, 2001.

Brooks, Laurie. *The Wrestling Season*. Woodstock, IL: Dramatic, 2000.

_____, and Russell Scott Smith. "Wrestling with Taboos: An Interview with the Playwright." *American Theatre* 17.9 (2000): 46.

Butler, Judith. *Gender Trouble: Feminism and the Subversion of Identity*. New York: Routledge, 2006.

_____. "Imitation and Gender Insubordination (1990)." In *The Judith Butler Reader*, edited by Sara Salih and Judith Butler, 119–37. Malden, MA: Blackwell, 2004.

_____, Peter Osborn, and Lynne Segal. "Extracts from Gender as Performance: An Interview with Judith Butler," 1993. http://www.theory.org.uk/but-intl.htm (accessed September 20, 2007).

Cart, Michael, and Christine A. Jenkins. *The Heart Has Its Reasons: Young Adult Literature with Gay/Lesbian/Queer Content, 1969–2004*. Lanham, MD: Scarecrow, 2006.

Chapman, Jennifer. *The Theatre Kids: Heteronormativity and High School Theatre*. Ph.D. diss., University of Wisconsin-Madison, 2005. Ann Arbor: UMI, 2005. ATT 3175579.

Coulbourn, John. "YPT's Closet Is Worth Getting Into." *Toronto Sun*, November 22, 1997. http://web.lexis-nexis.com/ (accessed July 11, 2007).

"CTM to Take a Few More Wacks at Children's Theater Mold." *Portland Press Herald*, October 14, 2001.

Davis, Glyn. "'Saying It Out Loud': Revealing Television's Queer Teens.'" In *Teen TV: Genre, Consumption and Identity*, edited by Glyn Davis and Kay Dickinson, 127–40. London: BFI, 2004.

Denizet-Lewis, Benoit. "Putting Tolerance to the Test; Canadian Playwright Hopes to Bring 'Other Side of the Closet' to Bay Area Students." *San Francisco Chronicle*, February 27, 2000. <http://web.lexis-nexis.com/> (accessed July 11, 2007).

Diamond, L. M. "New Paradigms for Research on Heterosexual and Sexual Minority Development." *Journal of Clinical and Adolescent Psychology* 32.4 (2003): 490–98.

Drukman, Steven. "Cootie Shots: Tolerance on Trial?" *American Theatre* 19.6 (2002): 15.

Figley, Allison. "Re: Speech and Debate." Email to the authors, December 14, 2007.

Filax, Gloria. *Queer Youth in the Province of the "Severely Normal*. Vancouver, BC: UBC, 2006.

Ford, Tom. "Play Vetoed; Jordan Drama Coach Quits." *Star Tribune* [Minneapolis], April 7, 2004.

Furstenberg, Frank F. "The Sociology of Adolescence and Youth in the 1990s: A Critical Commentary" *Journal of Marriage and the Family* 62.4 (2000): 896–910.
Futcher, Jane. "Novato Diversity Lawsuit Dropped." *Marin Independent Journal*, September 5, 2003. <http://web.lexis-nexis.com/> (accessed February 3, 2007).
Griffin, Christine. "Troubled Teens: Managing Disorders of Transition and Consumption." *Feminist Review* 55 (1997): 4–21.
Hartinger, Brent. *The Geography Club*. Unpublished play, 2003.
_____, "Re: Geography Club Productions." Email to the authors, November 1, 2007.
Hellman, Lillian. *The Children's Hour*. New York: Dramatists Play Service, 1953.
Karam, Stephen. *Speech and Debate*. Unpublished play, 2007.
Kaufman, Moisés, et al. *The Laramie Project*. New York: Vintage, 2001.
Kehde, Daniel, S. *A Service for Jeremy Wong*. Tallahassee, FL: Eldridge, 2000.
Lesko, Nancy. *Act Your Age!: A Cultural Construction of Adolescence*. New York: Routledge, 2001.
Letts, Will. "Queer[ing] Curriculum." In *Gender and Education* 1, edited by Barbara J. Banks, 327–30. Westport, CT: Praeger, 2007.
Levy, Paul. "Schools Cancel Tickets for 'Cootie Shots' Play." *Star Tribune* [Minneapolis], April 20, 2005.
Liner, Elaine. "The Wrestling Season Takes a Strong Hold on Tough Teen Issues." *Dallas Observer*, May 12, 2005. http://web.lexis-nexis.com/> (accessed February 3, 2007).
McKinley, Jesse. "A Prize Play, a Dispute and a Benefit." *New York Times*, June 14, 1999. http://web.lexis-nexis.com/ (accessed October 11, 2007).
"New Conservatory Theatre" http://www.nctcsf.org/opportunities.html (accessed October 19, 2007).
Noddings, N. "Global Citizenship: Promises and Problems." In *Educating for Global Awareness*, edited by N. Noddings, 1–21. New York: Teachers College Press, 2005.
Rowland, Marijke. "Teen Gay Issues Tackled by SF Troupe's Play." *Modesto Bee*, October 6, 2000.
Roy, Edward. "The Other Side of the Closet." In *Rave: Young Adult Drama*, 7–55. Winnipeg, MB: Blizzard, 2000.
Savin-Williams, Ritch C. *The New Gay Teenager*. Cambridge, MA: Harvard University Press, 2005.
Savran, David. "Queer Theatre and the Disarticulation of Identity." *The Queerest Art: Essays on Lesbian and Gay Theatre*, edited by Alisa Solomon and Framji Minwalla, 152–67. New York: New York University Press, 2002.
Sears, James T. "Gay Youth." In *Youth, Education, and Sexualities: an International Encyclopedia*. Vol. 1, edited by James T. Sears, 347–52. Westport: Greenwood Press, 2005.
Talburt, Susan. "Queer Theory." In *Gender and Education*. Vol. 1, edited by Barbara J. Banks, 63–70. Westport, CT: Praeger, 2007.
Wagner, Vit. "Plays about Teens Not Up to Challenge." *Toronto Star*, April 17, 1999. http://web.lexis-nexis.com/ (accessed July 11, 2007).
Warn, Sara. "Interview with Brent Hartinger, Author of Geography Club." In *After Ellen*, June 2003. <http://www.afterellen.com/archive/ellen/People/hartingerinterview.html> (accessed October 24, 2007).

Further Resources: Theater for Young Audiences (TYA) Plays with Gay and Lesbian Characters

Acito, Tim. *Zanna, Don't!: A Musical Fairytale*. PS Classics, 2003.
Anderson, Robert. *Tea and Sympathy*. New York: Samuel French, 1953.
Bowles, Norma, ed. *Friendly Fire: An Anthology of Three Plays*. Los Angeles, CA: A.S.K. Theater Projects, 1997.
―――, and Mark E. Rosenthal, eds. *Cootie Shots: Theatrical Inoculations against Bigotry for Kids, Parents and Teachers*. New York: Theatre Communications Group, 2001.
Brooks, Laurie. *The Wrestling Season*. Woodstock, IL: Dramatic Publishing, 2000.
Coo, Clarence. *Removing the Glove*. Boston, MA: Baker's Plays, 1994.
Guehring, Brian, and Tracy Iwersen, eds. *The Best of Pride Players*. Omaha, NE: Omaha Theater Company, 2004.
Hartinger, Brent. *The Geography Club*. Unpublished Play, 2003.
Hellman, Lillian. *The Children's Hour*. New York: Dramatists Play Service, 1953.
Karam, Stephen. *Speech and Debate*. Unpublished play, 2007.
Kaufman, Moisés, et al. *The Laramie Project*. New York: Vintage, 2001.
Kehde, Daniel, S. *A Service for Jeremy Wong*. Tallahassee: Eldridge, 2000.
Kiefer, Nancy. *Could Angels Be Blessed*. Woodstock, IL: Dramatic Publishing, 1995.
López, Josefina. "Food for the Dead." In *Food for the Dead and La Pinta: Two One-Act Plays*, 5–32. Woodstock, IL: Dramatic Publishing, 1996.
Mason, Timothy. "The Less than Human Club." In *New Plays from A.C.T.'s Young Conservatory*. Vol. 2, edited by Craig Slaight, 97–152. Lyme, NH: Smith and Kraus, 1996.
Moraga, Cherríe. "Giving Up the Ghost." In *Heroes and Saints and Other Plays*, 4–35. Albuquerque, NM: West End, 1994.
Roy, Edward. "The Other Side of the Closet." In *Rave: Young Adult Drama*, 7–55. Winnipeg, MB: Blizzard, 2000.

Crossing the Border
Irish Drama and the Queer American Character

David Cregan

American drama and American gay and lesbian issues have had a substantial impact on the world outside the geographical boundaries of the United States. Perhaps on the most obvious level, American playwrights, directors, and actors have shaped the development of genre, production technique, and acting style in the twentieth century, but American gay, lesbian, and transgendered culture and queer politics have had an even more powerful influence on the consciousness of artists in other countries. Subsequently, the politics and performance of gay and lesbian identities in the United States, both theatrical and political, have often served international theatre practitioners in their attempts to artistically liberate cultural heterosexism through the representation of indigenous gay identities. In this essay I will examine how the use of the American character in the writing of the Irish playwright Frank McGuinness functions as a queer interference in the conservative and homogenous culture of twentieth-century Ireland.

Irish theatre has its foundations in the revolutionary notions of early twentieth-century European nationalism, and is deeply woven into the issues of gender and identity, which, in turn, thematically preoccupy much of American gay and lesbian drama. As the Irish attempted to liberate their suppressed native identity from that of their British colonial occupiers, they reached deep within the experiences and memories of their own communities in order to identify the unique characteristics that represented "Irishness." Interestingly, the historian John A. Murray argues, "It was the American Irish rather the domestic Irish who increased the element of Anglophobia in Irish nationalism" (Murray 111), thus acknowledging the symbiotic political rapport between Ireland and the United States. Centuries of colonial oppression and suppression served as an artistic impetus for early Irish nationalist dramatists who saw the fiction of the stage as a safe place to represent these otherwise outlawed identities. Subsequently, the dramatic project of the retrieval of a separate Irish identity from that of the imposed British colonial one was revolutionary in its attempts to overturn false conceptions of the Irish as represented by the British. In order to do so, the Irish co-opted British social conventions and cultural classifications, upsetting colonial normativity in order to provoke political revolution through cultural representation.

Ideological connections between the project of Irish nationalism and the work of gay and lesbian theatre in the United States are not difficult to make. Colonial identities were traditionally marked out through gender and sexual identity and relied substantially on the essentialized notions of hegemonic homogeneity. The British demonized the Irish male as dangerous and animalistic, often representing the Irish in the nineteenth-century media as a cross between a monkey and a human being. This primal and "uncivilized" version of Irishness functioned as a metaphor for the Irish people themselves. British representation of the political idea of the island of Ireland was always female, Hibernia; Hibernia was portrayed as a delicate Irish woman in need of the cultured protection of masculinized Imperial Britain. Thus, colonial issues of drastic gender binaries parallel minority gay and lesbian identification by majority heterosexual culture and society. Irish theatre functioned as a form of artistic self-identification and political protestation against the reductive stereotyping that supports and upholds the justification of suppression through the threat of difference.

While the Irish dramatic tradition has spent most of the twentieth century preoccupied with the broader political liberation of Irish identity, one Irish playwright has continually introduced gay and lesbian identities into the cultural debates surrounding the issues of what it means to be Irish after eight hundred years of British colonial occupation. Irish playwright Frank McGuinness began his dramatic career in the early 1980s and has continually included gay and lesbian characters in his writing. McGuinness has artistically created ideological connections between postcolonial identity politics and gay and lesbian issues by explicitly engaging notions of citizenship and belonging in Ireland as played out on the stage through dramatic conventions.

Although the primary focus of this paper is on the use of the gay American character on the Irish stage, it is important to contextualize the intersection of drama and social debate in Ireland. To this day the theatre plays a significant role in social conversation in Ireland due largely to its rich legacy of historical roots in the revolutionary liberation of the nation itself. Although Dublin was traditionally a major stop on the touring circuit of any British theatre company, very little indigenous drama existed before the end of the nineteenth century. In the summer of 1897 the Nobel Prize winning poet and playwright William Butler Yeats planned the beginnings of what would become known as the Irish Literary Theatre with his mentor and friend Lady

Augusta Gregory. Along with their colleague Edward Martyn, the group began the most important theatrical movement in Irish history — an artistic association which would not only transform Irish theatre, but would contribute vastly to the revolution of ideas that would drive the British Empire off the island of Ireland forever.

Through the vision and inspiration of Yeats, Gregory, and Martyn, Irish characters and Irish themes were to take center stage in their theatre. This project would rescue the Irish character and narrative from the supporting, oftentimes antagonistic, role it consistently played on the British stage. Already one can make the connection between concepts of national identity and gay and lesbian drama as the Irish sought to represent themselves rather than be represented continually and reductively as the "other" in the theatre of dominant British culture and politics. In their revolutionary artistic manifesto outlining their plan for an Irish theatre, these early collaborators articulated their aesthetic vision: "We will show that Ireland is not the home of buffoonery and of easy sentiment, as it has been represented, but the home of an ancient idealism" (Gregory 20). A parallel purpose between the project of Irish national identity and gay and lesbian politics can be traced through the practice of reclaiming formerly demonized identities. Additionally, a common hope for political and social change is sought through the aesthetics of drama and performance.

The Irish Literary Theatre eventually evolved into the National Theatre of Ireland, or the Abbey Theatre. This theatre became a significant connection for the staging of gay identities in the plays of Frank McGuinness, and remained a regular site for domestic debates about acceptable representations of Irishness long after the British had left the Republic of Ireland. Although it would be decades before queer sexualities would be represented on the stage of the Abbey, heterosexual sexuality was hugely contentious in emerging Ireland as Irish people sought to identify themselves with the conservative values of Roman Catholicism. The Irish self-righteously defined their Catholic morality in opposition to what was widely held to be the civic immorality and theological error of British Protestantism. This stringent morality would serve to marginalize homosexuals in Irish society and even exclude them from the full rights of citizenship.

John Millington Sygne was an early dramatist for the Abbey, and the sexual energy of his play *The Playboy of the Western World* was the inciting force that actually caused riots in the auditorium of the National Theatre in January of 1907. In this play, Synge describes the female protagonist Pegeen in her shift, or slip, which was enough of a sexual innuendo to cause an audience eruption of indignation during the performance against what the early Irish audiences thought of as indecency.

Although remarkably modest to a contemporary audience, Synge's play is layered with a latent sexuality. In his book *The Politics of Irish Drama*, the renowned Synge scholar Nicholas Grene describes the erotic energy of *The Playboy of the Western World*, which served to offend those who did not like what was being implied about Irish character in its representations of Irishness:

> As the repressed physicality of the sexual was allowed to appear from under the normal decencies of its covering, so sex was proximate to violence and both made manifest the actuality of a specific location. Again and again distinctions, differences and the ideological labeling that went with them were jumbled in unsorted contiguity. Such contamination of confused categories was a deeply disturbing affront to the middle-class nationalist community whose self-image depended on such moral classification [Grene 86].

These social protestations against the idea of Irishness as represented on the National Stage indicate an important shift in Irish cultural politics, one that would impact the possibility of the emergence of gay and lesbian identities for decades to come. While early nationalism based its identity project on reconfiguring the negative British imagery of Ireland, post-liberation Ireland began to devolve into its own essentialization of the nature of the "true" Irish citizen, forcing the suppression of alternative life choices and marginalized identities through a civic conversation based on a catholic morality rather than the broad-based human rights of an emerging democracy.

These events of moral prudery and aversion to sexuality being theatrically represented, even in its most banal forms, are the historical antecedents that limited and prohibited Irish playwrights for decades. It is not until 1968 that the Dublin Theatre Festival produces a drama with an openly gay character. Thomas Kilroy's play *The Death and Resurrection of Mr. Roche* opened at the Olympia Theatre during the festival and was set in present-day 1960s Dublin. At the center of the play is the character of Kelly. Kelly is a country bachelor renting a basement apartment in Dublin. The action takes place between Saturday evening and Sunday morning, and portrays the weekly routine of a small group of friends who ritually drink the weekend away. Into these late night revelries comes the openly gay character of Mr. Roche, accompanied by a young man. Kilroy uses Roche's sexuality to articulate the latent sexual anxieties of Kelly. Kelly lashes out at Mr. Roche:

> KELLY: Get him away, away to hell. Dirty, filthy pervert. If you don't do anything about it I am telling you I will. I'm telling you that know. [*He exits to bedroom where at first he stands indecisive and nervous. Later he bends to look through and listen at the keyhole or walks about the room*] [Kilroy 28].

As events unfold, Kelly, predictably, admits to a previous homosexual encounter and his own sexual denial. But what is most interesting about this groundbreaking play for gay and lesbian issues in Ireland is its portrayal of the open homosexual character as object. Kilroy certainly represents the social anxieties surrounding homosexual identity in 1960s Ireland, but he does so as object rather than subject. The gay character is the antagonist, the problem, the source of the necessary dramatic conflict; an object of curiosity but nonetheless an object who is defined by the ideas and opinions of others around him rather than through his own articulation of self or experience.

It is during this same time period in Irish theatre that one of the most important links between Irish and American drama takes place. Brian Friel, the preeminent living Irish playwright, in his earliest attempts to move from his moderately successful career in short fiction writing into drama, accepted an invitation from Tyrone Guthrie to spend time at the theatre Guthrie had recently established in Minneapolis, Minnesota. Guthrie's work with Shakespeare and Chekhov heavily influenced Friel's future dramatic themes, but the time away from the culture and society of Ireland seemed to have had the greatest impact on his artistic vision. Friel describes his internship in the United States:

> Those months in America gave me a sense of liberation — remember this was my first parole from inbred claustrophobic Ireland — and that sense of liberation conferred on me a valuable self-confidence and a necessary perspective so that the first play I wrote immediately after I came home (*Philadelphia, Here I Come!*) was a lot more assured than anything I had attempted before [Roche 78].

It must be noted that Friel's work has influenced every Irish playwright to follow. His success both at home and abroad is unparalleled, and in a small dramatic community such as Ireland, intertexuality and aesthetic cross pollination are unavoidable. Consequently, it could be argued that Friel's time in the United States began to create new conditions for Irish dramatic writing and, as I would argue, also began to open the door to less conservative notions of representation in Irish theatre.

It is worth noting that in 1971 Friel introduces a gay character into his own writing in his play *The Gentle Island*. The play is set on the small island of Inishkeen off the coast of County Donegal in the North West of Ireland. The inhabitants of the island are emigrating due to fading resources with the exception of Manus Sweeney and his family. When two traveling strangers come to visit this remote island they become entangled in the fear and neurosis of this failing Irish family. Manus's son Philly becomes involved in a sexual relationship with one of the strangers, Shane, and is caught by his wife Sarah. The sexuality of this family is as dysfunctional as their interpersonal relationships, and Friel uses homosexuality to bring these frailties to a dramatic head. In the end of the play Sarah shoots and kills Shane. Homosexuality is again a point of conflict, an accusation, and an object of scrutiny in what Nicholas Grene calls "the social policing of sexual relationships" (Grene 211) in Friel's writing.

It is important to note that although entertainment in the United States was a huge influence on Irish culture during this period of the 1960s and 1970s, the sexual revolution in the U.S. was perhaps only stimulating the imagination of the general Irish population. While the civil rights movement in the U.S. was certainly inspiring to the Irish Republican Army (IRA) in Northern Ireland, it was impossible even to acquire contraception in the Republic of Ireland. After the events of Stonewall in New York in 1969 the organization the Gay Liberation Front (GLF) was formed and did, in fact, extend its influence into Ireland through Ireland's close proximity to the influential branch of the GLF working out of London. The manifesto of the GLF created a language through which gay and lesbian men and women could reconfigure their objectified identities:

> The emphasis was on pride and affirmation; these gay people were blatant, outrageous and flamboyant. Discarding an identity conditioned by notions of sickness and sin, they represented homosexuality as a revolutionary path towards freedom. They engaged in public displays of affection and violated gender conventions. Sexual expression was seen as a form of personal, political action that was subversive, liberating and a way of building solidarity. "Coming Out," the public affirmation of gay identity, became a key political act [Rose 5–6].

This important shift in queer language would ultimately influence Frank McGuinness, the first Irish dramatist to rescue the Irish homosexual from the assigned status of object to the self-defining position of subject.

As is often the case in Irish culture, important social or political issues frequently make their way onto the stage at the National Theatre. Although Frank McGuinness has woven gay and lesbian themes and characters into all his original writing, he did so with cautious and gradual "outings." It is not until his play *Dolly West's Kitchen* in 1999 that McGuinness explicitly "outs" a gay Irish character, and he does so with the help of an openly queer American.

Dolly West's Kitchen premiered at the National Theatre in Dublin on October 1, 1999, and was directed by Patrick Mason. The play is set in the town of Buncrana in County Donegal. Buncrana is not a fictional location and is, in fact, the birthplace of McGuinness himself. Buncrana is in the northeast corner of Donegal and is situated near the city of Derry. To be situated near Derry means that Buncrana is a border town. After the 1916 uprising in Ireland, which instigated the withdrawal of British colonial rule, a treaty was signed between the new Republic of Ireland and Great Britain. In this treaty the two parties agreed that six counties in the north of Ireland would remain under British rule and would become known as the political entity of Northern Ireland. The remaining twenty-six counties would be known as the Republic of Ireland and would be governed by the newly established Irish Parliament. However, while Donegal is considered the Republic, it is physically situated in the northeast corner of the geographical north of Ireland. Consequently, Donegal has always had a rather liminal position in Irish politics and culture as it has historically been the longest stretch of border between Northern Ireland and the Republic. Buncrana would be a rather isolated location and its inhabitants would find themselves crossing the border to the larger city of Derry regularly for supplies and whatnot; McGuinness uses this real location to cross ideological and sexual borders throughout this play.

Dolly West's Kitchen takes place during World War II and most of the action of the play is set in the kitchen of the West family. They are a comfortable middle-class family who would have enjoyed mild prosperity and a good education before the war began; this is not an archetypical Irish rural play depicting a country cottage and isolated peasantry. The father of the family has long since died, leaving behind his widow, Rima, two daughters Dolly and Esther, and a son, Justin. Rima is in her sixties, Dolly and Esther in their thirties, and Justin is in his twenties. Justin is an officer in the Irish Army. Since acquiring independence Ireland has defined itself as a neutral country and so, consequently, Justin is not heading to fight in the raging war on the continent.

Because the United States and Britain are political allies, an American military base was located near the city of Derry during World War II and served as a launching point for American troops into Europe. This historical reality allows McGuinness to introduce the two American characters, Marco Delavicario and Jamie O'Brien. The men are enlisted in the U.S. Army and are cousins from New York City. They are both in their twenties. In act 1, scene 2 Rima meets the two cousins in a local pub where her eldest daughter Esther spots her. Esther runs home to tell the others what she has seen and to warn them of the invasion of the Americans:

> ESTHER: She's a glass to her lips, drinking when I walk in there, with two young American soldiers. My mother is getting drunk with two GI's. I'm not — she is. She has also invited them back to eat with us. What is Justin going to say? [McGuinness 201].

We discover later in the play that Rima has, indeed, purposefully crossed the border with the express intention of using the Americans to help her son Justin, whom she suspects is gay, to come out of the closet.

Esther's bewildered announcement is shortly followed by Rima's arrival at the house with the boys in tow. Referring to the two Americans:

RIMA: ...They are wee angels. Well, big angels, Dolly, you'll love them. They are gods. Gods of men. Young fellas, come in—come in [McGuinness 202].

The language through which the Americans are introduced sexualizes them as well as defines them as physically large and thus angelic. Rima is titillating her daughters with the prospect of meeting these strapping young soldiers while simultaneously confessing that they are the perfect solution for her as yet unarticulated plan to sexually reawaken her rigid children by referring to them as heavenly.

As Marco and Jamie enter the West household, McGuinness immediately opens the closet and outs his American character. Marco is gay, and the first of the two Americans to speak, referring to his earlier encounter with Esther:

MARCO: Did you also tell her I hated you on sight?
ESTHER: May I ask why?
MARCO: The way you dress.
ESTHER: What's wrong with it?
MARCO: Nothing, if you're posing for the Statue of Liberty.
ESTHER: I've never seen the Statue of Liberty.
MARCO: It shows, honey.
ESTHER: I'm not your honey.
MARCO: My God, that woman's hair—was it suicide? [McGuinness 203].

McGuinness introduces this gay American to his Irish audience strategically, using a campy dialogue that allows those with the ears to hear the queer to identify Marco's orientation first.

In her seminal article "Notes on 'Camp,'" Susan Sontag describes camp as a sensibility. She asserts: "Camp is esoteric—something of a private code a badge of identity even" (Sontag 53). Marco disposes of the common courtesy of the politeness expected in first meetings, choosing, instead, to insult Esther in front of her family. In so doing, Marco violates normative social behavior, unbalancing the moment in order to make his queer presence known. Marco's unconventional attitude would appear rude, but to those who understand the language of camp, Marco's dialogue reveals the "badge of identity" of the homosexual. He immediately refuses the closet by his camp remarks and raises the stakes with each word he speaks:

MARCO: I am Marco Delavicario. This is my Irish-American cousin, Jamie O'Brien. We signed up together. Jamie brought the clothes he was standing in and a change of underwear. I brought one taffeta dress and a change of high heels. Who knows what might happen in the heat of battle? [McGuinness 203].

McGuinness creates a dramatic moment wrought with incongruities. These sexy American soldiers arrive making a colorful entrance, only to have one of them immediately confess to cross-dressing. Normativity is shattered in a strategic moment of camp's irreverent humor.

In his article "The Cinema of Camp (AKA Camp and the Gay Sensibility)," Jack Babuscio provides interesting insight into the type of social anarchy McGuinness evokes by introducing the camp sensibility into *Dolly West's Kitchen*. He defines camp as "a creative energy reflecting a consciousness that is different from the mainstream; a heightened awareness of certain human complications of feeling that spring from the fact of social oppression; in short, a perception of the world which is colored, shaped, directed, and defined by the fact of one's gayness" (Babuscio 118). Therefore, camp functions as a sort of protest to normativity and an ironic form of self-expression that arises out of both an awareness and a refusal of unjust marginalization.

For McGuinness, the combination of the camp aesthetic and the use of an American character carefully conflate to violate Irish moral sensibilities and to challenge social attitudes. He uses humor to destabilize the potentially threatening moment of representing a gay character, and he does so safely by distancing that character from any implication of Irishness. Marco is not only American but he is also Italian-American. His campiness allows an Irish audience to laugh at the social undercurrent of homophobia haunting his queer self-performance without being implicated themselves.

What is most strategic about the use of camp as a dramaturgical tactic is that it postpones confrontation, introducing contentious issues through laughter. Babuscio describes the camp strategy of humor as "a means of dealing with a hostile environment and, in the process, defining a positive identity" (Babuscio 126). Marco's outrageous introduction to the family is an example of how the gay character takes control of the situation through self-definition; he makes himself the subject rather than the object in an attempt to postpone or eliminate reductive homophobic judgment. His refusal to suppress his identity is a confrontation that rejects his imposed social stigmatization. "Camp can thus be a means of undercutting rage by its derision of concentrated bitterness. Its vision of the world is comic. Laughter, rather than tears" (Babuscio 127). McGuinness's play is filled with wit and laughter but, nevertheless, it is set in the middle of a devastating war that, in itself, stands as an analogy for the homophobic suppression of gay identity in Ireland and throughout the world.

But why did McGuinness choose to use a queer American in this play? Certainly it is to help the character of Justin come out of the closet, but could that not have been more easily achieved, and perhaps more realistically conceived, through an encounter with another Irishman or the more prototypical identity opposition of a British soldier? At this juncture it is essential to return to the notions of national identity that still permeate Irish culture and politics today. In fact, to the Irish the American is an ally where the British are the enemy, but this Irish-American pairing is, more critically, an accusation aimed at restrictive domestic Irish social policies.

In *Dolly West's Kitchen* McGuinness puts pressure on an Irish historical political reality. During World War II Ireland chose not to support her traditional allies, and remained neutral throughout the war. In their book *Ireland and the Second World War*, Geoffrey Roberts and Brian Girvin describe the history of the cultural and political myth of Irish neutrality:

> The Irish Free State's declaration of neutrality in 1939 was undoubtedly the wisest and safest course of action. It protected the Irish people from the perils of war, asserted the country's sovereignty and independence from Britain, and, crucially, maintained the unity of the state at a time of great national danger [Roberts 165].

The "unity of the State" is a type of code of normativity that imposes conformity for the sake of national security, thus articulating an inward looking social climate that rejects difference out of fear.

During World War II in the Republic of Ireland, "special powers were introduced to prevent the wearing of the uniforms on leave. Action was taken to prevent the collection of funds in the State on behalf of the British war effort (Roberts 89). The policies of censorship were established to neutralize Irish domestic life as well by limiting the possibilities of "the danger of disorder and disruption" (Roberts 89) within a state still struggling in the wake of years of conflict and civil war. Understood in this light, Irish neutrality can be interpreted as a political way of controlling moral positions in the name of social stability, or for the alleged greater benefit of the nation. The American stands free of traditional British/Irish struggles of opposition and therefore creates a new possibility of relationship.

McGuinness uses Marco and the legal prohibitions about the public wearing of uniforms to transcend these traditional tribal hatreds and to forge a new reality out of the stagnancy of history. The historical reality of restrictions on uniforms in Ireland during World War II becomes an essential element in exposing the queer in *Dolly West's Kitchen*. The uniform becomes a form of national identification, for what symbolizes citizenship and patriotism more than a man in uniform? Upon meeting Justin, Marco proceeds to teach him how to embrace his gay identity without the baggage of social restriction:

> JUSTIN: You've crossed the border.
> MARCO: Hasn't everyone?
> JUSTIN: I beg your pardon.

MARCO: Just being chatty.
JUSTIN: I never am.
MARCO: You can use your tongue for other matters.
JUSTIN: Than what?
MARCO: Chatting.
JUSTIN: Yankee wit.
MARCO: Yankee wisdom.
From this exchange to the end of the scene, Justin does not take his eyes off Marco [McGuinness 206].

In this exchange, McGuinness conflates Marco's gay camp performance with American identity, even going so far as to call it "wisdom." Borders have been transgressed in more ways than one; Justin, standing agape, finds himself still at home in Ireland but in a whole new world.

Marco's gay American wisdom has the anger of homophobic injustice just below the surface of the fun of camp. But McGuinness also employs the camp sensibility in *Dolly West's Kitchen* in order to confront social issues without alienating his audiences with overtly issue-oriented theatre. The fun of camp is an invitation to deal with serious issues in disguise. In order to engage an audience with contentious topics, camp approaches tough issues from alternative angles. While the Nazi threat to the West is certainly an important part of McGuinness's thematic use of this historical moment of World War II, so is the Nazi effort to eliminate homosexuals. McGuinness addresses this homophobic murder with a joke. In act 1, scene 3, Rima playfully accuses Marco of wearing lipstick and Marco responds:

MARCO: Madam, I am an American soldier. I am most emphatically not wearing lipstick. A little rouge, yes. No Nazi's going to bitch about my bone structure.
JUSTIN: Do you know what the Nazi's do to men like you?
MARCO: Why the fuck do you think I'm fighting them.
Silence [McGuinness 212].

In this moment the audience is introduced to the very real fear of denunciation by society, or state organized murder, at the heart of homosexual experience.

There is a delayed shock value that comes from combining real horror with calculated comic irony. Babuscio states:

Camp, through its introduction of style, aestheticism, humour and theatricality, allows us to witness "serious" issues with temporary detachment, so that only later, after the event, are we struck by the emotional and moral implications of what we have almost passively absorbed [Babuscio 128].

The flamboyancy of the American in this play is the entrance into the anti-homophobic message at the heart of the play. McGuinness does not choose to create a gay ghetto through which the homosexual can freely articulate his or her identity. Instead, he enters the center of public discourse by bringing together historical reality, social attitudes, and issues of national identity, using the fictional elements of drama to entertain and confront attitudes and assumptions.

McGuinness transcends the ideological issues of homophobia that filter through *Dolly West's Kitchen* through the phenomenology of the stage by representing the gay body. In his book *The Field of Drama*, Martin Esslin describes the actor on stage as "the iconic sign *par excellence*: a real human being who has become a sign for a human being" (Esslin 56). In this sense, the actor's body moves queer ideas beyond language into the much more explicit representation of the gay body. McGuinness cleverly uses the American character throughout the play to invite the Irish characters into an unveiled experience of homosexual pride, humor, and even anger. But that is not enough for a piece of drama aimed at breaking down the conservative social and cultural ideas of the homosexual in Ireland.

Esslin's concept of the actor as "a sign for a human being" is an interesting notion to explore in the specifics of production for *Dolly West's Kitchen* in 1999 in Dublin. The play took place as part of the annual Dublin Theatre Festival. During the festival the theatre receives a great deal of media attention and the actor playing Marco, Perry Ojeda, was interviewed several times. Ojeda was brought to Dublin from the United States to play the role. He is openly gay, and this became a fetishized focus in the media for the promotion of the play. In his article "Twisted, Mean, Sissy, Queen," Brian Finnegan of *In Dublin* magazine interviewed Ojeda:

> Ojeda has been especially imported from the Broadway stage to play the part of Marco. Dark and handsome in the matinee idol tradition, he aesthetically characterizes all that we have come to associate with the term American GI through countless nostalgic movies charting the time of the Yanks. His character's articulate and volatile homosexuality is a twist audiences might not easily accept, as they might also be affronted by his love scene with an Irish Republican Army Captain [Finnegan 32].

Later Finnegan quotes Ojeda: "As a gay man ... to have the opportunity to portray Marco is wonderful" (Finnegan 32). The article foregrounds Ojeda's American identity and his "real life" homosexuality. Finnegan warns potential audience members that as if the combination of American GI and gay is not bad enough, he actually has a love scene with an Irish person. Actor and character conflate in a queer cultural performance that exoticizes the homosexual as other and potentially threatening. Thus, stage and society engage as fiction and fact collide, providing for a more political discourse through the unique phenomenological aesthetics of drama.

As previously mentioned, McGuinness has continually represented homosexual subjectivity in his drama, so what makes *Dolly West's Kitchen* unique? In his most recognized play, *Observe the Sons of Ulster Marching towards the Somme*, McGuinness innovatively queered the Irish stage with the first kiss between two men. In fact, in this play McGuinness first used the idea of the soldier to represent an association with dramatic theme and national identity. *Observe the Sons of Ulster* tells the story of the 36th Division of the British Army who participated in the fateful Battle of the Somme in France during World War I. The play represents the memory of the protagonist Pyper, a tormented self-loathing Protestant homosexual who survives the deadly battle against all odds. Pyper is dangerous and seductive throughout. His hyper-sexualized attention is particularly focused on the character Craig, a Protestant working-class blacksmith. McGuinness dissolves all homosexual innuendo in a moment never before witnessed on the stage in Ireland: Pyper and Craig passionately kiss.

The kiss is the moment when the gay body is fully revealed and the idea of the homosexual gives way to a confrontation with the physical reality of homosexuality. This is what gay theatre scholar and playwright John Clum describes as "the relationship of body to word, action to dialogue, and actor to audience" (Clum 10). In the moment of the kiss the artifice of camp dissolves into the realism of two concrete human beings engaged in an act of social and sexual "deviance." Clum continues: "Sexual desire is not the only dimension of the homosexual experience, but it is the core of that experience. It is sexual desire and acting upon that desire that puts the homosexual into conflict with dominant power structures" (Clum 13). Theatre by nature goes beyond words or language. During the queer kiss the fiction of stage dissolves for an instant while many audience members are confronted with a physical reality that they may otherwise have comfortably denied through the humor of camp parody.

What distinguishes the gay bodies in *Observe the Sons* from those in *Dolly West's Kitchen*? The thematic engagement of the Battle of the Somme in *Observe the Sons of Ulster* is distanced from the Irish experience in its association with British history. The legend that surrounds the army regiment portrayed in this play and the way it was formed "is that, almost as one, the Protestant men of the nine counties of Ulster offered themselves for service in 1914" (This quotation is from the program note to the 1995 production of *Observe the Sons of Ulster Marching towards the Somme*, written by Kevin Meyers). McGuinness thematically employed a historical moment that was significant to the Protestant population of Northern Ireland, a population who predominantly identify themselves as British. In that sense, McGuinness again safely distanced the homosexual "deviant" from any real sense of

Irishness by costuming these men in the uniform of the British Army and thus signifying them as the "other" as indicated earlier in the complicated relationship between Britain and Ireland.

Enter the American. The heterosexuals in *Dolly West's Kitchen* receive Marco's camp humor and openly gay self-confidence more generously than the gay Irishman. The Irish homosexual, Justin, is still deeply within the closet and is cautious and suspicious of Marco. In act 1 the group decides to take a walk and, as is common in McGuinness's plays, the individual characters begin to move into pairs. As they leave the house Marco falls into line with Justin:

> MARCO: I shall refuse your arm, young man. I do not trust men in uniform.
> JUSTIN: What the hell are you?
> MARCO: An angel fallen from the skies.
> JUSTIN: Where are you from?
> MARCO: Paradise [McGuinness 208].

McGuinness's language in this exchange is redemptive and free of the accusations of homosexual self-hatred and social stigmatization. Again, Marco is depicted as an angel come from somewhere far away to save the angry tormented Justin from self-destruction. If actor and character are iconic signs, if they represent themselves as embodied presence and a fictionalization of social or cultural reality, then one might consider the symbolism of McGuinness's use of national identity.

Because of the rather symbiotic relationship between Ireland and the United States, one might ascertain that McGuinness is referring to American gay identity as a redemptive antidote to Irish conservatism and recent institutionalized homophobia. Although there has been a gay and lesbian rights coalition of one sort or another in Ireland since the 1970s, it was not until June of 1993 that a bill decriminalizing homosexuality in the country was passed. In 1977 the decriminalization campaign petitioned the High Court in Dublin to listen to their case. The politician and university lecturer David Norris advanced the case to end what he described as the "conspiracy of silence" (Rose 35) surrounding homosexuality. "The Government called not witnesses to back up its case but argued trenchantly that sexual relationships outside of marriage were unacceptable and that the state should do all in its power to stop the spread of homosexuality" (Rose 35). The High Court Judge, Mr. Justice McWilliams, found against the plaintiff on October 10, 1980, and he further defended his judgment by citing the Irish Constitution's Christian foundation; thus reinforcing the general consensus that homosexuality was itself immoral, and, consequently, homosexual people did not deserve legal protection.

In delivering the majority judgement, the Chief Justice began by stating that there were "a large number of people in this country with homosexual tendencies," and that after decriminalisation, the small number of people who were exclusively homosexual would entice this larger group into "more and more deviant sexual acts" to such an extent that such involvement may become habitual. So many more people, in the view of the Chief Justice, would have, as a result, to endure the "sad, lonely and harrowing life" of the exclusive homosexual man [Rose 36].

This shocking judgement indicates that as late as 1980 issues surrounding morality and ethics applied considerable tension not only on the Irish legal system but also on issues of diversity and equal rights to all citizens of the Irish Republic.

Eventually, the courts of the European Union forced Ireland to repeal their homophobic law. It was not until 1993 that Irish homosexuals were protected rather than prosecuted by the law. However, Ireland is not unique in the persistence of anti-gay judgments in the court. What is unique is the type of moralistic or ethical language that justifies the refusal of gay rights and, simultaneously, reinforces homophobic views in popular sentiment.

The demoralizing effect of such juridical language on the gay and lesbian community in Ireland is iconically concentrated into the Irish character Justin. Marco recognizes Justin's sexual orientation by the resentment he bears in carrying Irish attitudes toward who he is:

> *On the shore Marco takes Justin's cigarette from his lips. He lights his own with it.*
> MARCO: I like your hatred. Don't lose your hatred.
> JUSTIN: What would you know about it?
> MARCO: Everything.
> JUSTIN: What would you know about me?
> MARCO: What you've told me.
> JUSTIN: What have I told you?
> MARCO: Everything.
> *Marco touches Justin's face. Justin kisses Marco's hands.*
> JUSTIN: You'll tell no one else? [McGuinness 217].

The American homosexual is the catalyst of self-revelation, the place of safety, and the erotic point of release for the Irish character. Marco's very presence has an outing effect as he liberates Justin from captivity.

McGuinness uses the American character in this play to untangle the historical invisibility of the homosexual in Ireland and to relieve the fear of coming out of the closet for the Irish homosexual. In so doing, he taps into a vital difference of perspective between American and European thinking. In his article "The American Imagination," Denis Donohue provides insight into how fundamental differences in attitude between the United States and

Ireland allow the character of Marco to simultaneously release and empower the closeted Justin. He claims:

> The European mind defines itself chiefly in relation to the past as an anthology of gone occasions or perhaps to a general impression of those events as burden and responsibility, voices calling for response. The American mind takes that burden more casually, and turns its vitality toward a future which it construes as possibility. To the European, mistakes are definitive; to the American, mistakes are regrettable but not fatal — there is always a second chance. The American mind thinks itself a pioneer, and its best morality a matter of trials and errors [Donohue 70].

In act 2 the Irishman tells the American what he has done for him

> JUSTIN: Thank you. What was I like before I met you? Twisted, miserable git. I'm so ashamed [McGuinness 238].

McGuinness erases borders and transcends bigotry with a hopeful future-oriented American-style gay love affair.

The war in which this drama is set is integrated into the fight against homophobia and becomes the symbol of a shared gay identity that crosses borders. In act 2, scene 2, Marco is getting ready to leave for the war on the continent. Dressed in their respective national uniforms, symbols of their varying citizenship, Marco and Justin lie on the beach together, deferring Marco's eminent departure:

> *Justin kisses Marco*
> MARCO: Please, not here — not outside. Not when nobody's watching.
> JUSTIN: I don't want you to go.
> MARCO: When I come back, could we live in Italy?
> JUSTIN: Jesus, yes. I'd love that. I've a bit of money from my father. Yes, Marco, yes. Dolly can teach me Italian. You're on. Where — what part of Italy?
> MARCO: The Bronx?
> JUSTIN: That's in New York.
> MARCO: You poor boy, geography will be the death of you.
> JUSTIN: Marco, you're to come home safe.
> MARCO: Justin, I'm very frightened.
> *Silence*
> JUSTIN: You're to come home to me.
> MARCO: I will, yes. (*He kisses Justin's hand*) [McGuinness 241].

All of McGuinness's queer dramaturgical strategies combine in this moving scene. He indicates the inherent value in homosexuality through the transcendence of love. Through the kiss he contextualizes the otherwise hidden expression of gay sexual bodies within the common heterosexual experience of love and relationship. In a sense, he normalizes homosexuality by representing the shared qualities of concern, happiness, and tenderness that all human beings seek in relationships. In so doing he evokes empathy. John Clum describes it thus: "The kiss is an act that brings alien homosexual desire into the realm of the known and thus asserts a threatening parity between homosexual and heterosexual desire (Clum 14). The American character may have set forth the possibility of the queer, but when brought together with the Irish character, audiences at the National Theatre in Ireland are asked to see their own experiences of love and fear as exhibited by Marco and Justin's tender concern for one another.

Undoubtedly, the connections between the United States and Ireland remain strong through the links of heredity, politics, and economics. And yet, a gay, lesbian, and transgendered theatrical tradition beyond drag in Ireland lags behind its American counterparts, and is still in its earliest moments of gestation. Queer theatre practitioners in Ireland oftentimes remain isolated and have yet to combine their visions into a shared effort that might be described as "queer theatre." Academically, remarkably little work on queer studies exists in Ireland. Irish drama studies is often preoccupied with the notions of authenticity that advocate theatrical realism, thus leaving very little space for the value of the development of the non-naturalistic performance genres preferred by homosexual artists. Consequently, these conditions illuminate the need for international dialogue, and serve as a mandate to queer dramatic artists and academics alike to transgress the traditional limitations of far too often inward-looking production, and create alternative environments for queer aesthetics that cross the heteronormative borders that still consign and marginalize queer identities throughout the world.

BIBLIOGRAPHY

Babuscio, Jack. "The Cinema of Camp (AKA Camp and the Gay Sensibility)." In *Camp: Queer Aesthetics and the Performing Subject*, edited by Fabio Cleto. Ann Arbor, MI: University of Michigan Press, 1999.
Clum, John M. *Still Acting Gay: Male Homosexuality in Modern Drama*. New York: St. Martin's Griffin, 2000.
Donohue, Denis. "The American Imagination." In *America and Ireland, 1776–1976: The American Identity and the Irish Connection*, edited by David Noel Doyle and Owen Dudley Edwards. Westport, CT: Greenwood Press, 1976.
Esslin, Martin. *The Field of Drama*. London: Methuen, 1987.
Finnegan, Brian. "Twisted, Mean, Sissy, Queen." *In Dublin* October (1999): 7–20.
Gregory, Augusta. *Our Irish Theatre: A Chapter of Autobiography* [1913]. Gerrards Cross, UK: Smythe, 1972.
Grene, Nicholas. *The Politics of Irish Drama: Plays in Context from Boucicault to Friel*. London: Cambridge, 1999.
Kilroy, Thomas. *The Death and Resurrection of Mr. Roche*. London: Faber and Faber, 1969.

McGuinness, Frank. *Dolly West's Kitchen* in *Frank McGuinness: Plays 2*. London: Faber and Faber, 2002.
Murray, John A. "The Influence of America on Irish Nationalism." In *America and Ireland, 1776–1976: The American Identity and the Irish Connection*, edited by David Noel Doyle and Owen Dudley Edwards. Westport, CT: Greenwood Press, 1976.
Roberts, Geoffrey, and Brian Girvin. *Ireland and the Second World War: Politics, Society and Remembrance*. Dublin: Four Courts Press, 2000.
Roche, Anthony. *Contemporary Irish Drama from Beckett to McGuinness*. Dublin: Gill and Macmillan, 1994.
Rose, Kieran. *Diverse Communities: The Evolution of Lesbian and Gay Politics in Ireland*. Cork: Cork University Press, 1994.
Sontag, Susan. "Notes on 'Camp.'" In *Camp: Queer Aesthetics and the Performing Subject*, edited by Fabio Cleto. Ann Arbor, MI: University of Michigan Press, 1999.

Lisa Kron
Facing and Placing Lesbian Identity on New York Stages

Leslie Atkins Durham

Ideas about non-places and un-spaces have dominated the fields of cultural studies and performance theory for the last couple of decades. (See for example the work of Gaston Bachelard, Michel de Certeau, Michel Foucault, Herni Lefebvre, and Edward Soja.) As scholars have analyzed postmodern lived experience — in international airports, shopping malls, amusement parks, and cyberspace — they have variously articulated the sentiments expressed by Marc Augé in *Non-Places: Introduction to an Anthropology of Supermodernity*: "The space of non-place creates neither singular identity nor relations; only solitude and similitude" (Auge 103). Postmodern people spend ever-increasing amounts of time in transit through dehistoricized, commerce-driven placeless zones, and as a consequence both individuated subjectivities and their relationship to, and effect on, indigenous communities, are, according to such theorists, in extreme peril.

Against such an intellectual backdrop, the idea that Lisa Kron's dramaturgy has evolved in direct reaction to specific places in the New York theatrical landscape might seem more than a little old-fashioned. Kron, whose work plays with notions of a self that is created through performance — as a result of the telling and remembering of personal stories in concert with imagery re-appropriated from popular culture — fits cleanly within postmodernism, and her work might thus seem to demand an evaluation of place in keeping with the tenets of that experience and worldview.

But as much as Kron's work animates the ideas of postmodernism, her work has always clearly focused on her identity as a lesbian. And while postmodernism and its theorists may decry placelessness, the history of gay liberation and empowerment is grounded in a very specific place: The Stonewall Inn at 53 Christopher Street in New York's Greenwich Village. Lisa Kron is thus a post–Stonewall theatre artist in an important sense: she celebrates the importance of lesbian sexuality in creating an integrated, "well" self onstage, and she tells the stories about the voyage of forging that self from her encounters in very specific places. As Gay McAuley has written, "While theatre can take place anywhere, the point is that it must take place somewhere" (McAuley 2). Lisa Kron's theatre, like gay liberation more broadly, has taken place in a series of very particular "somewheres," and those places—the WOW Café, P.S. 122, the Public Theatre, and Broadway—rather than postmodern non-places have played a powerful role as she stages lesbian identity, giving it a particular face and place.

Voyage to Lesbos: The Five Lesbian Brothers at the WOW Café

One cannot hope to understand Lisa Kron's playwriting, performance and her innovative theatrical strategies in the first decade of the twenty-first century without reviewing her work with The Five Lesbian Brothers in the 1980s. In the Preface to their self-titled anthology of plays, the Brothers— Maureen Angelos, Babs Davy, Dominique Dibbell, Peg Healey and Lisa Kron—conclude their acknowledgments by thanking "all of the women at the Obie Award winning WOW Café where we were born and raised" (*The Five Lesbian Brothers*). Indeed, it is hard to imagine the genesis of the group or more particularly Kron as solo performer and playwright without this very particular performance venue.

The WOW Café itself was born from the inspiration of Peggy Shaw and Lois Weaver. Shaw and Weaver toured in Europe in the 1970s, where they experienced the power of women's theatre festivals. They decided it was time for one in the United States, so in October of 1980 they organized the first Women's One World (WOW) Festival in New York's East Village. Working without grants of any kind, and funded primarily by a summer's exhausting but educational work of throwing benefits, the women, along with Jordi Mark and Pamela Camhe, pulled together a remarkable festival—so remarkable in fact, that demand from local audiences and international performers prompted them to produce another one in October of 1981.

Between the festivals, the volunteers, artists, and audience who had gotten in the habit of gathering together continued to do so, making art and forming a community. This spirit only grew after the second festival, and Shaw and Weaver, with a little money in hand, sought a permanent base. They found their home at 330 E. 11th Street, and the WOW Café opened in March 1982. It was open from 3:30 until 11 P.M. daily, and in addition to functioning as a social club and community hub, it offered emerging female artists a space to perform. Alisa Solomon describes the Café's stage capacity as follows:

The stage, like the entire space is barely 10 feet wide. With its floor of octagonal ceramic tiles, patterned along one side, the room seems like it might have been someone's vestibule, or even earlier, half of a dining room. Now, impossibly narrow and maybe 20 feet long, it hardly contains a dozen or so rows of folding chairs. The homemade lightboard of household dimmers sits in the center of the room, controlling a handful of small, outdoor-type reflector lamps—all the electrical system can accommodate. The backstage area is a ten feet by ten feet jumble of old props, bits of costumes, and chunks of sets. The Café's original excuse, an enormous coffee maker, is stashed in a corner [Solomon 96].

Through the mid–1980s, anyone who wanted to perform could book the intimate, homespun space at the Café. Despite this egalitarian openness, several qualities emerged across the performances according to Kate Davy (in addition to being a major critic, Davy is the sister of Brother Babs Davy). She writes, "An unmistakable specificity is evident in pieces performed at WOW—the address is clearly lesbian. Freely borrowing from popular culture forms, WOW artists produce pieces based on scenarios from familiar, recognizable entertainment genres. In this work, they construct subcultural, under-the-text imagery, metaphors, and conventions derived from lesbian culture" [Davy 153].

When the Brothers came together in 1989, the WOW aesthetic was central in their self-creation as a group. Several of the Brothers had already worked together at WOW. When Kron staged her show *All My Hopes and Dreams*, for example, Healey, Dibbell, and Angelos played "Creamettes," sexy, black-clad back-up dancers, to Kron's star figure, or as she refers to herself in the show, "the lesbian Lola Falana." *Voyage to Lesbos*, the Brothers' first show, premiered at WOW on May 24, 1990, and balanced the power and stage time between Kron and the other performers. "We all liked the same dumb jokes," Kron remembers, and when Dibbell drew a cartoon of the co-collaborators based on the children's book *The Five Chinese Brothers*, the group had a name (Weisman 44). Like the booking of the space, the Brothers created the piece in non-hierarchical fashion. In the preface to the published version of the play, Moe Angelos describes a series of improvisations, Dada-inspired automatic writings, and the circulation of notebooks containing each Brother's thoughts and lists of source materials and other inspiration pertaining to the show, out of which, eventually, characters, songs and scenes developed. *Voyage* also embodied the characteristics Kate Davy outlines. The show is a campy send-up of the American musical formula, set in "Lesbos County, Illinois," in the early 1960s. Mimi, Connie, Evelyn, and Janet prepare for, and variously attempt to derail, the wedding of Bonnie, described in the list of the dramatis personae, as the character who "has sex with everyone in the play," to the never-seen Brad. Angelos explains that the title of the show "derived from the title of a fifties pop psychology book about a woman who goes into psychoanalysis because she has insomnia. She ends up being treated for queerness, and in the end she's not queer anymore but she still has insomnia" (*Five Lesbian Brothers* 4).

The Brothers' camp pop culture appropriations ultimately intervene in high culture by interrogating and reimagining comic structure. Peggy Phelan explains,

> *Voyage to Lesbos* explores marriage as both a social-political contract and as a theatrical plot. Since the time of Shakespeare, in order for a play to be considered a comedy, it must end with a marriage and the promise of fertility that heterosexual marriage conventionally represents. *Voyage to Lesbos* sets the terms for the subsequent development of the collective's preoccupations: How can we change the world without first changing the (marriage) plot? If "all the world's a stage," how can we restage the world to include the drama of lesbian lives? [*Five Lesbian Brothers* xvii].

As the Brothers seek to revise the marriage plot in *Voyage to Lesbos*, thus challenging comic conventions, the character, Mimi, played by Lisa Kron, is central to two scenes encapsulating the play's action, which both feature the literal and metaphorical grooming of Bonnie for her wedding and her sexual role. (I saw the performance on video at the Lesbian in Herstory Archives in Brooklyn. The taped performance had been staged at Dixon Place instead of WOW, but photos from the production published in *The Five Lesbian Brothers* anthology confirm that the setting remained the same at both venues.) Though all the Brothers' plays are collectively authored, Babs Davy notes that at the time of *Voyage*'s creation, "we were all writing characters for ourselves in those days and it was every woman for herself" (*Five Lesbian Brothers* 3). It is fair, therefore, to read Mimi as a character authored, not just acted, by Kron.

Mimi first appears in scene 2 of the play, along with the rest of the ensemble, to sing of the news of Bonnie's wedding day, but it is in scene 5 that the audience truly gets to know Mimi. The scene takes place in Mimi's house. As is typical of WOW productions, the setting is minimal. The roughly painted backdrop of Lesbos County has given way to some mismatched interior furniture—all that is necessary to set and critique the domestic scene. Bonnie is in her bra and slip getting fitted for her wedding dress, during which she sings, "I am so straight / Why don't they believe that I am? / Why do they think I'd rather be with a girl than a man?" (*Five Lesbian Brothers* 12). After, as the stage directions indicate, "Bonnie hugs Mimi's face to her crotch," Bonnie seeks marital advice from Mimi, since Mimi is the only character who has been married to a man. Mimi begins with a joke: "Never get in the habit of eating in front of the TV. That will kill the marriage faster than anything. That, and being a lesbian" (*Five Lesbian Brothers* 13). The joke is punctuated by the sound of a car crash off stage, and with that, Mimi's mood turns serious. As she "lathers up Bonnie's armpits and sharpens a straight razor on a strop," she has long monologue that includes the following:

> Like if I cut myself right now, maybe my feelings would come out and we could see them on the table. But that's the only way I know if I have them is if I can see them because I can't feel anything. And that's how I know I'm dead. It's pretty lucky that I can still stand up even though I'm dead, right? I think that's pretty lucky. I think that's about the only lucky thing that's happened to me for around twenty years. That I'm dead but I'm still alive enough to take out the trash and clean the blender. That blender is a classic model. See how it shines [*Five Lesbian Brothers* 13–14].

In this scene, trademarks of Kron's style are emerging. Kron takes the mundane and makes it sensual and funny at the same time. In a bad wig and snug, frumpy house dress with a garish print, Kron makes the perfect imperfect housewife imparting the rules of the game to fresh-faced and firm-bodied Bonnie, played by Peg Healey, Kron's longtime partner onstage and off. Somehow, Kron's Mimi conveys to the audience that she knows what she is supposed to be—how her body is supposed to be groomed and what that groomed body should desire (kitchen appliances instead of another woman's body)—but she just can't execute the effect that she doesn't truly enjoy. She has the blender, and it's shiny clean, but she sees the absurdity of the scene she's forced to play in the gloss of the enamel and helps her audience see it too.

In scene 20, the play's final scene, the ensemble is grooming Bonnie a final time. After Bonnie has played a scratched and warped version of Perry Como's "The Hawaiian Wedding Song" on a child's record player, Mimi leads the group in a ritual preparation of Bonnie's body for the wedding. The stage directions read as follows:

> Mimi picks up Bonnie and takes her to a chair. Connie and Janet enter and take off Bonnie's dress, revealing her nuptial bra and panties. They put on her veil. Connie resets the needle back to the beginning of the song. They ritually wash Bonnie with moist towelettes. They stand her on the chair and line up to kiss her pussy good-bye. The song ends and they let the record play, the needle stuck in the groove makes a scratching and popping sound [*Five Lesbian Brothers* 36].

When the ritual is complete, Bonnie puts on her wedding dress and walks downstage, with a plastic smile and streaming tears, to strains of Mendelssohn's "Wedding March." The last line of the play is Mimi's: "Good-bye, Bonnie. Forget all about pussies now. But don't forget the smell" (*Five Lesbian Brothers* 37).

In this scene, elements of Kron's style also surface, but here we see the importance of the place of performance in shaping her style. Lesbian eroticism is physicalized and verbalized in ways that Kron does not do in less specifically lesbian venues. At WOW, her gifts for physical humor can playfully extend to another woman's body, and her language can express sensually, unabashedly, and comically the joys of physical intimacy between women. As Kron recalls in her essay "Straight Line,"

> I learned to be a lesbian at WOW. Through our plays and variety nights and rent parties and fashion shows and retreats and staff meetings full of lesbian "process" and lots of lesbian drama, we made a place in the world where it was taken for granted that girls like other girls and we could drop the explanations and justifications and become fully human [www.lisakron.com].

WOW taught Kron to be a central, proudly and raucously lesbian figure at the center of her own drama. When she leaves the protected sphere of her early home at WOW, the ways she can perform her relationship with Healey and her characters, while never entirely absent, must shift to fit a heterosexual venue.

101 Humiliating Stories at P.S. 122

The mid 1990s found Lisa Kron continuing her work with the Five Lesbian Brothers—the group would attain its greatest mainstream and critical success in 1994 with *The Secretaries*, a dark, satirical tale of Slim Fast swilling secretaries in Big Bone, Oregon, which garnered them an Obie Award. But Kron was also continuing to develop as a solo artist, with work like *101 Humiliating Stories*, which premiered at P.S. 122 in January of 1993. Kron had worked at P.S. 122 in the mid–1980s, performing in the venue's Avant-Garde-Arama cabaret series (one such performance is available on tape at Lincoln Center's Performing Arts Library), and performing *All My Hopes and Dreams*. *101 Humiliating Stories* marked a difference nonetheless. This show premiered at the downtown, experimental, but not specifically lesbian venue, and thus presents another opportunity for exploring the way performance space and place shaped Kron's writing and playing of an onstage persona.

101 Humiliating Stories is Kron's hilarious account of her impending return to Lansing, Michigan, for her twenty-year high school reunion, at the request of Debby Downs, a former classmate, who wants her to perform there. The story weaves back and forth among various "humiliations" occurring during Kron's imagined performance at the reunion, her struggle to decide whether to accept the invitation, and her current interaction as her performing persona with her live theatre audience. As the time frames and locales collide, so do the various versions of Kron.

Before looking at the text, we need to examine P.S. 122 and its character as a performance space. Located at 1st Avenue and E. 9th Street in the East Village, P.S. 122 resides in the old, brick elementary school that its name memorializes. The school was built in 1894, and by the late 1970s, the City of New York had closed the school, considering it obsolete. After a group of visual artists had started using the abandoned classroom as studio spaces, a group of performing artists also began using the building, first for rehearsal and workshops. The group's founders—Charles Moulton, Charles Dennis, Tim Miller, and Peter Rose—expanded P.S. 122's offerings with the institution of the still-running Avant-Garde-Arama. In 1983, Mark Russell became the space's first artistic director, curating the various offerings and turning the venue into a year-round performing space that would, for more than two decades, become one of the prime locations for developing alternative theatre talents and some of the most innovative performances in America.

The first performances at P.S. 122 took place upstairs in the school in a room that used to function as an auditorium. In the mid–1980s, according to Charles Tarzian, the space looked thus:

> It is vast and sparse, with a high ceiling punctuated by four mock-Corninthian [sic] pillars.... The dark wood of its ornate façade climbs to an apex halfway up the wall, ending in a square frame in which a stained glass window is inlaid, making the atmosphere more like a church than a school. The space is almost as deep as it is wide, offering many playing possibilities, though most performers take as the starting point for their "stage" the southern or northern walls, which are banked by high windows. They extend the playing area out from the wall 17 feet to about the half way point, and restrict the width of the stage to the 15 feet between the pillars. The audience fills in on three sides around the circumference [Tarzian 87].

Despite the possibility for flexible staging, like WOW, P.S. 122 had a particular aesthetic for which it was known and that seems to have influenced artists who developed there. Tarzian describes it as follows:

> The structural part of their aesthetic is informed by television: the time span, non-linear breaks, the short story form, understanding the limits of attention spans, and image work. They are the television generation doing theatre, unaware of theatre's constraints. Yet, whereas the creators of Happenings in the 1960s abandoned plots and story structures, the foundation of traditional theatre, these artists have, in various ways, sought to reclaim story by using the performance format. Though the stories tend to be non-linear, they are there nonetheless [Tarzian 88].

Tarzian goes on to note the frequent use of autobiographical material in the stories that are performed, surmising, that the strategy is part "of an overall intent to engage the audience on a more emotional, intuitive level" (Tarzian 90).

Elements of P.S. 122's aesthetic are easy to spot in *101 Humiliating Stories*. As Ben Brantley wrote in his *New York Times* review, the show is "a chain of artfully paced narratives of excruciating moments recollected in, well, not exactly tranquility, but with the modulated control of a master comic eternally poised between ingenuousness and irony" (Brantley, "Retelling of Life's Abashing Moments"). Kron moves between her stories— short story narratives of humiliation — quickly and artfully. She never lets her audience, who was of course raised on television, get bored, as she flips the channels of her memories, lighting on everything from a misguided effort to dress in calico like Laura Ingalls Wilder when she was in elementary school, to scaring Sigourney Weaver at a cocktail party. The fragments of autobiography, arranged in nonlinear fashion, are deeply engaging, but in Kron's hands, her own story does more than chronicle an individual's path in the world; she charts the way a lesbian identity is constructed and negotiated against those memories.

Perhaps the part of the show most telling about the art of lesbian self-construction within a particular locale can be found in the four versions of the speech she will make to her high school classmates. The first reads as follows:

> I work as a solo performance artist in the East Village of NYC. I am here today with my committed partner of five years Peg Healey. She is my lover. And she and I are in a theater company together called The Five Lesbian Brothers and we're based in the lesbian theater collective, the W.O.W. Café [Kron *2.5 Minute Ride* 64].

In this version of the speech, Kron is very out and proud. She foregrounds her lesbian identity and the places in the world where she can stage it openly. It is well worth noting, however, that in this, Kron's most forceful articulation of her sexuality, her lifestyle, and her art in the piece, she is considerably more conservative than she was playing a character other than herself— Mimi — at the WOW Café. Gone are both the physical expressions of lesbian desire and the frank wording to describe lesbian pleasure. Perhaps as she invokes WOW, audiences who know the range of her work will be able to picture this other version of Kron's lesbian performance and judge this performance persona against it. But within the piece, without the Brothers, and in the context of P.S. 122, the nature and manner of performance have changed.

In the next version of the speech, Kron keeps the same general contours of the address— describing her work and venue, and introducing Peg Healey — but how she fills the form has changed radically:

> I live in New York City, and I work as a solo performer, doing one-woman shows ... uh, it's Off Off Broadway! Um ... I'm not married. Although I do have a room-

mate and she's here with me today. She and I are in a theater company together, actually, The Five Le ... made up of five women, and we're based in a women's theatre collective ... a big group of women who just like to hang out together, I guess, I don't know what else they'd be doing together [Kron *2.5 Minute Ride* 64].

Wherever Kron had been out in the first speech, she retreats to the closet, however comic, in the second. The second speech's relationship to other stories in the show is crucial to this change in attitude. The story immediately preceding the second speech involves Kron's acceptance of a prize for her picture, "An Old-Fashioned Christmas" in Santa's Art Gallery. Kron talks of her love for old-fashioned things, and why this motivated her to enter the contest. Upon accepting her honorable mention, she was required to sit on Santa's lap, "whom as a Jew, I knew to be a fraud" (Kron *2.5 Minute Ride* 63). Thus, performance of an inauthentic self is clearly a linking device. But Kron also talks of her obsession with pulling her skirt down while sitting on the fraudulent Santa's lap. She remembers, "I had learned to keep my dress down from Ms. Hildreth in first grade. Before that time I had not known this was a thing one needed to be concerned about. But one day I was sitting in the reading circle folding my dress up into a neat little roll and Mrs. Hildreth yelled at me to pull my dress down, and so I credit her with teaching me shame" (Kron *2.5 Minute Ride* 63–64). Shame, and the metaphorical need to keep one's dress down, are clearly evident in the second speech. The pain of this second self-construction — and its narrative placing — is crucial to the show. Kron makes clear that it is not just a present-tense place or performance space, but an accumulated history of places and personae, that shape lesbian self-presentation.

Kron retreats from the pain of the second speech with satirical self-aggrandizement in the third. She seems to dip back into her well of staged personae, retrieving the "lesbian Lola Falana" of *All My Hopes and Dreams*. Highlights from this speech — which break from the patterned content of the other three — include, "Come on, give it up for Debby Downs. Let me tell you something about this little lady. She is a real trooper. It wasn't easy for her to track down my manager and find a little window of time in my schedule when I was available to come here and perform for all of you, and let me tell you I am so pleased that I could work this in. I'm sorry ... (to Debby) Didi, can you get me a Pellegrino?" It is quite simply fun to see Kron try on this effervescent persona after the pain of the second speech. But as pleasurable as the interlude is with its celebration of "shows and shows and touring and Europe a couple of times, it's been a whirlwind" (Kron *2.5 Minute Ride* 69), the audience knows as surely as they did in the second monologue that this is Kron in another form of comic disguise. We hunger for something more genuine, especially toward the end of the speech when her own self-construction and aggrandizement come at the expense of her imagined audience: She shifts her attention to the member of the audience who didn't move away from Lansing. You said, "See the world, adventures ... it's not important to me. I'm going to stay right here in Lansing" (Kron *2.5 Minute Ride* 69).

The show's penultimate segment is the fourth installment of the graduation address. The first three speeches offered extremes of self-presentation: bold fearlessness, memory-induced shame, and escape into glib, inconsiderate stardom. But the fourth speech, generated in part by all the stories that have come before, reads as follows:

> I've never been on TV or anything. I'll never be on TV. Because I'm a big lesbian. Although, maybe that's just an excuse. Maybe I'll never be on TV because I don't really have any talent and I just use being a big lesbian as a big ... crutch. I don't know. So I'll tell you a little about what I do. I live in New York City and I work as a performer and I do a lot of shows, but I still have a job as a word processor. And it's really exhausting.... So, I'll just do a little of what I do. I tell stories. No big New York production like you might have been expecting, just story after story after story [Kron *2.5 Minute Ride* 71–72].

In the final speech, self-doubt and self-understanding are balanced. Kron doesn't hide who she is—including the insecurities that persist even for a performer of her stature. Here she also names her power: she tells stories, stories in a line, that retrace the past but that valiantly keep on going, seeking a place in the present. As powerful as this revealing moment is, it is nonetheless disappointing that Healey has disappeared from this version of story and self.

In addition to the storytelling strategies that would evolve into Kron's most recent, most acclaimed, and most well-known work, her characteristic use of stage space was also materializing in *101 Humiliating Stories*.

Just as Kron's construction of character is based on accumulation rather than a seamless or solitary picture, so too is her construction of place. She finds the power in dividing the stage into two areas—one a present performance space and the over an ever more flexible space that morphs as her memories evolve. In the second space she uses only the lightest touches a podium to mark a high school or a lipstick and compact to build an office—to map the changes in locale. Surely a remnant of her work at W.O.W. as well as the P.S. 122 aesthetic, which Tarzian notes, featured "a desire to discard the use of objects in favor of a more direct relationship with the audience" (Tarzian 90), this fractured, minimal space also allows the various selves, and the memories that make them thus, to drift easily among the places. The divided stage, featuring places of memory, as well as making plain the theatre itself, will appear in *Well*, regardless of where the play is performed.

Well at the Public Theater and on Broadway: Big Stages and Crowded Living Rooms

By the time *Well*, Lisa Kron's most ambitious and most well-known play, opened at the Public Theater on March 16, 2004, George C. Wolfe had already announced that he was stepping down as Artistic Director after ten years of service. But understanding the context in which Kron created *Well* and where it first opened means understanding the theatre Wolfe had created at the Public. As has long been the case at the Public, the artistic director's persona forged the image of the place and had a strong effect on the work that premiered there.

The first person to define the Public was, of course, the legendary producer Joseph Papp. Papp founded the New York Shakespeare Festival in 1954, first staging Shakespeare in a Lower East Side church. He then took Shakespeare to East River Park, the five boroughs of New York in The Mobile Theater, and eventually to Central Park, where he would found the Delacorte Theater. In 1966, Papp secured a year-round home for the New York Shakespeare Festival — the old Astor Library Building, the city's first public library, at 425 Lafayette Street. In 1967, the Public Theater began producing work, "a year-round program of contemporary plays at popular prices" ("Re-Public" 147).

When Papp selected the plays for his season, he was deeply committed to reflecting the diversity of the city in which his theater was located, so much so in fact, that forty years after its founding, this continues to be a hallmark of the theatre. Papp's widow Gail described for the *New York Times* the expectations that come with a position at the Public: "Part of that has to do with socially conscious work and diversity. That's a major part of the theater and what makes it unique" (Brantley, "The Public Faces Life without Its Dynamo").

When George C. Wolfe took over as producer at the Public in 1993 — Joanne Akalaitis held the post for less than two years immediately following the death of Papp — he continued this commitment to diversity in new play development. Among the talents who had their work produced at the Public during his watch were Suzan-Lori Parks, Anna Deveare-Smith, Jose Rivera, Jessica Hagedorn, Diana Son, and Tony Kushner. While Wolfe was entirely skillful at maintaining this part of the Public's mission, he was perhaps less successful at pairing adventurous innovation in staging, for which the theatre had also been known in its heyday in the 1970s and '80s, with this new material. No previously unknown director got his or her start at the Public during Wolfe's tenure and like many other nonprofit theatres, the Public was, according to the *New York Times*, under increasing pressure to "produce more mainstream fare with Broadway potential" (Pogebrin).

So as Kron was developing *Well* for a premiere at the Public, she must have found herself inhabiting a complex landscape. On the one hand, her performance history and her sexuality made her a prime candidate for continuing the diversity for which the Public was known and for which Wolfe famously worked. Though she was moving uptown from her theatrical roots, she had arrived at a place that despite five acting spaces and an unequaled pedigree in American theatre, did according to its mission, promote a "philosophy of inclusion" (see the Public's mission statement at *www.publictheater.org*). Audiences at the Public were used to hearing diverse voices—both in terms of race and sexual orientation. On the other, her innovative structure of creating a metatheatrical solo show with other characters that intentionally turns in upon itself, might have appeared challenging to people who were looking for shows that could transfer to Broadway with only minimal retooling. As it turned out, *Well* would follow the very path that was so desired at the end of Wolfe's tenure, though the journey was not entirely smooth.

As the lights come up at the beginning of *Well*, a narrator named "Lisa," played by Lisa Kron, enters and introduces her audience to the themes of the show they are about to see. She says, "The play we're about to do deals with issues of illness and wellness. It asks the question: Why are some people sick and other people are well?... What is the difference between those people?" (Kron, *Well* 11). She also introduces the audience to a woman sitting in a La-Z-Boy recliner in the midst of what looks like a crowded living room stage left. This woman is the character, "Ann Kron," Lisa's mother, who in the Public Theatre and Broadway productions of the play, is played by Jayne Houdyshell. "Lisa" says, "This play is *not* about my mother and me" (Kron, *Well* 11).

Reviewers of the show have been quick to point out *Well*'s similarity to the work of Luigi Pirandello. And indeed, the comparison is apt. *Well* deals with an author attempting to stage a play, about what it means to be well and sick, both for an individual and a community, but she is frequently interrupted and redirected by her own creations. Her characters talk back, contradict her, and refuse to stay confined within the structures she defines. The play and its onstage author and star performer seem fixated on the work's metatheatricality and the implications of that quality. But it is also worth noting, in reference to the quoted line above, a kinship that *Well* has to the work of Rene Magritte, perhaps most notably his work "Ceci n'est pas une pipe" (1926). On Magritte's famous canvas, the image of pipe is captioned with a line that reads "This is not a pipe." Like Magritte, Kron presents an image—of herself and her mother—but uses the linguistic mode of storytelling to make her audience question the act of representing this relationship, onstage in particular, and how language, storytelling, and image work together to parse reality and memory, the real and the representation, as an individual works to create a healthy self.

Kron uses the set design to physicalize this exploration. Like *101 Humiliating Stories*, she once again employs a fractured stage space. This stage is larger, filled with more objects and people, but her earlier stage strategy, which had evolved as a result of the previous stages on which she worked, is nonetheless present. As noted above, there are two halves to the stage. One is Ann Kron's living room, and the other, as the stage directions indicate, is "the theater in which it's being performed." This second area is flexible — it becomes the Allergy Unit where Lisa was treated during her college years; the site of neighborhood meetings from Lisa's childhood, during which her mother worked to organize her Lansing, Michigan, neighbors, protecting the area and developing an integrated neighborhood; her childhood neighbor Oscar's backyard; and the site of a 4th of July parade. The second half of the stage gives Kron a place where she can re-enact her memories.

Throughout the show, the reality and artificiality of the theatre and the domestic interior are juxtaposed and negotiated. Until the end of the play, Lisa inhabits the world of the theatre. She is often the one making the changes in the flexible space — stripping beds in the Allergy Unit, rolling on folding chairs and the like, sometimes because she is in control of the action and sometimes because the other characters in the play — referred to in the printed script as "A, B, C and D," and onstage by the name of the actor who is playing the role in the particular staging — are distracted by Ann and/or are refusing to help Lisa.

She also frequently retreats to what the script refers to as her "special light." In the Public's staging of the show (the show has been preserved on video and is available for viewing for research purposes at the Theatre on Film and Tape Archive at Lincoln Center), there was a long, rectangular box of light with a bright white downstage area and a darker, grey upstage one. From the "special light," Lisa would often adopt a confessional tone with her audience, behaving as though Ann, mere feet away, could not hear her. This device allowed her to discuss the differences between her mother's version of events, particularly in regard to her time in the Allergy Unit, and her own. She reveals that she's sharing things with her audience that she's never discussed with her mother, though she continues to deny that the play is about her mother. She says, "This is a theatrical exploration of universal issues. But that's what is so incredibly helpful about this convention of interior monologue. It will allow us to explore these issues in a professional, theatrical context" (Kron, *Well* 18).

The sanctity of the "professional, theatrical context" is challenged throughout the evening, as is the version of events generated there. In addition to Ann's interjections from the static space of the living room, a character from Lisa's past, a ten-year-old child named Lori Jones, appears onstage against Lisa's wishes. After Lori bursts through the scrim in the flexible space to confront Lisa, Lisa tries to tell her, "You know what? You're not in this. (Pulling her note cards out of her pocket.) Look. See? (Shows Lori her cards.) You're not in this. See?" (Kron, *Well* 40). Lori proceeds to knock the cards to the ground, further destroying the stage order Lisa has created, saying, "I don't care about those. Me and Belinda and Pam and Carol and Antoinette want to see you dance. Go on." Thus Lori shifts the gears of the show, causing Lisa to veer away from her stories about allergy testing and off into a memory about dancing with the neighborhood children and being unaware of the music, such as Stevie Wonder's "Superstitious," that they found cool.

In addition to reordering the storyline, Lori also threatens the show's narrative by posing questions about Lisa's version of the story of her neighborhood's integration. Lisa wants to pair her mother's inability to get well physically with her mother's efforts to create a healthy, integrated neighborhood. Lori embodies the problems she wants to forget — not everyone knew or liked the same music and not everyone got along. When Lisa is anxious to ban Lori from appearing in any more scenes so she can rescue her tidy construction, Ann sees right through her. Forced out of her living room space by a physical confrontation between Lori and Lisa, she scolds Lisa, "Kick Lori out of the play for acting like a crumb if you want, but not because she's not an appropriate 'representation'" (Kron, *Well* 56). Ann has metaphorically left her narrative space and physically left her stage space, and begins commenting on the construction of events in the theatre.

Though the stage might have initially appeared to be the "real" place and the living room the represented one, the proximity of the fractured spaces, and the ways that what happens in one area affects what happens in the other, skews this neat division. Echoing Magritte's *This Is Not a Pipe*, Ann's half of the stage seemed to read "this is not reality." But over the course of the performance, Kron shows her audience that memory and metatheatrical art are not independent planes of self-presentation. Both places involve purposeful kinds of staging, and reality in both places can be threatened by the intrusion of disobedient images.

Unlike her earlier work, when Kron presents herself to the audience, she does not discuss her sexuality directly until late in the show. She is performing in a theatre where a lesbian audience or perspective certainly cannot be presumed, but one should also note that by 2004, a play by a lesbian does not have to treat sexuality as the primary focus. The multiple dimensions of lesbian lives — how a woman relates to her mother, how she remembers her childhood, how she makes her art — are, as Kron demonstrates through example, important and stage-worthy. Remembering the creation of *Voyage to Lesbos*, Dominique Dibbell stated, "Lesbian feminism of the 1970s and 1980s had placed a heavy emphasis on 'positive images of lesbians.' But by the late eighties the emphasis had become a mandate. No good art can come of a mandate, so we incorrigibly did the opposite of what we were told: we instinctively returned to the image of lesbian as pervert" (*Five Lesbian Brothers* 4). Mandates for what defines lesbian theatre have changed markedly over the course of Kron's career and her recent work reflects the freedom that that change allows.

But Kron does not disguise or deny her sexual identity onstage in *Well*— this is not another version of *101 Humiliating Stories'* high school address in which she erases her lover, her performance venues, the specific nature of her theatrical achievements, and her own desire. Instead, her sexuality emerges, if a return to the old Aristotelian terms can possibly be appropriate given the play's imaginative and complicated structure, right at the moment of recognition. Retreating into her special light after her mother has urged her just to say whatever it is she's so afraid to say to her, Lisa remembers visiting a man she had known in the Allergy Unit many years before. When he wants to know how she got better, she tells the audience,

> I looked down and shrugged and I said, "I don't know." But I was thinking — it's sex. I've got this girlfriend who's cured me with sex. It's therapy, I moved to New York and got into therapy. I left Lansing and started to eat better food. I studied theater so I learned how to breathe and stretch ... I started to learn how to inhabit my body — that there is an alternative to dragging your body around like a stone and wishing it would disappear. That it is possible to integrate your physical self with the rest of you [Kron, Well 69].

Kron heralds the virtues of therapy, theatre, and organic food — and later in the monologue the value of shopping at Target instead of Kmart — but she begins her realization about the integration of body and mind with sex and, though she doesn't name her directly, Peg Healey. Though this statement lacks the campy flourishes and the outrageous theatricality of her work with the Five Lesbian Brothers, it remains one of Kron's most powerful statements about sexuality, the body, and lesbian identity. Of all the versions of herself that she's presented on various New York stages, we find at the moment of recognition, a self that is well, with body and soul integrated and united.

The play ends with Lisa reading a letter that Jayne has found that Ann wrote for one of her neighborhood meetings. The final lines of the show are as follows: "This is the purpose of integration. This is what integration means. It means weaving into the whole parts that are uncomfortable or don't seem to fit. Even the parts that are complicated and painful. What is more worthy of our time and love than this?" (Kron, *Well* 76). The final image is of Lisa holding the paper out, offering it to the audience. The lights fade as "Superstitious" plays. As she's staged an integrated self, Kron shows that she also fully integrated lesbian identity in all its richness as she own her place on the Public stage.

When *Well* moved from the Public Theatre to Broadway, expectations were high. The show had enjoyed a successful intermediary run at San Francisco's American Conservatory Theatre where it had been tweaked and refined. The critics had loved *Well* at the Public, and that didn't change when the show moved uptown to the Longacre Theatre in March 2006. Beyond simply calling the show "sparkling," Ben Brantley of *The New York Times* wrote,

> But more than any other monologuist I can think of, include Mr. [Spalding] Gray, she uses autobiography to point out the limitations of the artificial forms we naturally impose on memory. Even better, as she acknowledges those limitations, she tries to break out of the circularity of public introspection.... Lisa Kron may understand, painfully and regretfully, that we can never really know someone else. But the loving vigor with which she tries to do so here turns the natural selfishness of the memoir into a glowing act of generosity [Brantley, "Lisa Kron's *Well* Opens on Broadway"].

Kron herself knew that the move to Broadway was a big leap for her show, no matter how strong and polished her material had become. Before the previews began, Kron told *American Theatre* interviewer Wendy Weisman, "Everyone involved knows it's a risky choice bringing this play to Broadway. It's not a musical and we have no stars. It's a really brave choice on the part of the producers" (Weisman 44). And while the move was brave, it proved not to be profitable. Robert Simonson of *Playbill* reported that the show would close on May 14, 2006—after 23 previews and 53 performances—and confirmed Kron's statements about the show's move as prescient. He wrote, "Though it opened to some of the best reviews for any play this season, *Well*—bereft of a name actor, star playwright, or Pulitzer Prize (such as the hit play *Doubt* has)—struggled to find an audience. Audiences in recent weeks have hovered around one-third capacity" (Simonson). Kron and Houdyshell would both garner Tony nominations—the kind of adulation that can entice prospective audience members—but the nominations would not be announced before the show closed.

Though *Well* did not turn a large profit, it did accumulate many other marks of what industry insiders regard as excellence: it earned stellar reviews, it moved from a celebrated Off Broadway theatre to a major Broadway house, and its performers were recognized as being among the best on stage in the year in which it was first produced. Though large audiences did not follow her on her first voyage to the Great White Way, Kron's achievement in telling a personal story from a lesbian perspective with a complex, multifaceted structure on Broadway should earn her an important "place" in the history of American theatre.

Conclusion

Over the course of a varied, celebrated, twenty-year career that is showing no signs of slowing down, Kron has tested the limits of how a lesbian can inhabit the stage and play her self. While touring some of New York's most significant and varied performance venues, Kron used the distinct character of those very particular stage places to her advantage as she's faced her audiences, her memories, and the culture that's influenced both. She's made the outrageous and the campy, the alternative and the avant-garde, and even the mainstream and commercial part of who she is and the sites that cater to these tastes a place where lesbian representation can feel right at home. Place rather than placelessness matters to Lisa Kron, her performance persona, and her playwriting, because claiming a variety of particular, public places for lesbian performance is essential for continued empowerment, liberation, and integration.

BIBLIOGRAPHY

Auge, Marc. *Non-Places: Introduction to an Anthropology of Supermodernity*. London and New York: Verso Press, 1995.
Brantley, Ben. "Lisa Kron's *Well* Opens on Broadway, with Mom Keeping Watch." *New York Times*, March 31, 2006.
_____. "The Public Faces Life without Its Dynamo." *New York Times*, February 21, 2004.
_____. "Retelling of Life's Abashing Moments." *New York Times*, June 23, 1994.
Davy, Kate. "Reading Past the Heterosexual Imperative: Dress Suits to Hire." *TDR* 33:1 (Spring 1989).
The Five Lesbian Brothers (Four Plays). New York: Theatre Communications Group, 2000.
Kron, Lisa. *2.5 Minute Ride and 101 Humiliating Stories*. New York: Theatre Communications Group, 2001.
_____. *Well*. New York: Theatre Communications Group, 2006.
McAuley, Gay. *Space in Performance: Making Meaning in the Theatre*. Ann Arbor, MI: University of Michigan Press, 1999.
Pogebrin, Robin, "Much Ado about a Vision." *New York Times*, October 18, 2000.
"Re-Public: The Cine." *Theater* 35:5 (2005).
Simonson, Robert. "*Well* Runs Dry: Lisa Kron Play to Close on Broadway May 14." *Playbill*, May 8, 2006.
Solomon, Alisa, "The WOW Café," The Drama Review: TDR, Vol. 29, No. 1, East Village Performance (Spring, 1985), pp. 92–101.
Tarzian, Charles. "Performance Space P.S. 122." *TDR* 29:1 (Spring 1985).
Weisman, Wendy. "The Importance of Lisa Kron." *American Theatre* 23 (March 2006).
www.lisakron.com.

The Last Gay Man
Raised in Captivity *and* Hurrah at Last

ROBERT F. GROSS
For Jim (d. 2001) and Phil (d. 2007)

This disease will be the end of many of us, but not nearly all, and the dead will be commemorated and will struggle on with the living, and we are not going away. We won't die secret deaths anymore. The world only spins forward. We will be citizens. The time has come [Kushner 148].

—Whatever Happened to Gay Theatre? [Roberts 175].

Two quotations. The first, from Prior Walter's curtain speech in *Perestroika*, at the conclusion of the most widely noted theatrical event of the 1990s, Tony Kushner's *Angels in America*. The second, the title of a thoughtful article by Brian Roberts in *New Theatre Quarterly*. Only seven years separate the first quotation (1993) from the second (2001), from a triumphant assertion of visibility to an interrogation of it. What happened, indeed? Why did *Angels in America*, which seemed at the time of its international success and instantaneous canonization to herald a new great flowering of queer drama, quickly appear to have marked the end of an era? Why does the assertion, "The Great Work Begins" (Kushner, 148) now seem to induce more wistfulness than enthusiasm in me when I read it?

To understand what happened, I am going to put the much-discussed *Angels in America* aside and examine two plays that have largely been ignored by scholars. Small-scale pieces in the tradition of John Guare's dark domestic comedies, plays with modest Off Broadway runs, these plays have attracted little critical comment and have not been scrutinized for evidence of the development of American gay drama in the second decade of the AIDS epidemic.

The two plays: Nicky Silver's darkly comic *Raised in Captivity*, first performed at the Vineyard Theatre in 1995, in a production directed by David Warren, with Peter Frechette playing its impoverished, gay, traumatized writer-hero, and Richard Greenberg's darkly comic *Hurrah at Last*, first performed at South Coast Repertory in 1998 and receiving its New York premiere at Gramercy Theatre a year later — a play directed by David Warren, with

Peter Frechette in the role of the impoverished, gay, traumatized writer-hero. One certainly need not go far to find similarities between these two plays.

And the longer one looks, the more the similarities increase. In both plays, the gay protagonist is situated in a milieu that is almost exclusively marked as heterosexual; there are no gay friends or community to which the protagonist can turn in his traumatized state. In both cases, the protagonist turns to his biological family, whose primary representative is his sole sibling, a neurotic sister caught in a troubled marriage. The family is troubled at the least or, in the therapeutic lingo of the '90s, "dysfunctional" at worst, but it provides a haven for the recovering gay man. Dramaturgically, both plays undermine the certainties of what has hitherto been a domestic realism geared up to a comic pitch by presenting events from the point of view of their protagonist's increasing delirium. As one loses blood after a near-fatal attack and the other succumbs to a mysterious disease, the audience is shown events that defy realistic verisimilitude and is treated to revelations that are bizarre and unascertainable. The physical traumatization of an already damaged character erupts in expressionistic delirium. And yet, *Hurrah at Last* is not simply a repetition of *Raised in Captivity*. It is a substantial revision of the earlier work, and the terms of that revision reflect important developments in the treatment and perception of HIV/AIDS that took place between 1995 and the end of the decade.

Early in *Raised in Captivity*, Sebastian Bliss explains his current situation to his sister Bernadette, who desperately craves some evidence that his life is not "perfect" (18):

> I'm forty-five thousand dollars in debt. I haven't sold anything since that *Vanity Fair* piece you disparaged. I live entirely off of credit cards. I charge my rent and my food and I pay the minimum on one card with a cash advance from another. I haven't had sex in eleven years. I haven't held or kissed or cared for anyone, in anything but the most superficial way, in so long that I no longer know if I know how [19].

Sebastian is suffering trauma from and uncompleted mourning for the death of his lover, Simon, who died of AIDS eleven years previously, in the early years of the epidemic: "It was GRID in the beginning, AIDS at the end," Sebastian explains (66), and, in a harrowing monologue, he describes Simon's physical deterioration and the care he took of him.

In "Mourning and Melancholia," Freud distinguishes between mourning as a process of gradual libidinal withdrawal from the deceased, and melancholia is a status in which the mourning process is blocked, leaving the survivor to identify with the deceased in a state of death-in-life. The greater the ambivalence the survivor feels toward the deceased, the more likely the chance that mourning process will be frozen into melancholia. Sebastian's eleven years of melancholia, from a Freudian perspective, hints at massive ambivalence.

Sebastian's sole enthusiasm, mounting to an obsession, is Dylan, a murderer serving a life sentence in a southern state penitentiary. For Sebastian, Dylan becomes an imaginary figure of concern, fascination and sexual desire. The closest Silver comes to explaining Sebastian's obsession with Dylan comes in the last moments of the play, when Sebastian reveals that his late lover knowingly had unprotected sex with people after he knew he was infected with HIV, and caused their deaths. This revelation not only provides an explanation for Sebastian's uncompleted mourning and extreme melancholia — his relationship to Simon is simultaneously one of both great affection and moral horror — but also explains his obsessive relationship with the murderer, Dylan. Dylan provides the locus for a displacement of Sebastian's conflicted feelings toward Simon. Only when Dylan terminates his correspondence with Sebastian, and Sebastian can admit the roots of his conflicted feelings about Simon, can he begin to mourn — "I miss everyone.... I miss Mother" — and the play can come to its conclusion (114).

Sebastian's dire financial situation resonates off his emotional desolation, but it must be understood against the background of '90s affluence. In a decade in which the Dow Jones average went from around 3300 in early 1993 to 11000 by August 1999 and spiked again before the year was out, upward mobility seemed to be the norm, however dogged by the specters of increasing disparity between the rich and poor and ongoing worker insecurity (Morton 13). While one of the dominant gay stereotypes of the decade was the gay man or couple who participated in that boom, Sebastian functions as its opposite. In fact, his movement from his biological family to gay existence is from the first as impoverishment: "I walked away from servants and swimming pools to live on complimentary peanuts and cashews in cocktail lounges," he recollects (7). While his sister can assure her husband Kip that she has the financial assets to support him no matter what (111), Sebastian is indigent.

Sebastian's movement from extreme melancholia to the beginnings of mourning is also charted against a movement from estrangement from his family, the sole surviving member of which is his sister Bernadette, to reincorporation within the family. Sebastian's story is set into action by his meeting with Bernadette at their mother's funeral, where the numbed Sebastian — "inertia given human form" (24) as he calls himself — encounters his raw-nerved and emotionally hyperbolic sister. "She's insane, obviously," Sebastian observes, "and unhappy, I think. But she obviously participates! She clearly feels things" (24). Although it might seem that a play that begins with the death of a parent would be one of charting a movement away from biological family, the funeral not only provides an occasion for the siblings to re-encounter each other, but to mysteriously put Sebastian back into the currents of life. When Bernadette sings "This Could Be the Start of Something Big," the choice is at once amusing in its ghastly indecorousness, and quite apt, even prophetic. Soon after, Sebastian breaks his totally dysfunctional relationship with his psychotherapist, Hillary McMahon, and makes a tentative, albeit disastrous, move toward interaction with a hustler, Roger. This pattern of renewal in the aftermath of the mother's funeral is not confined to Sebastian. Kip leaves dentistry, an occupation that depresses him, to become a painter, and Bernadette finds satisfaction in motherhood. Like his sister, Sebastian finds a new purpose through domesticity. He moves into his sister's home, becomes obsessed with her newborn baby, and offers to take the place of the father when Kip leaves. The play ends with brother and sister playing mother and surrogate father, and Sebastian suggesting that the hitherto unnamed child should be called "Simon."

Raised in Captivity reverses a common narrative of modernity — one that recounts the emergence of the individual out of a stifling and inhibiting world of domesticity (think of *A Doll's House, The Breadwinner, In a Garden, Street Scene, The Silver Cord, The Glass Menagerie*, and *Picnic*, to name only a few examples). This narrative reflects the loosening of family ties that coincided with and contributed to the creation of urban gay identities (Sinfield 7). The emergence of the individual out of a constricting domestic world found particular resonance within the coming-out narrative. Indeed, *Raised in Captivity* can be seen as an inversion of that delicately closeted proto-coming-out drama, *The Glass Menagerie*. Silver's play not only makes an explicit reference to Williams's canonical and immensely influential pre-gay drama — when Bernadette describes her brother saying "He lives in a fantasy world of glass animals" (78), but the structure of the Bliss family — hardworking mother, absent father, hysterical daughter and melancholic writer-son who runs away — echoes that of Williams's play as well. But whereas Tom Wingfield leaves home in pursuit of his desire, Sebastian renounces desire and returns home. The movement out of the heteronormative unit into a gay world has been obliterated by eruptions of the death drive. (Not only was Simon seemingly responsible for the deaths of other gay men, but Sebastian almost bleeds to death when slashed by an emotionally unstable hustler. Sebastian's sole, hesitant movement toward sexual activity in the play turns out to be close to lethal.) Sebastian is incapable of supporting himself, incapable of healing himself (four-and-a-half years of psychotherapy with Hillary have proven to be utterly unproductive for him), and there is nowhere to go but home. Home is depicted as a flight from the world and a regression — Sebastian stays home in his pajamas, sleeping and spending his days in the nursery with the baby. In his fantasies of the child's brilliance and precocity, he almost enters into the narcissistic grandiosity of the child. Brother and sister wind up providing a sexless parody of husband and wife, almost as if "playing house." Domesticity may be queered by such a move, but, at the same time, queerness is desexualized.

If *Glass Menagerie* can be described as "pre-gay," in that it begins to sketch out a coming-out narrative without the language, concepts, or political tools of a post–Stonewall gay awareness, *Raised in Captivity* can be described as a moment that is "post-gay" in that it represents gay culture as obliterated, traumatized, and presenting no opportunities for sustenance or healing. Outside Sebastian, who can hardly be put forth as a figure of gay culture at its most robust, the characters identified with male same-sex desire are dangerously pathological, each marked at once as both victim and victimizer. Simon suffered horrifically from AIDS and was its fatal, conscious disseminator. Roger tells a tale of sexual and physical abuse, drug addiction, and forced separation from his lover, but also slashes Sebastian with a shattered wine glass, almost killing him. Dylan may well be the victim of the justice system, but is also a brutal murderer. There is no model of gay nurturance aside from Sebastian, who is given no gay figure to reciprocate his generous impulses.

Furthermore, these figures pose a more subtle dramaturgical threat. Drawn within the circuit of Sebastian's delirium, we are never certain whether their statements are the true assertions of autonomous agents or whether they are merely the projections of Sebastian's consciousness. Dylan's observation "that it takes a special strand of pearls" to set off his prison coveralls (41) or the revelation that he has changed his name to Ruth (49) may well be more a part of Sebastian's sensibility than that of a southern homicide. The overlapping of Sebastian's account of Simon's death and Dylan's account of the murder committed is the clearest indication that Dylan dramatically functions more as an expression of Sebastian's subjectivity than he does independently. Roger, who first introduced himself as "Alfonzo," (55) offers his tale of misfortune in response to Sebastian's desire to write about him, and it is delivered enigmatically. Silver tells us Roger/Alfonzo "*seems to become quite sad, but there may be an odd flatness to it*" (59). Is that flatness the result of emotional damage or fabrication? There is no way of telling. Even Sebastian's ultimate revelation that Simon knowingly infected sexual partners with HIV is presented as a surmise. "I think he meant to," is as close as we come to certainty (114). Throughout the play there is no foundation of shared truth on which to build a gay community.

It is always easier to argue from a presence in a text than from an absence, but the absence of a gay community in *Raised in Captivity*, along with the repeated linking of traumatization, violence, and uncertainty, can best be understood by recourse to Kai Erikson's work on collective trauma. While research on trauma has primarily been focused on psychological studies of individuals, Erikson, working with communities that have been under severe and prolonged stress, has observed trauma as a sociological phenomenon. Trauma can sever the most basic bonds in a community. He explains:

> The collective trauma works its way slowly and insidiously into the awareness of those who suffer from it, so it does not have the quality of suddenness normally associated with "trauma." But it is a form of shock all the same, a gradual realization that the community no longer exists as an effective support and that an important part of the self has disappeared.... "I" continue to exist, though damaged and perhaps permanently changed. "You" continue to exist, though distant and hard to relate to. But "we" no longer exist as a connected pair or as linked cells in a larger communal body" [233].

Simon is the caretaker/survivor—"He died. And I didn't" (68)—the melancholic and traumatized collateral damage of AIDS in gay America.

From this cultural perspective, Sebastian's acute melancholia is not simply the result of psychological ambivalence. Studies of mourning in the 1990s, sensitized by clinical interactions with gay men grieving the loss of partners and friends to AIDS, put new emphasis on the social context of mourning, substantially complicating Freud's psychodynamic model. Martha R. Fowlkes argued that the difference between mourning and melancholia also needed to be understood as the result of a social differentiation between a loss that is socially legitimated and one that is not. The socially conferred role of mourner helps to validate and support the griever's experience of loss and functions to minimize the long-term social alienation of the mourner (Fowlkes 534). Gay men, by and large, not having been granted the role of mourner by American society at large, were among those particularly prone to melancholia. A 1992 volume on AIDS counseling, bearing the eloquent and revealing subtitle *Intervening with Hidden Grievers*, sets out its thesis: "Survivors of AIDS deaths experience prejudice, stigma, devastation of large numbers of relatively young people, confrontations with mortality and multiple losses on a large scale, all of which exacerbate the normative grieving process" (Dane & Miller 45). In the United States, the primary criterion for socially condoned mourning is kinship. Given American society's general refusal to accept queers into the kinship system, the authors conclude, "there is no legitimacy and no public acknowledgment of the grievers" (157).

Sebastian's experience must be understood in the context of this disenfranchised grief. His account of Simon's death includes no references to any family, friends, or community offering assistance or support. Sebastian cleans his ailing partner when the nurses refuse to, and spends the last minutes of his partner's life in the company of an anonymous member of the hospital staff. In the second decade of the AIDS epidemic, he finds himself totally apart from a society of gay men, which only appears to persist in traumatized and dangerous fragments.

In the absence of social alternatives, the return to the biological family seems to be the only recourse. This return distinguishes *Raised in Captivity* from Silver's earlier work. There, as Robert J. Andreach has pointed out, sexually idiosyncratic characters are often agonized by their "rejection by a family that should be supportive and the confusion of a sexuality that seeks an expression at odds with society's norms" (57), while here, the family, however flawed and psychologically damaged, still winds up being supportive. The resultant tone is gentler and the disapprobation of society-at-large is correspondingly muted.

But this is not to say that Silver has transformed the family into the irreproachable seat of all positive values. The Bliss family—their surname an intertextual reference to the egomaniacal artistic clan of Noël Coward's *Hay Fever*—have no history of closeness or mutual support, and when the mother, Miranda, appears in Sebastian's bloody delirium to explain its origins, the story is grim indeed. Sebastian and Bernadette are, we are told, the result of rape and Miranda, rather than kill the offspring that were conceived in violence and traumatization, resolved to feel nothing for them. Rather than the charming but feckless Wingfield father whose photo still graces the family home, and the well-meaning but smothering mother, Silver's *Raised in Captivity* menagerie is one of crippling parental distance, in which the father has been kept a mystery and the mother refuses to feel. The home owes its origin and its dynamic to traumatization. Psychoanalyst Peter Shabad has analyzed how a physically present but emotionally absent parent like Miranda can traumatize a child by degrees, leading to a pattern of emotional detachment in later life (110–11). Absent father, absent mother, absent partner— Sebastian's story is one of absence doubled and redoubled. Whether Miranda's appearance is understood as a revelation form beyond the grave or a delirious invention, Sebastian's understanding of his upbringing is one of emotional starvation.

There is no evidence of Miranda's steely distance being played out in her offspring; if anything, Sebastian and Bernadette swing to an opposite extreme of feverish, even delirious, immersion. The baby becomes enthusiastically adopted as the way to remedy the psychological woes of both brother and sister. For Bernadette, the infant provides a long-sought identity: "I'm a breeder!" she exults (74). For Sebastian, the child provides an alternative to his Thanatos-saturated obsession with a convicted killer. One can only cringe at the long-term results of such desperate immersions in parenting.

The Child emerged as an increasingly important figure in the '90s gay imaginary. As Lee Edelman shows at length in *No Future: Queer Theory and the Death Drive* (in an argument far too intricately Lacanian to be successfully summarized here), the Child has become the embodiment of the Future, a pure, bright-eyed trope that conservatives and liberals alike can exploit in their appeals on a range of issues, and that is repeatedly placed in contrast to the figure of the gay man, a figure not of the Future, but of death-in-life. Ignoring the rebirth of the parent's narcissism through the child (Freud "On Narcissism" 91), parenting is figured as the ultimate in selflessness, while non-reproductive sexuality is narcissistic.

Nowhere in '90s gay discourses was the trope of the Child more unabashedly present than in discussions of gay parenting. As one gay adoptive father of the decade expressed it in the pages of *The New York Times Magazine*, "Many of us have decided that we want to fill our time with something more meaningful than sit-ups, circuit parties and designer drugs. For me and my boyfriend, bringing up a child is a commitment to having a future" (Savage 95). Parenting is presented as the alternative to sit-ups (narcissism), circuit parties (social exclusivity), and designer drugs (hedonism), in short, to all the popularly perceived excesses of post–Stonewall gay life. "Having" a child becomes a way of ensuring futurity, in contrast to a future-less gay existence. *Raised in Captivity* participates in the discourses of gay parenting by having the newborn baby first appear onstage only a moment after Miranda validates her son's love for Simon ("You're lucky to have loved at all," she tells him [68]), and then progressively substituting Sebastian's involvement with the baby for his obsession with Dylan. The baby provides a home and a future for Sebastian.

Even if the origins of the Bliss family actually are acts of rape and traumatization, *Raised in Captivity* ultimately exorcises those origins in favor of an affectionate and wacky domesticity in the tradition of *You Can't Take It with You* and *Auntie Mame*. The more immediate threats are gay melancholia, alienation, and violence, from which the biological family provides a haven.

The pace quickens, the rhythms grow more frantic, the comedy becomes more farcical, and even the shattered remnants of gay community dissolve in Richard Greenberg's *Hurrah at Last*. Although it premiered only three years after *Raised in Captivity*, it reveals evidence of collective traumatization far beyond Silver's play, in that the protagonist has no gay community, however dangerous, to which he can turn.

Although Sebastian has not had sex in eleven years, we do feel his impulses of desire as he turns toward Dylan and Roger. Compared to Greenberg's Laurie, Sebastian is a sexual dynamo. Laurie's libido seems nonexistent. He admits that he is sexually attracted to men but bored by the way most of them think, and prefers the asexual company of women. His novels, we are told, are populated by characters who "practically don't have bodies" (235). Characterized by an absence of animating desire, he is presented as a eunuch, a feminized presence from infancy: "the only *boy* ever named after a character in *Little Women*" we are told (251), who now writes novels "like the novels *English* ladies write—where after two hundred pages they've poured the tea" (235). With a homosexuality that seems to have verged on asexuality at the best of times, it is no wonder that his sex drive completely vanishes as he succumbs to a mysterious ailment. When his self-proclaimed heterosexual friend Oliver strips himself naked in Thea's kitchen for Laurie's benefit at the Christmas party, it can be seen as the remnant of a sexual fantasy of Laurie's, but the titillation of the strip-tease is deflated and takes a comic turn since Laurie makes it clear that he is less interested in seeing his friend naked than knowing how much money he makes. With *Hurrah at Last*, the traumatization of the gay figure is physicalized and recontextualized.

In a 2006 interview, Greenberg revealed that the play was inspired by his own health crisis with Hodgkins Lymphoma in 1992 (Witchel 2006), but the play is unforthcoming with any clear diagnosis. Presented with a seriously ill gay man, a '90s audience would inevitably entertain an HIV-related complication or opportunistic infection as a likelihood, and the play enigmatically engages that possibility. Thea tells Laurie that he has disappointed the doctors who were "so excited when they thought you had AIDS" (258). Thea's report is qualified by more than a touch of comic perversity and inverted expectations. To begin with, one would expect the doctors to be weary of AIDS cases by 1998 and would be pleased to find something other than HIV. Yet her statement also functions metadramatically, chiding every audience member who has automatically diagnosed Laurie as HIV positive, and thus immediately consigned *Hurrah at Last* to the genre of "AIDS play." Gay men, Greenberg reminds us, can die from other causes. And yet the very denial of AIDS brings the disease to mind. Is this a Freudian *Verneinung* on Greenberg's part, *denying* it is an "AIDS play" when in fact it is? In the world of dramatic fiction, of course, a disease can simultaneously be AIDS and not AIDS, or be AIDS and something else as well, especially in this dramaturgy of delirium. After all, it is never clear whether we are to take Thea's statement as a realistically depicted statement, or a hallucination. It is clear, however, that the moment admits the existence of HIV as an element in the lives of gay men even as it denies it.

Laurie is not given Sebastian's detailed biography. Not haunted by the past, his dilemma is completely in the present. On the verge of being evicted from his apartment because he cannot pay the rent, Laurie is known as "a writer's writer," which, as he explains to his mother, means "I'm a failure" (251). At a Christmas Eve party in his sister Thea's posh loft, Laurie has what at first seems to be a nasty cold. It becomes what seems to be an increasingly high fever, sending the first act into an increasing delirium in which it becomes impossible for the spectator to distinguish between objective reality and hallucination. The confusion continues to intensify in the second act, set in Laurie's hospital room, as family and friends visit and share increasingly extravagant confessions, heightening the invalid's anxiety.

As an impoverished writer in the boom time of late '90s Manhattan, Laurie becomes fixated on the money he cannot hope to earn. Money, not sex, is what fascinates him, and information about money is withheld from him more assiduously than information about sex is. The bank account replaces the closet as the privileged site of bourgeois secrecy and reserve. Laurie exists on the fringes of the economy of the play; the best he can hope for is a "trickle-down" from his fabulously wealthy and generous brother-in-law Eamon or his father. The society is not going to change, and it is clear that there is little hope for him but to become a charity case within his own family. Laurie's poverty and financial dependence reflect his total lack of agency.

Michael Feingold pointed out in his insightful review that *Hurrah at Last* is very much a play about the artist who is condemned to poverty in an age of affluence, in which a respectable living can only be made by those who can conform to the visions of vast mass media concerns. Laurie's mother notes that John Grisham is a terrible writer but a financially successful one and suggests to Laurie, "You could write as badly as he does if you tried"; Laurie not only admits that he can't, but further admits in what Greenberg describes as *"flat; a confession"*—"I've tried" (249). Feingold's observation is very apt, but it is also interesting to note that the set of economic concerns—impoverished artist in an affluent, late capitalist society—gets mapped onto a gay man in a heteronormative society, one that defines itself through the nuclear family and childbearing. Laurie's sexual orientation renders him as marginal in the domestic realm as his writing does in the economic realm.

As Laurie's mysterious illness develops in the second act, the relationships around him are revealed to be increasingly desperate and hostile. His mother is not only impatient for him to die, but wishes Thea would as well. Oliver, despite his success, his envious of Laurie's talent and eager to steal his ideas. His brother-in-law is so immersed in his own neurotic quest that he behaves irresponsibly toward Laurie, and his sister Thea believes that his life is so meaningless that it matters little whether he lives or dies. Death, she explains, is "just the loss of life. And you can only *lose* as much as you *have*.... Darling, you have nothing to worry about.... I mean, what is your life, really? Take-out dinners and Nick-at-Night?" (273). The proximity to physical death mirrors a proximity to a meaningless and barely lived existence. Laurie's position in the world has become totally superfluous, and the play's fundamental comic strategy — a cruel one — is that of repeatedly revealing the inability and indifference of the other characters to respond to the protagonist's traumatized state. In *Hurrah at Last*, a man must either make money or sire offspring. Laurie, who has neither money nor heterosexual drive, is a double nought in this economy.

With libido absent in Laurie, it makes fugitive appearances in reputedly straight characters. Laurie is bemused by his friend Oliver's homoerotic side (242) and shocked by his father's admission of moments of same-sex desire (285). Given that Laurie has never come out to his father, this abrupt, seemingly unmotivated, and immediately disavowed coming-out is a comic moment insofar as it functions as a non sequitur, both in the dramatic situation and the character, but also in that it is the gay son who is suddenly taken off guard and astonished by his father's revelation. Yet, like the reference to AIDS, it functions as a denial. Sumner insists that his moments of same-sex attraction do not add up to a gay identity. In both Oliver and Sumner, moments of desire exist neither as significant determinants of character nor as indications of gay identity. In fact, even Laurie's gay identity is weakly and intermittently marked. Laurie is characterized more frequently as a writer, ill, and penniless, than gay.

Laurie's existence resembles Sebastian's life in its physical celibacy and psychological inertia. In both plays the gay protagonist flounders at the edge of virtual nonexistence. Laurie, however, does not share Sebastian's regeneration through surrogate parenthood. He is deeply suspicious of the drive to find salvation through parenthood — "are they [children] redemptive, or, as it usually turns out, merely repetitive?" (279). He observes that his sister and brother-in-law are not "capable of having children in the old way, and too self-important to adopt," and depend entirely on Eamon's fortune to buy them offspring through the latest reproductive technology (274). In the affluent milieu of this play, procreation itself has become a luxury item, but although Laurie envies affluence, he does not envy fertility. In fact, by being strangely indifferent to affluence, fertility is the item that shows up the limits of affluence. It is not the simple process presented in *Raised in Captivity*. While Oliver and Gia unreflectively produce offspring at an improbably accelerated rate, Eamon and Thea find even the most expensive reproductive therapies not only ineffective but deleterious to their intimacy as well.

Laurie may be returned to the biological family, but its farcical delirium offers little support in his recuperation. His mother and father have been at loggerheads for as long as Laurie can remember, and his sister is too self-absorbed to pay attention. Laurie's father, Sumner, articulates the failure of the family as an institution, and, by extension, all social relationships as a source of meaning and sustenance. For Sumner, hell is other people; solitude is bliss. "I never had my own room," Sumner laments. "In my whole life. I lived at home. Then the army. Then home again. Where did I have my own room in that?" (286). Resisting this dramatic universe's desperate drive toward fertility, in which Thea is always trying unsuccessfully to become pregnant, while Oliver's wife, Gia, always seems to be pregnant, Sumner concludes, "Marriage is merely a prison: children the *abyss*" (287).

Both *Raised in Captivity* and *Hurrah at Last* inscribe a similar plot trajectory, with a traumatized gay protagonist moving toward death, the extreme verge of that movement marked by a possibly hallucinated encounter with a parent who reveals the lovelessness of the union within which the child was conceived. In *Hurrah at Last*, Laurie's parents existed within a marriage of convenience. In *Raised in Captivity*, Sebastian is told he was the result of a rape.

In both cases the gay man learns of the lovelessness of his origin — he was not wanted. The gay man is the unintentional product of the reproductive process. The fundamental traumatization, it is implied, is not the death of Sebastian lover, or Laurie's mysterious illness, but the realization that although the hero may return to the family, his place in the family from the first has been without love. The ambiguities of representation in both plays make it impossible to tell whether the revelation is objectively true, but, either way, it reflects back on the lack of love in the gay protagonist's life. Note that although both families contain a heterosexual daughter and a gay son, it is only the gay son who is marked by sterility, inertia, poverty, melancholia and alienation. The parent's turning away from the child is presented dramatically as turning away first and foremost from the gay son. In the dreamlike logic of these unloved son/parent scenes, one is led to wonder if the inability to love is presented as the origin of the gay son, or if it is a displacement of a more brutal insight — that the son cannot be loved by the parent insofar as he is gay. In either case, it is not the heterosexual daughter but the gay son who is made to face the revelation that he is conceived in lovelessness, the product of a mere sexual act — in effect, marked by "emotional celibacy" from birth. After this crucial revelation, the hero is returned to the family. Curtain. Happy ending? It's hard to tell. In both cases, the gay man who is returned to the family by the end of the play is a gay man without desire. Melancholia is removed in every respect *but* the resurgence of libido. The ultimate alternative in the plays' deep structures is a disturbingly familiar one: same-sex desire *or* incorporation within the family. But the viewer does not experience that alternative directly, since same-sex desire has been marked with traumatization and becomes melancholia, so the alternative presented in the surface structure is: melancholia *or* incorporation within the family.

In the play's third and final act, we seem to be back in Thea's loft for an Easter party, but the delirium of the preceding acts has undermined our confidence in the truth of what we see and hear, and there are elements in the final act that undercut our assurance that we have returned to realism and Laurie has returned to health. Illness has released a delirium that reaches out and infects the entire play. A Christmas party for a Jewish family seemed slightly odd in the first act, but a Jewish Easter party is definitely much odder. The loft has sprouted multiple rooms, and an Old Master painting is on display.

Has Laurie recovered, or sunk deeper into his moribund state? Oliver announces that he and Gia have named their latest offspring after Laurie, who notes that in the Jewish tradition one only names children after the dead (299). Is this a perversely and cruel gesture in life, or something witnessed from beyond the grave? How do we know when we are looking at comic extravagance, and when hallucination? Laurie returns, supposedly cured, but we are told that he suffered, as did a number of celebrities, from "the most curable form of cancer known to man" (294), an explanation that rings false, of course, since there is regrettably no cure for cancer yet, let alone a "most curable" form. The use of the superlative here merely increases the impossibility of this claim. Laurie's diagnosis, something we expect to hear in a realistic play, is kept from the audience, leaving it a mysterious and extreme form of somatic and psychic traumatization that creates its own world, that of *Hurrah at Last*, which never offers us a stance completely and clearly outside Laurie's subjectivity from which to interpret the action confidently.

While *Raised in Captivity* presented the gay project as traumatized, *Hurrah at Last* shows it approaching dissolution in a swiftly moving vortex in which it only circulates as lack of meaning. If both Sebastian and Laurie have to be hospitalized, it is not because of the old pathological model of same-sex desire as sick, but because the lack of desire marks the gay hero as (to use a word applied repeatedly to Laurie in the second act of *Hurrah at Last*) "moribund" (271) in a world of otherwise desiring subjects. Gay desire, and with it, gay identity are dissolving in *Hurrah at Last*, but not into some postmodern, polymorphously perverse play of liberated desire. Only same-sex desire attenuates: heteronormativity remains intact.

In both *Raised in Captivity* and *Hurrah at Last* the return of the protagonist to his sister's home is presented in an energetic comic register, but the comic tone does not eliminate the problems of the return. Although *Raised in Captivity* is far more often dark and anguished than *Hurrah at Last*, its conclusion is the more hopeful of the two. Sebastian finds a place as surrogate father, forges a relationship with his sister, loses his obsession with Dylan, and begins at last to mourn Simon. The return is in part regressive; Sebastian uses the baby as a blank screen on which to project images of intellectual and developmental precociousness and unconditional love, and even his desire to name his nephew "Simon" may indicate that the mourning process still has a long way to go. The overall movement of the play is one from death to life, albeit a life inevitably colored by neuroses (this is, after all, a Nicky Silver play), but sexual desire is ultimately erased in favor of domesticity.

The return is even more enigmatic in *Hurrah at Last*. Although the last act ostensibly marks Laurie's return to health, we are not sure whether we are looking at a return to health or a deeper sinking into delirium, maybe even death. All the extravagances of fertility and finances are merely ratcheted up another notch from what we have seen earlier, the delirious energy increases and there is no attempt whatsoever to address what Laurie's experience has meant. Although he at first asserts that he sees life with such clarity now that he has been restored to health, he soon loses any shred of it in the familial circus that ensues, and the curtain goes down on, as the final stage direction has it, "Mayhem. Chaos." (305). The difference here between delirium and life is, in the final reckoning, indeterminable. Both are mere plays of phenomena.

Both *Raised in Captivity* and *Hurrah at Last* show the gay man as traumatized, poverty-stricken, unsuccessful, isolated from a community of gay men, and forced back into the bosom of the family as a last healing resort. The family is marked by a deep ambivalence toward the gay man — in both plays he is welcomed with open arms *and* told he was not loved by his parents. He is welcomed in, but as a completely isolated figure who, in his return to the family, renounces the possibility of reciprocated gay desire. The injured subject is allowed to heal, but only under the sign of castration. The heroes, and perhaps the playwrights, are too battered and exhausted to register any strong protest against the terms of their re-inclusion in the realm of domestic comedy. For Silver, there is no alternative but retreat and regression; for Greenberg, immersion in the chaos of other people's selfish desires. But for both, the representation of male same-sex desire comes to bear a crucial silence — but this time not because it *dare* not speak its name, but because it has been exhausted by isolation, trauma and the burden of carrying its own desire. A depressed libido becomes both a symptom of illness and a grounds for acceptance.

In 1996 gay columnist Andrew Sullivan argued that it had been AIDS that has facilitated the acceptance of gays into mainstream culture, creating bonds across boundaries that had hitherto not been traversed. "The victimization of gay men by a disease paradoxically undercut victimization by a culture" (56). As I look around me in 2007, I do not see the degree of social acceptance that Sullivan claimed to witness over a decade ago, and I do not remember having seen it then, but his claim is echoes in the terms of gay assimilation dramatized in both *Raised in Captivity* and *Hurrah at Last*. The embrace of the traumatized gay man in these plays, with nowhere to go but his family, can be taken as a figure of the assimilation process. What the plays register, however, and Sullivan's claim does not, are the tensions of an acceptance that comes out of traumatization.

The return to health from the brink of death appears as a motif in both Silver's and Greenberg's plays. In *Hurrah at Last,* however, it gains a particular shading from advances made in the treatment of HIV in the late 1990s. The most important development in gay life between *Raised in Captivity* in 1995 and *Hurrah at Last* in 1998 was the announcement at the 1996 World AIDS Conference in Vancouver of the efficacy of protease inhibitors for many HIV+ patients. With the development of these pharmaceuticals and combination therapies they made possible, many patients who were in bad health and on the verge of death were finding themselves suddenly enjoying a reprieve that they had not anticipated. No more a cure for HIV infection than the illusory cure for cancer that restores Laurie, these therapeutic regimens were responsible for what came to be referred to in the late '90s as the "Lazarus syndrome," in which the HIV positive patient, having decathected from most objects in anticipation of death, suddenly is faced with the challenge of recathecting to the world as a degree of health is restored, and the predicted date of death, once terrifyingly close, is moved further into the future. The reprieve, therapists found, was not without its own anguish and difficulties (France). HIV-positive men found themselves struggling with debt and credit card problems, dislocations in personal relationships, conflicted feelings about the resurgence of libido, and relapses into substance abuse (Rofes 115). Although Laurie does not suffer from a textbook case of Lazarus Syndrome after his recovery — he seems almost disconcertingly buoyant — he is nonetheless confused by his return to normalcy. The question of reconnection with life after the death of a partner in *Raised in Captivity* becomes the question of reconnecting with life after facing one's imminent death in *Hurrah at Last*.

The cover of the November 10, 1996 issue of *The New York Times Magazine* read, in oversize letters, "WHEN AIDS ENDS," announcing an article in its pages by Andrew Sullivan. Both the cover and the essay sparked controversy for their hyperbole, and now, more than a decade later, it all seems pathetically premature. But they are an important evidence to how, after more than a decade of increasing horror, trauma, and exhaustion, the introduction of protease inhibitors and combination therapies did constitute a major step forward in the treatment of HIV infection and at last provided some occasion for hope, even desperate fantasy.

Sullivan describes the power of these new drugs for many users, the psychological wrenching of the return from death's door, and, most important for an understanding of *Hurrah at Last*, the social impulse to ruthlessly banish any awareness of ongoing HIV infection. He regards the hyperbolic aesthetics of the circuit party as driven by a desperate desire to forget the horrors of the recent past (which are, of course, still ongoing for many). He relates the anecdote of a bodybuilder with Kaposi's sarcoma lesions on his torso, dancing shirtless at a circuit party, who was approached by another reveler with the demand, "Would you please put your shirt on? You're ruining it for everybody else" (57). Such behavior, Sullivan observes, would have been unthinkable only a short time earlier.

Certainly the late '90s showed an eagerness to launch a new era for queer men, seen in such titles as Eric Rofes's 1998 *Dry Bones Breathe: Gay Men Creating Post-AIDS Identities and Cultures* and Alan Sinfield's volume of the same year, *Gay and After*. For some, like Andrew Sullivan, the new era was a sign of newfound maturity and acceptance. For others, like John Weir, it was a capitulation to the affluent materialism displayed in Greenberg's play. "I'm post-gay," asserted Weir in a 1997 essay (225). "I'm not gay any more. I'm not even queer. I'd rather be mistaken for a registered Republican," he fumes. "After all, there is no distinction anymore between conservative Republicans and self-identified homosexuals" (258). For many, whether left, right, or center, the terms to define gay experience since Stonewall had proved inadequate, and the moment became post. Laurie's mysterious malady reflects this post–AIDS moment: shadowed by the spectre of AIDS, it disavows it. Laurie himself, at once gay and without desire, assimilated and oddly invisible, is symptomatic of this post-gay moment.

Both Sullivan and Weir interpret the frenzied gay revels of the '90s as acts of denial, and where recognition is denied, mourning is impossible. While *Raised in Captivity* charts the movement from melancholia to mourning, *Hurrah at Last* completely erases the loss. Laurie has not lost anything; he is presented as never having had anything from the outset. Grief has been so thoroughly disenfranchised that it never makes its presence felt. While Silver constructs his play toward the revelation of the causes of Sebastian's suffering, Greenberg presents a "fascinoma" (258) (a medical anomaly that intrigues because of its seeming uniqueness) that departs as mysteriously as it appeared. It is yet another inexplicable event in a world of frenzied affluence, desperate attempts at procreation, stripping friends, lurching dogs, and crashing glassware. Greenberg replaces mourning with manic delirium.

In her 1940 essay, "Mourning and Its Relation to Manic-Depressive States," Melanie Klein amended Freud's theory of mourning by noting that the mourning process not only includes depression but moments of manic elation, in which the mourner grandiosely imagines being invulnerable to the loss (353). These moments of fantasized omnipotence momentarily impede the work of mourning (355). In both Sullivan's account of the circuit party (55) and Weir's of the gay march (255), we can see Klein's moment of manic disavowal at work. *Hurrah at Last* can be understood as the reflection of the same dynamic and historical moment, though construed in different terms. For Sullivan and Weir, gay mourning is effaced by a seemingly erotic spectacle of delirious excess, while Greenberg displaces both mourning and sexuality with consumerism.

In *Hurrah at Last*, the gay man disappears as a sexually desiring subject to emerge as a consumer. In his hospital bed, Laurie yearns for a "nice blue suit" (260), and, once recovered, he sports one. The fascinoma departs and gives way to the illusion of affluence. Physical traumatization, financial woes, and alienation are so closely linked that all three vanish at once in both plays. The gay man disappears into that unit of late-capitalist consumption, the family (Lowe 93), vanishing into the mainstream as he purchases the suit that bears no mark of sexual orientation. Diminished in his hospital bed to accepting money from his "daddy" (292), something Laurie had refused to do earlier, the line between the gay man and the Child is almost erased. Both the closet and the ghetto have been supplanted by the consuming family, and difference vanishes.

In the early '90s, David T. Evans already lamented the commercialization of gay culture, seeing it as creating a space "through which self-preoccupied people pass, commodified and de-politicised" (90), and that process has only increased in the years since. What Evans misses, and *Hurrah at Last* does not, is that self-preoccupation, commodification, and de-politicization were not unique of markers of gay life in the '90s, but have become elements of American middle-class culture at large. Indeed, they may be prerequisites for full acceptance in the mainstream. Donald M. Lowe has argued that a sexual lifestyle based on consumption has replaced a sexual identity, based on orgasms, in late-capitalist America (127–33). From Lowe's perspective, Laurie's initiation into consumption can be seen as more widely illustrative of contemporary American society overall, and not exclusively gay. It is a sign of the complex overdetermination at work in *Hurrah at Last* that it figures simultaneously both as a reflection of a general late-capitalist sensibility and of gay experience more specifically.

At the conclusion of *Angels in America* Prior Walter invokes a vital sense of a collectivity that keeps alive a memory of the deceased. The collectivity has largely disappeared in *Raised in Captivity*, to be replaced by a wilderness of traumatized loners and an insular domesticity modeled on the nuclear family, and the memory exists primarily in Sebastian's solitary, disenfranchised mourning for Simon. In *Hurrah at Last*, both gay collectivity and memory have vanished. Laurie not only suffers from a fascinoma, he himself *is* a fascinoma because he is presented as a figure untouched by history. The figure who appears in a new blue suit seems little more than a cipher. Even in his most bland and inoffensive form, however, he encounters intense resentment, and lacks the critical awareness that would allow him to understand it. While he is a fascinoma to his physicians, the negativity he encounters remains a fascinoma to him.

An examination of these two plays in the context of their decade does not lead to a repudiation of the widely accepted narrative of gay progress that predominates in our culture, but it suggests that the narrative needs to be made more complex and nuanced. Looking at them, we can see how the increasing collective traumatization of gay culture in the '90s led to increasing fragmentation, how the introduction of protease inhibitors, while introducing hope and health to many, also had the unintended consequence of sharply curtailing mourning, and that consumption increasingly became both a substitute for sexual desire and an entry into the mainstream. They also challenge us to consider the extent to which gay theatre of the last decade, and gay culture more widely, have been enfeebled and trivialized by their tendency to turn away from their losses rather than incorporate and revisit them in their collective memory. Loss that is left unacknowledged remains, and it may be that we have not even begun to realize the cost of its disavowal from the '90s to today.

Bibliography

Andreach, Robert J. "*The Maiden's Prayer*: Nicky Silver's Chekovian Play." *American Drama* 11:2 (Summer 2002).
Dane, Barbara O., and Samuel O. Miller. *AIDS: Intervening with Hidden Grievers.* Westport, CT: Auburn House, 1992.
Edelman, Lee. *No Future: Queer Theory and the Death Drive.* Durham, NC: Duke University Press, 2004.
Edelstein, David. "Hi, Ho, Silver!" *Village Voice*, March 7, 1995.
Erikson, Kai. *A New Species of Trouble: The Human Experience of Modern Disasters.* New York: W. W. Norton, 1994.
Evans, David T. *Sexual Citizenship: The Material Construction of Sexualities.* London: Routledge, 1993.
Feingold, Michael. "Screen Testiness." *Village Voice*, June 15, 1999.
Fowlkes, Martha. "The Morality of Loss: The Social Construction of Mourning and Melancholia." *Contemporary Psychoanalysis* 27:3 (1991).
France, David. "Holding AIDS at Bay, Only to Face 'Lazarus Syndrome.'" *New York Times*, October 6, 1998.
Freud, Sigmund. "Mourning and Melancholia." In *Standard Edition*, Vol. 14. London: Hogarth Press, 1957.

---. "On Narcissism: An Introduction." In *Standard Edition*, Vol. 14. London: Hogarth Press, 1957.

Greenberg, Richard. *Hurrah at Last*. In *Three Days of Rain and Other Plays*. New York: Grove Press, 1999.

Klein, Melanie. "Mourning and Its Relation to Manic-Depressive States." In *Love, Guilt and Reparation, and Other Works, 1921–1945*. London: Vintage, 1998.

Kushner, Tony. *Angels in America. Part Two: Perestroika*. New York: Theatre Communications Group, 1993.

Lowe, Donald M. *Body in Late-Capitalist USA*. Durham, NC: Duke University Press, 1995.

Morton, Donald. "Pataphysics of the Closet." In *Marxism, Queer Theory, Gender*, edited by Masu'd Zavarzadeh, Teresa. L. Ebert, and Donald Morton. Syracuse, NY: Red Factory, 2001.

Odets, Walt. *In the Shadow of the Epidemic: Being HIV-Negative in the Age of AIDS*. Durham, NC: Duke University Press, 1995.

Roberts, Brian. "Whatever Happened to Gay Theatre?" *New Theatre Quarterly* 16:2 (May 2001).

Rofes, Eric. *Dry Bones Breathe: Gay Men Creating Post-AIDS Identities and Cultures*. New York: Haworth Press, 1998.

Savage, Dan. "The Baby," *The New York Times Magazine*, November 15, 1998.

Shabad. Peter C. "Vicissitudes of Psychic Loss of a Physically Present Parent." In *The Problem of Loss and Mourning: Psychoanalytic Perspectives*, edited by David R. Dietrich and Peter C. Shabad. Madison, CT: International Universities Press, 1989.

Silver, Nicky. *Raised in Captivity: A Play*. New York: Theatre Communications Group, 1995.

Sinfield, Alan. *Gay and After*. London: Serpent's Tail, 1998.

Sullivan, Andrew. "When Plagues End." *The New York Times Magazine*, November 10, 1996.

Weir, John. "Going In." In *Gay Men at the Millenium: Sex, Spirit, Community*, edited by Michael Lowenthal. New York: Putnam, 1997.

Witchel, Alex. "A Dramatic Shut-In." *New York Times Magazine*, March 26, 2006.

The Soundplay's the Thing
A Formal Analysis of John (aka Lypsinka) Epperson's Queer Performance Texts

JOE E. JEFFREYS

Have you ever done this?— pretended to be blind? I don't mean to offend those of you in the audience who are blind — physically blind, that is — though there are seldom many of you at plays — blind: *deaf, yes: blind seldom; which surprises me, since most good plays come at you "by the ear," so to speak; but then again, so do a lot of bad ones — by the ear.*
—Edward Albee, The Play about the Baby

John Epperson is a playwright like no other. Since the mid 1980s he has created and performed nearly a dozen unique works that have enjoyed successful and critically acclaimed extended runs Off Broadway as well as national and international tours. His queer performance texts are aural formalist masterworks that tackle subjects from the pressures and pitfalls of fame to the nature of gender and performance itself.

Yet despite his formidable playwrighting skills, Epperson is ironically best known as the character for whom he has written most of his plays— Lypsinka. Lypsinka is Epperson's drag alter ego in his solo plays. A mix of one-name fashion models Dovima and Verushka with further inspiration coruscating from Broadway star Dolores Gray, Lypsinka and Epperson's uber-precise performance of her have deflected attention away from the remarkable scripts he painstakingly creates. Further, the performance texts that Epperson authors, while tightly constructed with words and songs, do not leave behind a traditionally publishable text that can be studied and analyzed. Additionally, his performance texts are based in a bastardized and marginalized art form. As the name Lypsinka suggests, Epperson's plays are elaborate soundtracks that he lip-synchs to.

This brief analysis of Epperson's soundplays thus only teases out some of the formal elements in their construction. Like the blind at the theatre, this non-illustrated essay keeps the image of Lypsinka from dominating Epperson's performance texts (unless perhaps you have seen him perform or in photos elsewhere). The same printed word, however, is also deaf and falters in conveying a listener's response to his soundplays as half-remembered bits of movie dialogue or a familiar-sounding female voice plays.

Born in 1955 in Hazlehurst, Mississippi, John Epperson took years of piano lessons as a child and knew there was more than his red hair that marked him as different from the others. After graduating from Belhaven College, Epperson began using his piano skills to make a living playing for dance classes. While he had dressed in drag for Halloweens and was fascinated by the local drag scene in the state capital of Jackson, considering it a type of absurd theatre, he was not yet ready to put himself out there as a performer.

Epperson moved to New York City in 1978 and recalled in a *Re/Search* interview, "I was as 'green' as they come ... for a 23 year old from Mississippi ... who was insecure and shy (with all the baggage that comes from growing up in the South), moving to New York seemed like a major achievement" (Vale 155). He soon began working as a pianist for the American Ballet Theatre and for the next 13 years traveled the world with the company.

When Epperson arrived in New York, the simmering East Village art scene of the 1980s was just beginning to percolate. In 1979 he attended a screening of *Beyond the Valley of the Dolls* at Club 57, Ann Magnuson's early performance bar that would soon be joined by similar establishments like the Pyramid Club, Club Chandelier, the Limbo Lounge, King Tut's Wah Wah Hut, and 8 B.C. Located in a church basement at 57 St. Mark's Place, the club's crowd interacted and talked back to the movie. Club 57 was the environment Epperson had been looking for in which to launch his drag career. He soon began performing lip-synched drag numbers there at such events as John Sex's "Acts of Live Art."

Sex urged Epperson to get a gig at the Pyramid and in the summer of 1984 he did, with one gig leading to the next in an ever-expanding series of venues like the Boy Bar and Gusto House. He began to appear under the single moniker Lypsinka with its Slavic-inspired spelling and develop her look, act and backstory. By the mid–1980s he was an established entertainer of the drag-happy East Village demi-monde that included such luminaries as RuPaul, Ethyl Eichelberger, and Lady Bunny. It is also the scene that birthed the outdoor drag festival Wigstock.

His first two serious stage works, outside the brief lip-synch numbers he was performing on the bar scene, were traditional format musicals. Composer, lyricist and book writer, Epperson's *Ballet of the Dolls* (1985) and *Dial "M" for Model* (1986) constitute the first phase of his playwrighting career and are parody musicals of the ballet and fashion worlds crossed with *Valley of the Dolls* and other 1960s pop.

Now for a deeper look at just one aspect, a few formal structural elements found in the performance texts, of the second phase of Epperson's playwrighting career. This phase comprises 8 soundplays. Epperson's most recent work, and the third phase of his playwriting career, is in more traditional formats. This last phase includes writing and performing an autobiographical cabaret performance, *Show Trash*; writing and staging another traditional pen-and-paper play, *My Deah* (*My Deah* was staged Off Broadway by the Abingdon Theatre Company in NYC in 2006. The script is available through Samuel French and Epperson has recently completed a sequel); and writing a version of *Medea* set in the South and a screenplay *Happy Everything*.

His eight soundplays for Lypsinka include: *The Many Moods of Lypsinka* (1988), *I Could Go on Lip-Synching!* (1988), *The Fabulous Lypsinka Show* (1991), *Lypsinka! Now It Can Be Lip-Synched* (1992), *Lypsinka! A Day in the Life* (1992), *Lypsinka! As I Lay Lip-Synching* (1994), *Lypsinka Must Be Destroyed* (200?) and *Lypsinka! The Boxed Set* (1997). His latest soundplay, *The Passion of the Crawford* (2005), is also of this school but somewhat outside the Lypsinka box. (He does not perform this work in his Lypsinka character but rather creates an impression of Crawford.) In programs for these works Epperson is credited as the performer of Lypsinka as well as with "soundtrack production, creation and design." He does not credit himself as a playwright. Epperson clearly, however, is the architect of these sound collages just as a playwright puts words and actions in unique sequences that merit authorial claim.

Epperson's soundplays employ the audio byte as their primary building block. Each is all quotes and draws on his large record collection and vast knowledge of film. Averaging one hour and ten minutes, the collaged clips derive from a range of mostly pre–Stonewall movie stars and entertainers from cabarets and Broadway stages to Las Vegas lounges. In many ways, Epperson's soundplays are similar in construction and effect to the works of queer playwrights including Jackie Curtis and Charles Ludlam. Both wrote crazy collage plays colliding snippets of text from high and low, classical and pop sources. Ludlam's *Conquest of the Universe,* for example, is a play built largely by cutting and pasting direct quotes from Marlowe's *Tamburlaine,* Shakespeare's *Julius Caeser, Titus Andronicus* and *Hamlet* as well as drawing from Hitler's speeches, TV commercials, Chaucer, and the newspaper help wanted ads. These works challenge the audience as half-familiar snatches go by and challenge the actor to connect the emotional and logical dots between and among the quotes. Of his Lypsinka soundplays, Epperson told Philadelphia's *City Paper,* "I felt it had to be rooted in tradition. When I say tradition, lip-synching is a very traditional gay form. The Irish dance jigs, Native Americans do tribal dances and gay men get in drag and lip-synch. It's just something that happens. But I've tried to push it to extremes" (Kasrel).

In these soundplays parts of songs from female vocalists including Mimi

Hines, Eileen Rodgers, Ann Henry, Karen Morrow, Julie Wilson, Doris Day, Pearl Bailey, Neile Adams, Gisele MacKenzie, Patti "Cupcake" O'Mason, Libby Morris, Kay Thompson, and Kaye Ballard are inter-cut with bits of patter from live lounge acts. Epperson contrasts the patter, and heavy brass and percussion show-stopping musical numbers, with spoken sections sampled from classic Hollywood films and stars. The themes are often dark and disturbing and include unrequited love, fame, paranoia, hysteria and sexual and substance abuse.

While he says he has never counted the bits and pieces that compose his expressionistic and hallucinatory one-act audio wonders, it is well into the thousands for each show. Working at first with just his home tape recorder and pause button, today he creates his auditory psychodramas with computers and studio sound engineers. A playwright who writes and edits with Pro Tools or Sound Tools instead of Word or WordPerfect, he likens the process not to that of creating a radio drama but to another medium. "It's like making a film," Epperson told the *Gay City News*. "Nancy Walker once made a terrible film called *Can't Stop the Music*. Later she said, "Making a movie is putting little bits of shit together" (Tallmer).

The pieces of "shit" that Epperson puts together are far from simple mixtape-like compilations. Epperson's sampled soundworks create more than moods and themes. They also achieve narrative threads, emotional arcs and tight structural patterns.

While Epperson would have happily granted an interview for this analysis, it was determined that, like his soundplays, this essay would be made only of bits and pieces of him as already found on record. Epperson graciously provided me copies of two of his soundplays on CD: *Lypsinka! As I Lay Lip-synching* and *Lypsinka! The Boxed Set* for this paper.

Below are transcribed examples of how he uses patter and musical numbers in highly sophisticated and unexpected ways to build themes and narrative. *Lypsinka! As I Lay Lip-Synching* begins with a brief sound montage opening sequence that includes the sound of a siren and ringing telephone (more later on the importance of phones in his work). Lypsinka then launches into two upbeat musical numbers. The first patter Lypsinka mouths cleverly introduces one in a string of meta-commentaries Epperson's soundplays and performance style deftly juggle. Here is part of this patter from *As I Lay Lip-Synching*: "I'm not very good in the talking department. But I'd like to stop singing long enough to tell you that I feel very peculiar." This is the first time in the all lip-synched performance that the audience sees Lypsinka "speak" as opposed to "sing." It also serves as a meta-commentary as it flirts with the notion of Lypsinka's inability to speak. This bit of patter is Ethel Merman from her Las Vegas lounge act and is followed by part of "There's No Business Like Show Business" from her infamous disco album. Mostly Epperson mismatches patter and song, as in this example from *As I Lay Lip-Synching*: "Just about here every night we change and sing something romantic and a little bit mushy, cause we like mushy songs, like this one." A wild bongo number that is far from mushy or romantic blares. Here's another example of mismatched or juxtaposed patter and song for surprise or contrast effect from *Lypsinka! The Boxed Set*:

> Thank you ladies and gentlemen. A few weeks ago I heard an LP called Nina Simone at the Town Hall and I must say I've become a tremendous fan. I'd like to sing for you two of her numbers. Here is one of them.

Fay McKay's inebriated "12 Daze of Christmas" follows and couldn't be more unlike a Nina Simone number. Patter sets expectations up for one thing and then cuts to something totally unexpected. In another example, a performer talks about the song he sang on the Academy Awards featuring in *Lypsinka! The Boxed Set*:

> A few months ago I was most delighted to be able to take part in one of the most important events in our show business—the presentation of the Academy Awards. And on that evening I was also very happy to sing this song.

Libby Morris' epic demolition of "Tea for Two" is the mismatched follow-through. After the comic number, we hear this, also in *Lypsinka! The Boxed Set*: "Let's talk about the Academy Awards. I think everyone tried to have the cutes and each one who came after the couple before tried to be funnier."

The voice is Joan Crawford's and it is from a 1973 Town Hall public interview in which she goes on to reproach Marlon Brando for his "behavior" as she calls it at that year's awards. (Epperson uses this recording extensively in his *The Passion of the Crawford*.) A new type of structure is at work. Crawford's talk of the Academy Awards links back to the patter before "Tea for Two," that likewise mentioned the Academy Awards, framing the song and this section of the show.

Sampling extant patter also helps Epperson construct beginning, middle, and end horizontal structures. Near the end of *Lypsinka! The Boxed Set* he uses this Dolores Gray lounge act patter:

> Thank you very much. I think you will all agree here tonight that girl singers do work hard. Thank you. You have been an artist dream of an audience tonight. I am very very deeply grateful to you. It means so much as you know. But would you please extend some of the warmth and sweetness that has filled this room tonight to some of the other people who work so hard to give you a nice evening. All the people at the front of the house on the lights and all the very nice people backstage who contribute a great deal. We thank them I'm sure. But my last few little words are from me just for you.

The performer, like Lypsinka's show at this juncture, is clearly winding down her act and once again there is the dramatic juxtaposition of patter with song, in this case the patter cuts to the climax of "This Is My Life." Meta-gender and meta-performance commentary rest in the clip's talk of "girl singers" and all the front of house and backstage folks. The sound of applause seamlessly links many of the patter/song pairings together and Epperson's sound mix often starts the opening strains of the upcoming song under the mismatched patter's conclusion to further smooth auditory transitions.

Between patter/song pairings are spoken sections built around direct quotes from classic Hollywood films and stars. Here is an example from *As I Lay Lip-Synching*:

> I had a thing with the doctor in Spain. I love doctors. He said to me, "Shall I undress you like a doctor?" He was very good looking, very hard working. Six children, busy. The waiting room was full of patients. We could hear them on the other side of the wall. We had to whisper but it didn't matter. They couldn't hear his lips. They couldn't hear him touch me and caress me. He was so gentle when he touched me. He was panting. He was panting. Panting. We got down our knees to pray for strength. I smelled the whiskey on his breath. He took me. He took me with the stink of the rot house whiskey on his breath. All that dirty touching with his hands on me. All over me. And I like it. I liked it. He let me sit on his lap. He let me hug him. He told me I was beautiful. He stayed in that house for one week and taught me more about evil than any thirteen year old girl in the world knew. You haven't heard the worst of it yet. I loved it. Every awful moment of it I loved. *Sound of scream.*

Spoken sections such as this one are distinct from the patter sections and explore Lypsinka's interior monologue and struggles. In the transcribed clip a dark theme of sexual abuse and molestation is built through sound clips from Piper Laurie in *Carrie* to Elizabeth Taylor in *Butterfield 8* and *X, Y and Zee*. Epperson maintains the original or places musical underscoring beneath these dialogue sections. He ingeniously sets up one of these surreal sections using an Ethel Merman clip: "I had a dream. I had a dream. I had a dream" with cheesy fade to dream sequence music underneath.

The most frequently recalled dialogue sections of Epperson's soundplays are his telephone sequences. They can run 5 minutes or longer and are trademarks of a Lypsinka show, just as phone routines became closely associated with performers including Bob Newhart, George Jessel and Shelley Berman. Audiences expect and anticipate them and there may be more than one such phone sequence in a show. For a character who cannot truly speak but only mouth the words of others, the auditory nature of the phone is a perverse device to build a bit around. Here from *As I Lay Lip-Synching* is an excerpt from one:

PHONE RINGS. SOUND OF RECEIVER PICK UP: You must go to some very bad plays.
PHONE RINGS. SOUND OF RECEIVER PICK UP: With a man over twice your age. Now get out'a here.
PHONE RINGS. SOUND OF RECEIVER PICK UP: And you were the one who was going to help me. Help me. Help me!
PHONE RINGS. SOUND OF RECEIVER PICK UP: Barbara, please. Please, Barbara.
PHONE RINGS: I tell you it's funny.
PHONE RINGS. SOUND OF RECEIVER PICK UP: She's my daughter.
PHONE RINGS. SOUND OF RECEIVER PICK UP: She's my sister.
PHONE RINGS. SOUND OF RECEIVER PICK UP: She's my daughter.
PHONE RINGS. SOUND OF RECEIVER PICK UP: She's my sister.
PHONE RINGS. SOUND OF RECEIVER PICK UP: She's my sister and my daughter.
PHONE RINGS. SOUND OF RECEIVER PICK UP: Why I'm not teaching logic at Columbia I'll never know.
PHONE RINGS. SOUND OF RECEIVER PICK UP: Barbara, please.
PHONE RINGS. SOUND OF RECEIVER PICK UP: You dragged me into that. I didn't drag you.

With audio samples here including Elizabeth Taylor in *Butterfield 8*, *Suddenly Last Summer*, and *X, Y and Zee*, Faye Dunaway in both *Mommie Dearest* and *Chintown*, and Joan Crawford from *I Saw What You Did*, it is easy to drown in the flash flood of references at the expense of the intricate tripartite structures Epperson has created. Meta-theatrical themes are again evidenced in Taylor's comment about bad plays.

The juxtaposition of sound bites often answer each other like a telephone conversation. The clip ending with the angry words "now get out'a here" is answered by the pleas of the voice at the next phone pick up, "you were the one who was going to help me." The sound bites also respond or comment on each other in complicated meta-textual means. Dunaway's over-the-top Crawford cry of "Barbara, please" is followed by a ring interrupted version of her equally over-the-top *Chinatown* sister/daughter monologue. Elizabeth Taylor comments between the two, in case you miss the point, that "it's funny." Note that there is no receiver pick up sound before Taylor's comment, thus breaking the pattern and drawing attention to the statement that follows. To further highlight this distinction, Lypsinka speaks these Taylor lines out to the audience and not to the person on the other end of the phone line as with the clips that contain both a ring and receiver pick up.

Here's a short moment from another a phone sequence, this one largely built around samples from *Hush, Hush, Sweet Charlotte*. Similar call-and-response structures and meta-commentary themes are employed, as in *As I Lay Lip-Synching*:

PHONE RINGS. SOUND OF RECEIVER PICK UP: What do you think I asked you here for? Company? I thought you were gonna help me.

PHONE RINGS. SOUND OF RECEIVER PICK UP: There's nothing like a new dress to make you feel like a new man.
PHONE RINGS. SOUND OF RECEIVER PICK UP:: My dress. Somebody slashed my dress.
PHONE RINGS. SOUND OF RECEIVER PICK UP: Wasn't me that ripped your dadburned old dress.
PHONE RINGS. SOUND OF RECEIVER PICK UP: I don't believe it.

This time Epperson also works with a linking structure, picking up the word *dress* from one line to the next like Gertrude Stein's "a rose is a rose is a rose" landscaping technique. Additionally, the idea of a "new dress [making] you feel like a new man" functions as a comment on Epperson's drag performance.

What is briefly outlined here only begins to scratch the surface of the complex structures and patterns that Epperson creates in his expressionistic audio works. It doesn't even start to tackle the history and perception of lip-synching or how Epperson's performance, stagings and various production elements, like lighting, bolster the ornate structures of his scripts. It should be pellucid to all, however, including the blind or deaf, that Epperson's eight soundplays for Lypsinka are beyond post-modern and are the quintessence of queer performance texts.

BIBLIOGRAPHY

Kasrel, Deni. "Lypsinka: Grandes Dames." *Citypaper.net*, Sept. 14–21, 1995. www.citypaper.net.

Tallmer, Jerry. "Lypsinka Unplugged." *Gay City News*, August 22–28, 2003.

Vale, V., and Andrea Juno, eds. "Lypsinka." In *Re/Search: Incredibly Strange Music*, Vol. 1. San Francisco: Re/Search Publications, 1993.

A note on this essay: *A version of this essay was presented by the author at the Association for Theatre in Higher Education conference in San Francisco, California, in July 2005 as part of a panel "The Queering of New Plays: A Look at the Innovations in Content, Structure, and Audience Relationships in the Work of Contemporary Playwrights." In presentation, the paper was entirely lip-synched. A prerecorded cassette tape was made with a female actress, Joan Marie Moossy, reading the paper's text and I lip-synched to it. On the tape I read Epperson's quotes to distinguish between what he had said about his work and what I had written. To further this distinction, in performance I merely opened and closed my mouth like a ventriloquist's dummy during the reading of his quotes and made no attempt to match the prerecorded reading of his words. While this essay transcribes the examples used from* Lypsinka! The Boxed Set *and* Lypsinka! As I Lay Lip-Synching, *in presentation these sound clips were cut into the tape. No attempt was made to perform to these show samples and they simply played. Both text and image PowerPoint slides were also used as part of the paper's meta-presentation.*

The (Fe)Male Gays
Split Britches and the Redressing of Dyke Camp

PAUL MENARD

Although homosexuals have always been part of the theatre, most assuredly since its cross-dressed inception in ancient Greece, one has had to look very carefully to find them. Just as one may read a series of unspoken cultural signs to identify someone as gay — or at the very least "queer" — the theatre similarly subscribes to performative semiotics of sexuality. Of course, homosexuality has reared its lavender head throughout the course of theatre history, with varying degrees of blatancy. But by the time of Oscar Wilde, and under the tyrannical installment of the closet, homosexuality had developed a stage language of its own — a language of dual coding and outrageous queerness sheathed in prophylactic irony. Camp, the performative style of ludicrous exaggeration, became most closely aligned with gay men. An inversion of what the heteronormative would consider "normal" and delivered from an outsider perspective, camp's secretive and coded sense of subversion resonated with the gay community. In the mid–1960s, a period of growing gay rights tension that exploded in the 1969 Stonewall riots, camp became less secretive and more subversive. And even though queer theatre was kicking down the closet door while simultaneously inscribing its own oppression, drag camp performance remained virtually a gay boys' club until the 1980s.

At its most basic linguistic level, the language of camp is performative rebellion. The diametrically opposed stances of insider/outsider replicate the dialectic of the closet, evidencing itself through the duality of irony. Ironic wit functions only when one is fully immersed in a (sub)culture (as to gain insider understanding) but can also completely distance themselves to comment upon it. Gay men and lesbians, one may argue, are unable to truly assume the position of the "subject" within a heterosexist linguistic system. Therefore, any attempt at articulation within that system is to be deprived of the true possibility of actual "speech" and, as Judith Butler states, "to speak at all in that context is a performative contradiction, the linguistic assertion of a self that cannot 'be' within the language that asserts it" (Butler 116). Playing upon the semantic contradiction of the closet — both its dependency and its oppression — camp's first site of performative subversion is through language. By reappropriating and subverting normalized categories of sexuality and gender performance through terms such as *butch*, *femme*, *sissy*— or the parodic reclaiming of *fag*, *dyke*, or *queer*—camp reorients language itself to destabilize and redefine once-derogatory gay and lesbian identifiers. This contradictory and performative language — the foundation of camp — naturally lends itself to the theatre through performance and role-playing. Susan Sontag, in her famous "Notes on 'Camp,'" observed, "Camp sees everything in quotation marks ... to perceive Camp in objects and persons is to understand Being-as-Playing-a-Role. It is the farthest extension, in sensibility, of the metaphor of life as theater" (Sontag 56). This role-playing, not unfamiliar to homosexuals living within an oppressively heterosexist world, is the most basic extension of camp's linguistic foundations. When making the leap from the spoken to the active, camp becomes embodied in the artificiality of role-playing, highlighting the sheer constructiveness of even the most basic of identities (such as, of course, gender). Again, both contradictive and performative, the essence of staged camp is to refute anything natural, or at least commonly considered by society as a given. There should be little surprise that the staging of the "unnatural," and the desire to create new realities is so closely aligned with the queer sphere, where sexual practices— and subsequently, the basic tenets of identity— are condemned as "crimes against nature." Therefore, the ideology of the queer camp theatre is to subvert reality, constructing a world of artifice where normalcy can be transgressively reinscribed. But through the reappropriation of traditional sexual roles and other elements of heterosexist oppression (including language), camp creates yet another duality. Through irony, it eradicates the power structure of heterosexist realist models and articulates homosexual agency — yet through the same methodology, it reinforces and further inscribes gay oppression. Therefore, in addition to being a simultaneously critical and reflexive device, queer camp, through its parodic reappropriation of heteronormativity, creates a tension based on the dialectic of assimilation/subversion. This final duality takes queer camp full circle, past the critical staging of straight oppression, and out of the theatre. The assimilation/subversion dialectic, a thorny cornerstone of the gay rights movement since the 1960s, turns the critical mirror of camp back onto the spectator, and the larger gay community itself.

By the early 1960s, camp's subversive elements were bubbling up from the gay male underground and adopting an almost propagandistic approach. And while Andy Warhol's alternative cinema and Jack Smith's film *Flaming Creatures* caused some shock waves, camp was still generally seen as a somewhat harmless rebellion against aesthetics, dismissively defined as "it's good because it's awful" (Sontag 65). But in 1965, when John Vaccaro founded the Playhouse of the Ridiculous, camp quickly became a theatrical weapon against heteronormative oppression. Focusing on ludicrous exaggeration and male-to-female drag, the Playhouse of the Ridiculous achieved success in the 1970s and 1980s under the guidance of Charles Ludlam who, after a split with Vaccaro, renamed the troupe the Ridiculous Theatrical Company. Under Ludlam's guidance, the Ridiculous Theatrical Company achieved fame for its camped-up and crossed-dressed reappropriations of classical films, plays, and operas, establishing itself at the frontline of subversive queer camp theatre. But the genre was still male dominated. In the 1970s, feminist theatre exploded, but lesbian performance was frequently viewed as the wicked stepsister of the women's movement. Pejoratively dubbed the "Lavender Menace," lesbians were kept relatively silent within the feminist movement, and women's theatre most often concerned itself with reproductive rights and other subjects that did not directly affect lesbians. By the mid–1970s, theatre troupes specifically dedicated to lesbian performance began to appear, stepping out from the silencing umbrella of "feminist theatre." But the approach of female queer theatre was distinctly different from the queer camp aesthetic defining Ludlam's Ridiculous and other gay male troupes. Women loving women meant gentler, non-violent, nurturing relationships and a rejection of male-imposed roles and masculine-type power hierarchies. That is, until 1981, when the lesbian company Split Britches formed, redefining queer theatre and effectively articulating "dyke camp."

Lois Weaver became a founding member of Spiderwoman, a multi-ethnic feminist theatre company, in 1975. Peggy Shaw, originally inspired to pursue a life in the theatre after seeing Charles Ludlam's *Bluebeard* in 1970, was a member of the gay male cabaret Hot Peaches. Weaver and Shaw met in 1977 when both companies were touring in Berlin. Spiderwoman's costumes were lost in transit and, upon hearing that another American troupe was playing in town, the ensemble ended up borrowing costumes from Hot Peaches. Weaver noticed how the sequined gowns of Hot Peaches' drag queens added a new contextual layer to Spiderwoman's radical, multiethnic feminist theatre. This reappropriation of feminist political performance and crossover with gay-male subculture would prove integral to Split Britches' future articulation of a "dyke camp" aesthetic. Shaw left Hot Peaches to work with Weaver on Spiderwoman's next show, bringing with her the camp aesthetic of the gay male drag group. After collaborating on several influential projects, Weaver and Shaw left Spiderwoman to form Split Britches in 1981. Although ethnic and sexual differences led to the Spiderwoman split (co-founder Gloria Miguel was reported to have said, "Some of the women who were lesbian wanted to make Spiderwoman an all-lesbian group ... and — over our dead bodies" [Case 5]), it was indicative of the fractioning of feminism in the early 1980s. Working with writer Deb Margolin, Weaver and Shaw developed *Split Britches*, a piece based on Weaver's family history and set in the Blue Ridge Mountains of West Virginia. The title came from the pants women wore while working in the fields, allowing them to urinate while standing and thereby, work continuously. They adopted the company name Split Britches to symbolize continued laboring in the arts, punctuated by personal and private "leaks"; the name also connotes both the reappropriation of masculine behavior and the fissuring of male gender wear. Following the success of their second collaboration, *Beauty and the Beast* in 1982, the group opened the WOW (Women's One World) Café, a community-based performance space that quickly became one of New York's best-known venues for women's theatre. It was also one of the few available spaces for openly lesbian material.

But how does the work of Split Britches operate in the world of camp? And, more specifically, how does it differ from the gay male camp of troupes like the Ridiculous Theatrical Company? How does Split Britches hold the performative, constructionist aspect of lesbian identity in tension without erasing the historical and material realities of lesbian lives? Split Britches subscribes to the belief that camp "involves a new, more complex relation to 'the serious.' One can be serious about the frivolous, frivolous about the serious" (Sontag 62). This tenet became the manifesto for Ludlam's Ridiculous Theatrical Company, the idea of treating a dangerous and serious idea in a madly farcical way. Split Britches also embraces this camp theory, as evidenced through the contradictions of homophobia and racism told through the fairy tale genre of *Beauty and the Beast*, or the class issues satirically addressed by the Manhattan trailer trash of *Upwardly Mobile Home*. The duality of camp irony — the juxtaposition of contradictions — is at the center of Split Britches' work. Similarly, the ridiculous paradoxes set up by their characters — such as the effeminacy of *Belle Reprieve*'s Stanley or *Beauty and the Beast*'s rabbi in toe shoes — follows in the vein of gay male camp. They present characters who they love or admire alongside those whose politics or behavior they find reprehensible. Furthermore, Split Britches exploits the concept of "instant character" by using stereotypes to create a camp duality. According to Lois Weaver, "Stereotypes are very theatrical. They are also useful. Sometimes you have to recognize and embody the stereotype before you can create a new representation" (Weaver 196). The work of Split Britches, like all camp, is highly performative — using vaudeville, self-conscious theatricality in both text and staging, and distancing techniques such as direct address and dance breaks. But Split Britches hones in on the essence of female performativity, or rather, queer female performativity. Granted, the acts of performance and subversion through ironic assimilation are straight from gay male camp theatre. But, for Split Britches, the role of the performative takes an additional queer reading by placing lesbians on stage; there is a female transcription of queer camp. It may be argued from a feminist perspective that simply placing a woman on stage — expressing her desire to speak or to achieve agentic articulation — is a radically political act. Therefore, the mere visibility of a (queer) woman onstage in command of her own language achieves a slightly different goal than that of the male camp theatre. Coded language — and the amusement of ironic gay assimilation that goes with it — is lessened. Instead, Split Britches strives to define how "lesbian" identity is articulated through performance: how lesbian address is constructed, how it is uniquely received by a lesbian audience, and the dynamics of lesbian desire, role-playing, and camp within this system of representation. For Split Britches, lesbianism and politics are inseparable; in their work, the politics of performativity become integral to both lesbian identity and female queer visibility.

Where dyke camp, as articulated by Split Britches, clearly diverges from gay male camp is in its use of drag. Cross-dressing is an essential element to queer camp, as a method of combating the specious linking of gender to sexuality and the dehumanization/desexualization of the homosexual body by the straight majority. But, to theorize that male-to-female drag is the same as female-to-male would be rather naïve. Although both strive to subvert and destabilize traditional gender roles — and reinscribe reality through visibility — the power dynamics and methodologies differ greatly. At its simplest level, female-to-male cross-dressing (also known as drag king performance) borrows much from its male-to-female cousin. The theatricality of costuming and the performativity of gender role-playing dovetail with the camp aesthetic. But when female-to-male cross-dressing is viewed as a misogynistic defense against femininity and the phallic lack it signifies, as some scholars would argue, it leaves little room for the lesbian camp equivalent. Rather, cross-gendering aims to critique, not the opposite gender, but the coded language through which it speaks; drag attacks both the sign and the socially signified. And while drag queens use irony, insult, and inversion to affirm dominant forms of femininity, drag king culture strives to create a counterpublic space where heteronormative (and often white) masculinities and power structures are criticized and replaced by new minority masculinities. Through exaggeration, parody, and mimicry, female-to-male drag subculturally explodes and produces masculinities that challenge the authenticity and primacy of dominant masculinities. Perhaps that is why, as Peggy Shaw states, "there's not a built-in cultural humor to women being what the audience perceives as a man" (Davy 1005).

But cross-gendering in Split Britches goes beyond simple drag king performance; it operates within the butch/femme aesthetic. Derived from the heteronormative role- playing of pre–Stonewall lesbian couples, the butch/femme tradition has long been a source of controversy within the lesbian community. Not coincidentally, the debate centers around the same audience-criticizing dialectic operating at the basis of queer camp theatre — the question of assimilation/subversion. The butch/femme drag aesthetic is key to Split Britches' reclamation of queer camp, in effect, re/dressing the traditional gay male genre as dyke camp. Just as gay male camp depends upon the oppressive dialectic of the closet, dyke camp — as re/dressed by Split Britches — depends on the same duality, but set within the lesbian community. Of course, butch/femme is just one piece of the overarching camp aesthetic of role-playing (and extreme exaggeration), challenging and subverting traditional gender and sexual roles. But within the context of Split Britches, butch/femme constructs agency through the rigidity and performativity of its roles. Notions of gender binaries and "the female body" are redefined as these roles are played through semiologies rather than ontologies. Thus, the extremity of gender-play in butch/femme permits an agentic subject by allowing at least two options for gender identification. In the case of works such as *Belle Reprieve* (where lesbians played Stella and Stanley, and gay men played Mitch and Blanche), the crossed-dressed performance of gender roles is further complicated by a second performative dimension: the visible signifiers of sexual orientation. But the sheer performativity of butch/femme redefines reality through the fiction of role-play, transgressively reinscribing heterosexist narrative into dyke camp. This imaginative, ironized theatrical space subverts the oppressive authority of realism and, by realizing the extremes of masculinity and femininity, permits Split Britches to turn the politics of desire upon itself. With a woman in possession of the "male" gaze, ostensibly consuming femininity, the butch/femme sphere of desire resembles the heterosexual world but, through its ironic distancing and contradictions, freely creates its own reality.

When operating within the worlds of coded language and minority reappropriation of majority signifiers, audience identification and reception can problematize queer camp. And when dealing with a doubled minority (such as homosexual *and* female) and the specific language of butch/femme, the reception of dyke camp can be doubly problematic. Arguably, the work of Split Britches is most successful when presented for a homogenously lesbian audience, or at least the mostly lesbian audience of the company's own space, the WOW Café. (Charles Ludlam once remarked that "the worst thing that ever happened to camp" was its co-optation by the straight world: "Then you get something that has nothing to do with camp" [Ludlam 226–27]). But the question of reception — a "for us, by us" sort of spectatorship — arose with the work of Split Britches, specifically the Holly Hughes penned collaboration *Dress Suits to Hire* (1987). Originally staged at PS 122, which Hughes herself described as "miles away [from WOW] on the cultural map" (Hughes 19), *Dress Suits* was the first Split Britches project to be placed before a more heterogeneous audience. But it was the performance of *Dress Suits* at the University of Michigan, Ann Arbor, that proved problematic. Feminist scholar Kate Davy observed that "'in a conventional theatre setting, in the legitimate (and legitimizing) institutional setting of a major university, the work's potential to subvert dominant ideology was seriously undermined.' Sue-Ellen Case, who had admired Split Britches' *Beauty and the Beast* (1982), also thought this: she saw the Michigan audience for *Dress Suits* being gleefully entertained, consuming and erasing the specificity of lesbian lives and desires" (Sinfield 336).

But is the supposed "failure" of dyke camp in front of a mostly straight audience due simply to camp's inability to communicate to a heterosexual spectatorship? Has the oppression of the closet leaked into the sacred space of the auditorium? Assuredly, WOW Café has patrons who are either straight, male, or both — but they are in the minority. At WOW, tickets are sold at a discounted price to lesbians, transgenders, and students; one might argue that for at least the duration of the performance, every spectator has (to varying degrees) aligned themselves with lesbian identity. Rather, one might examine the impact of lesbian spectatorship on the creation of dyke camp. Bette Borne of Bloolips once noted the relationship between the WOW spectatorship and the unique aesthetic of the work produced there. Peggy Shaw recalls that "he described it as an aesthetic that comes from certain type of community, certain types of thinking, or lesbian thinking" (Davy 1004). Furthermore, the impact of community — not simply upon the textual or aesthetic creation of dyke camp, but also upon the temporality of the performance itself — cannot be overlooked. In performance, Split Britches will reference the audience, going beyond direct address by hurling insults into the house or encouraging active participation. At WOW, the audience is a collective performer. "I learned from the old Hot Peaches days that the gay audience is a loud, vocal, supportive audience," said Lois Weaver. "Consequently, WOW has become that sort of space where there's screaming and hollering and vocal support for the performers. That's something that's very important; it's a big part of the interchange with the audience. We always get some immediate response to the show.... I think that's predominantly a gay phenomena" (Davy 1003).

So then, if queer camp — and especially dyke camp — is most successful when presented before a homosexual audience, what purpose can this subversive art form have when safely nestled in queer spectatorship? The coded language of camp and the identities operating therein establish and reinforce queer community. But beyond community building, queer camp functions as a utopian force. The word *utopia*, as coined by Thomas More, literally means "no place"; already, there is a sense of linguistic irony and contradiction that aligns it with a camp aesthetic. Moreover, camp's embracement of the performative and its rereading of "the real" symbolizes its utopian performativity. Specifically, the work of Split Britches strives to create a utopian sphere, not merely by surrounding itself with *communitas* (as the ancient Greek theatre did) and allowing that community to actively contribute to the art, but also through its subversion of heterosexual norms. By disrupting the gender regime, Split Britches creates a utopian alternative space within the patriarchal order. Through these utopian performatives, as defined by Jill Dolan, "theatre and performance can articulate a common future, one that's more just and equitable, one in which we can all participate more equally, with more chances to live fully and contribute to the making of culture" (Dolan 455).

Split Britches has done more than simply reclaim the legacy of gay camp; the troupe has, in effect, reappropriated elements of gay male camp and re/dressed it to create a medium unique to the needs of lesbian performance. Influenced by the gay male camp of Charles Ludlam, Hot Peaches, and Bloolips, as well as of feminist performance (Spiderwoman), Split Britches opened up the camp genre to other lesbian artists such as Five Lesbian Brothers and Holly Hughes. But it is through their use of butch/femme, effectively re/dressing the sometimes-sticky issue of drag, that Shaw and Weaver constructed a form (and a specific language of Sapphic codification) that culls from historical queer theatrical subversion while speaking to an expressly lesbian representation. Furthermore, in the dyke camp of Split Britches, the multiplicity of roles and the fluidity of narrative signal a further feminist reading: the potency of lesbian agency. But since the genre requires the oppression of the closet, its existence is somewhat paradoxical; in a world without homophobia and sexism, dyke camp would fail to exist. It is dependent upon its own irony. So while dyke camp subverts the heteronormative oppression of the patriarchal world, its doubly coded linguistics (queer and female) are problematized through reception. But through the WOW Café, Weaver and Shaw have cultivated a utopian space where the sheer concept of lesbian visibility — especially though the aggressive and queerly "masculine" form of dyke camp — subverts oppressive normality. Split Britches have rediscovered the sacred and dangerous language of theatre: role-playing. By shifting the most basic and grounded identities (gender and sexuality), Split Britches and its articulation of dyke camp remains a uniquely subversive force forever bound to the live stage. For, as Peggy Shaw states, "The danger of theatre ... is in the power of presence, in the power of the transformations it makes possible" (Dolan 469).

BIBLIOGRAPHY

Butler, Judith. *Gender Trouble: Feminism and the Subversion of Identity*. New York: Routledge, 1990.
Case, Sue-Ellen, ed. *Split Britches: Lesbian Practice/Feminist Performance*. New York: Routledge, 1996.
Davy, Kate. "Peggy Shaw and Lois Weaver: Interviews (1985, 1992, 1993)." In *Modern Drama: Plays/Criticism/Theory*, edited by W. B. Worthen. New York: Harcourt Brace, 1995.
Dolan, Jill. "Performance, Utopia, and the 'Utopian Performative.'" *Theatre Journal* 53.3 (2001).
Hughes, Holly. *Clit Notes: A Sapphic Sampler*. New York: Grove Press, 1996.
Ludlam, Charles. *Ridiculous Theatre: Scourge of Human Folly*, edited by Steven Samuels. New York: Theatre Communications Group, 1992.
Sinfield, Alan. *Out on Stage: Lesbian and Gay Theatre in the Twentieth Century*. New Haven: Yale University Press, 1999.
Sontag, Susan, "Notes on 'Camp,'" In *Camp: Queer Aesthetics and the Performing Subject*, edited by Fabio Cleto. Edinburgh: Edinburgh University Press, 1999.
Weaver, Lois. "Performing Butch/Femme Theory." In *Acts of Passion: Sexuality, Gender and Performance*. New York: Hawthorn Press, 1998.

"Ladies and Gentlemen, People Die"
The Uncomfortable Performances of Kiki and Herb

JAMES WILSON

"Running the World"

At a recent performance in Joe's Pub at the Public Theater in New York's East Village, forty-something Justin Bond, as the "boozy chanteusey," seventy-something Kiki, and thirty-something Kenny Mellman, as the "dependable codependent" piano player Herb (also in his seventies), presented their version of "Running the World." (Bond and Mellman appeared as Kiki and Herb for several dates in November 2006 at Joe's Pub, and from January to May 2007, they performed there most Sunday evenings at 11:30 P.M. During this engagement, I saw them perform at Joe's Pub on January 7 and May 27, 2007.) Jarvis Cocker's alternative rock song would appear to be less than an ideal choice for the septuagenarian duo, whom, one would think, would lean closer to the show tune and popular music repertoire of another famous lounge couple, Steve Lawrence and Eydie Gorme. Yet for most of the song, Kiki and Herb perform it as if the song were a traditional pop ballad. Near the end of the number, Kiki, tapping into the glamour of her former showgirl persona, gracefully sits on the stool next to the piano. With almost balletic elegance, she crosses her impossibly high-heeled left leg over her equally impossibly high-heeled right while simultaneously waving her right arm around her body to land voguishly on her hip. Clutching a microphone in her left hand, she is the image of sophistication, and at that moment it seems as though she should be performing in an upscale New York cabaret like Feinstein's, the Carlyle, or the Algonquin rather than the self-consciously plebeian Joe's Pub. Her delivery is sincere and heartfelt, and Herb's gentle tinkling of the keys makes the song seem like a Broadway standard even though the anti-capitalist lyric is anything but.

At first Kiki addresses the audience directly, but she maintains a respectable air even as the words become yet more politically pointed and accusatory toward the "cunts," who are driven solely be greed of the cost free speech and moral decency.

The sophisticated façade gradually drops away, and Kiki's face begins to contort. She rises from her perch and threateningly skulks to the audience while growling and wailing about the "cunts" at the political helm.

She becomes more desperate, twisting her mouth around the hard "c" in "cunts" and angrily punctuating the final "ts." Through repetition, the refrain becomes a primal scream, and she stomps across the small stage waving her arms and fists in a frenzy. Herb is pummeling the piano keys and baying as if in a trance at the spotlight hanging over the piano, shouting, "They're running the world! They're running the world!" No longer the elegant cabaret artist she was at the beginning of the song, Kiki has the ferocity of a glam rock star of the 1970s. She is pounding her fist in the air, violently snapping her head forward and back, chanting, "Cunts! Cunts! Cunts! Cunts!"

By the end of the song, both Kiki and Herb have regained their composure and they are once again the image of cabaret respectability. The song ends sadly, quietly, and reflectively. Even before the number has officially concluded, Herb graciously acknowledges the audience, and Kiki, channeling the quintessential lounge-act and cabaret diva, looks up at the crowd and earnestly says, "Thank you very much, ladies and gentlemen." She takes several deep and gratifying bows as she receives the accolades as if she were Judy Garland making a triumphant comeback at the Palace Theatre on Broadway.

Kiki and Herb's performance of "Running the World" encapsulates the ways in which the pair destabilizes traditional associations of theatrical drag, gay camp, and autobiographical performances. Bond and Mellman's multilayered shows and meticulously drawn characterizations bring together elements of cabaret, theatre, rock concerts, and performance art, while parodying the conventions of each form. They offer a postmodern, hipster rejoinder to mainstream drag artists of the 1980s and '90s, such as Charles Pierce, Charles Busch, Lypsinka (John Epperson), and RuPaul (Andre Charles) whose camp references included silver-screen goddesses, popular women singers of the 1930s through '50s, and high fashion super-models. Bond and Mellman replace these associations of Hollywood allure, show music, and mass cultural glamour with badly applied makeup, drunkenness, and covers of songs by Eminem, Kate Bush, and Radiohead. Justin Bond's Kiki is anything but "ladylike," and the character revels in *trash*, making her a close cousin to Divine, star of John Waters' films such as *Pink Flamingoes* and *Polyester*. In addition, the anachronistic music selections and incongruent physicality and choreography consistently remind the audience that Kiki is a character (not a "real" woman), distinguishing the act from some drag performers who strive for an absolute illusion of their gendered creation or an impression of iconographic women performers, such as Judy Garland, Barbra Streisand, or Bette Davis. (Performer Jim Bailey, who famously recreates performances of Judy Garland and Barbra Streisand explains, "From the first minute on stage when I am Barbra Streisand, I look like her, talk like her, I have her mannerisms and sing like her.... I am Barbra, not an imitation, lip-syncing or a witty impression" [Bailey].)

Unlike many cross-dressing entertainers, of whom David Román says provide a space for "apolitical nostalgia" with their Technicolor vision of the world and "romanticized days of gay life before AIDS" (that, as Román points out, never really existed), Bond and Mellman's work is overtly political (Román 99). At the same time, they self-identify their work as "queer," incorporating and often pushing beyond the limits of political correctness around issues associated with race, class, and sexual orientation. Indeed, nothing seems to be off limits for Kiki and Herb, who have made such serious and often taboo subjects as religion, pedophilia, rape, and cancer the targets of their mockery. Applying both Brechtian distancing techniques and Artaudian theatre of cruelty elements, the act savagely critiques and undercuts political ideologies and traditional theatre practices. In short, if one assumes that queer theatre concerns lesbian, gay, and transgendered identities, and the verb form *to queer* means to subvert, then Bond and Mellman *queer* queer theatre.

"It's Not Unusual"

Bond and Mellman's Kiki and Herb act has its roots in performance art, avant-garde theatre, activist street protests, and Las Vegas nightclub lounge acts. Bond and Mellman began working together in 1992, and Kiki and Herb were born shortly after. Bond, hailing from Hagerstown, Maryland, moved to San Francisco in 1988 to find an alternative to the "classical acting" in which he was trained, and Mellman, who studied music composition at Berkeley, had recently transferred to San Francisco State to focus on poetry (Ross 90). Bond had worked with transgender author and performance artist Kate Bornstein in *Hidden: A Gender* (1989), and then began developing an act around the deep-voiced, somewhat androgynous Julie London. A mutual friend introduced Bond to Mellman, and the pair began working on a musical lounge act called *Dixie McCall's Patterns for Living*, a show built around London's character in the 1970s hit television series *Emergency!* In addition to appearing in *Dixie*, Bond and Mellman performed out of character, playing a number of gay and straight clubs and performing indie, punk, and alternative rock music sets.

Around the same time, Bond began to create another character, a tough-talking, world-weary former showgirl who worked in a costume shop in Las Vegas. The character, who later became the basis for Kiki DuRane, was inspired by a close friend's mother, a one-time burlesque dancer and singer in the 1950s. She was dying of cancer when Bond met her in New Jersey in the early 1980s, but her strength and outspokenness were very much in evidence. Bond remembers:

> She was a real *broad*. I took her worldview, which is a very leftist political worldview. She called it like she saw it. And she could be very intimidating and aggressive intellectually with her political views. So I then came up with this conceit: What would she have been like if she had never given up show business? So I started doing this character around town, just going and singing, and just being really chaotic [Wilson].

At the same time, Mellman began experimenting with a character of his own. Like Kiki, Herb was based on a similarly colorful individual, a pianist at a San Francisco nightclub called Athens by Night. The lonely piano player drank tequila through the night, and in the course of the evening, he'd get drunker and drunker and sadder and sadder as he played songs and talked about his only companion, his recently deceased cat. By the end of the night, the man would be weeping uncontrollably in his tequila.

The night of Gay Pride in 1992, Bond and Mellman had a gig at San Francisco's Café du Nord. Bond told Mellman that because his voice was shot from shouting all day during the parade, he wouldn't be able to sing well, so he suggested they do their material as Kiki and Herb. Bond's ragged voice, they agreed, would be perfectly suited to the hard-drinking, heavy-smoking sound of a (then) sexagenarian. (The strident voice is an essential element of Kiki's character for as Bond once described her, she is an "alcoholic battle-axe with a throat full of razor blades" [Cripps 53].) In order to help them get into character, they had several drinks, deciding that Kiki's drink of choice would be Canadian Club ("C.C. for Kiki"), and Herb's Dewar's (Veltman). Just before and during the show, Bond began devising biographical details associated with Kiki and Herb's traumatic personal lives and rocky professional careers. They received a standing ovation, and within a short time, the act became a fixture in the underground clubs throughout San Francisco.

The fictionalized backstory of Kiki and Herb continued (and continues) to develop, but their chronicle is a collage of familiar scenes from the show business autobiography genre. First, the story satirizes sentimental tales of sexual abuse and childhood poverty. For instance, Kiki, sexually molested by her father and in constant competition with her mother's favorite child Candy, had been sent away to a government-run "institutional" because her family, financially ruined by the Depression, could not afford to support two children. Kiki and Herb met as children at the institutional where they were diagnosed as "retarded" and became fast friends since they were both disliked by the other children. The tale also parodies coming-of-age, coming-out experiences. At the institutional, Herb, as Kiki tells the audience, had it particularly difficult because as a homosexual and Jewish youth, he was taunted and beaten by the other children. As Kiki reminds the audience, "When we were growing up, it wasn't trendy to be a gay Jew tard like it is today" (Gates E4). Next, they ascended the ladder of show business as they began to perform together, first for war veterans and then professionally in nightclubs across the country. Recordings followed, such as *Kiki and Herb: It's Not Unusual*; a spoken word-record, *Kiki and Herb: Whitey's on the Moon*; and a disco album, *Kiki and Herb: One Last Chance to Blow*.

Unsurprisingly, in this show business memoir, estrangement, alcohol, and personal tragedy derail the successful career. Kiki has been married once, to the brutalizing boxer Ruby, and they had a child Coco. When the marriage ended badly, she returned to show business and had a tryst with Aristotle Onassis. While satisfying her sexual desires below deck of Onassis's yacht, Coco fell to her watery death. Struggling with the emotional scars and guilt, she implores, "Ladies and gentlemen, where the hell can a kid go on the deck of a boat?" (The story, as with much of the backstory, is recounted on the recording *Kiki and Herb Will Die for You: At Carnegie Hall*.) She also has a son, Bradford, the result of a rape when she was sixteen. Now a gay travel agent living in San Francisco's Russian Hill, Bradford will not speak to his mother after a disastrous drug and alcohol intervention. She also had her own "miracle," a "menopausal baby" named Miss D, at age fifty. Miss D's father is Yasaweh, a loving African American man who worked at Popeye's Chicken, but Kiki lost touch with him when he went to prison, and she had to get back on the comeback trail. Miss D, who, as Kiki likes to remind her audience, is "biracial" (which according to Kiki is "a much sexier term than 'high yellow'" quoted in *Kiki and Herb: Coup de Théâtre*, which played the Cherry Lane Theatre in Summer 2003]), and she now lives in Baltimore with her foster family. For years Kiki had not seen Miss D, who had been taken away from her by Social Services, but the mother and daughter have recently been reunited (at Carnegie Hall of all places). In short, Kiki's traumatic life is marked by the vicissitudes of the varying demands of being a woman, a mother, and a show business legend. It is no wonder that she drinks.

Kiki and Herb's fictional autobiography offers both a send-up of *authentic* celebrity autobiographical performance conventions and a critique of them. In recent years, celebrity autobiographical shows have become staples of mainstream theatre. In Spring 2002 alone there were three such shows on Broadway, including Elaine Stritch's *At Liberty*, Bea Arthur's *Just Between*

Friends, and John Leguizamo's *Sexaholix*. Jesse McKinley noted this trend in his "On Stage and Off" column in *The New York Times*, pointing out that in addition to the autobiographical performances, other one-person shows were prominently featured on Broadway that season, including Barbara Cook in *Mostly Sondheim*, Kevin Bacon in *An Almost Holy Picture*, Patrick Stewart in *A Christmas Carol*, and Simon Callow's *The Mystery of Charles Dickens* (McKinley E2). Since then, Broadway has seen Billy Crystal's huge commercial success *700 Sundays* (2004) and Suzanne Somers' now infamous commercial failure *The Blonde in the Thunderbird* (2005). Mario Cantone's *Laugh Whore* (2004) and Chita Rivera's *A Dancer's Life* (2006) mixed biographical elements with stand-up comedy and variety show-type musical numbers, respectively. (The genre has even been parodied in Broadway shows by Barry Humphries, including *Dame Edna: The Royal Tour* [1999] and *Dame Edna: Back with a Vengeance* [2004], and Martin Short in *Martin Short: Fame Becomes Me* [2006].)

Although these shows have a good deal in common with autobiographical performance art of the 1990s, the Broadway theatres and touring houses do not allow the same kind of intimacy between performer and spectator that Tim Miller, Holly Hughes, and Deb Margolin, to name just a few, enjoyed. Those performances generally developed in small community-based and geographically marginalized venues like New York's WOW Café, PS 122, Los Angeles's Highways, and San Francisco's Theatre Rhinoceros. And unlike performance art, celebrity autobiographical shows are intended for mass audiences and commercial success. Autobiographical celebrity performance has much in common with autobiographical performance art, but the differences are significant. The first tends to be produced for mass cultural consumption and capitalizes on the individual's fame (based on television, film, or theatre credits). Autobiographical performance art tends to be directed toward a smaller arts community and name recognition evolves from the performer's connection with a particular community. On one hand, these shows feature recognizable names that may help fuel audience interest, and on the other, the productions, which usually feature a single performer (and in some cases, a small group of backup dancers and/or singers), are relatively inexpensive to produce.

While the producers capitalize on the notoriety of the individual celebrities, the shows themselves usually emphasize the individual's survival through adverse conditions that could strike anyone. Struggling with alcoholism and diabetes, coping with a parent's death at a young age, or coming to terms with child abuse, to name just a few, are posited as great levelers of famous people and everyday audience members alike. The goal of these performances is to make the audience feel empowered, or at least willing to talk about the issues, so that they too can handle misfortune in their own lives, and many performers see their shows as having a social benefit. Actress and writer Mary Pat Gleason, for example, presented an Off Broadway one-person show involving her experiences with bipolar disorder. In an interview with *The Villager*, she said, "My belief was that the theater does heal. Sometimes people in the audience see things on the stage that they are not able to talk about that they've experienced, or it's a forbidden subject in the family, and it opens up a conversation for them" (Harrah).

The performers also strive to connect directly with the audience and create a sense of unity among those in attendance. In this regard, celebrity autobiographical performances have a good deal in common with autobiographical performance art. As Meiling Cheng explains, the performance "centrally revolving around an individual self may have the power to cohere a spectatorial community" and make the audience feel that their own experiences are being addressed by the performer (Cheng 448). Carrie Sandhal explains that autobiographical performance is far more successful in this regard than fictional plays, because the emphasis on lived experience as presented by the one who lived it "lends performance art monologues the air of authenticity" (Sandhal 29). Thus, there can be a significant degree of comfort in knowing that one's own experience is, when it comes down to it, not all that dissimilar nor more unbearable than Billy Crystal's, John Leguizamo's, or Chita Rivera's.

From the outset, attending a Kiki and Herb performance is different from a standard autobiographical show. The "moral" to be gleaned from Kiki is pithily stated, "Ladies and gentlemen, people die. That's all you need to know." The genre hallmarks, such as personal loss, disease, and the emotional toll of a life in show business, are generally all present, but the inauthenticity of the narrative produces a different experience. The excessiveness of Kiki's troubles borders on the ridiculous, and the audience is allowed to laugh at her misfortunes. The parody of the current mania for public confessional also points to the inherent voyeurism that contributes to their appeal rather than the potential unity of celebrity and noncelebrity. The performer holding the stage is not an average person, and no matter how earnest she or he is in reaching out across the footlights to connect with an audience, the social distinction is always present. Justin Bond mocks the disingenuousness of celebrities equating their lives with those of the decidedly unfamous audience members: "[Kiki] is a show business casualty, as so many of us are" (Downie 54).

Nevertheless, because of the act's roots in political activism and queer theatre, there are numerous opportunities for building community in a Kiki and Herb performance. There are elements in Justin Bond's monologue that might strike a familiar chord with the predominantly queer audience that Kiki and Herb attract. Kiki is scorned by society, but she rises above the ridicule and societal contempt, and Herb's gay bashing experience would certainly resonate with many of the gay, lesbian, bisexual, and transgendered people in attendance. In addition, the act uses political theatre methods to construct a sense of solidarity among the audience while identifying and ridiculing the enemies of the community. Kiki is unsparing in her assault on right-wing politicians and evangelists, and her verbal attacks have the power to shock even the most liberal-minded. For example, blaming Ronald Reagan for every single AIDS death ever, Kiki once stated, "The saddest day in America was when John Hinkley *missed*" (Carnegie Hall recording). Referring to Pope Benedict XVI in his stylish red robe, she said it confirmed, "The devil *does* wear Prada" (*Kiki and Herb: Alive on Broadway*, August–September 2006). And days after the death of Jerry Falwell, Kiki raised a glass to his demise, calling Falwell "a fat, dead fascist" (Joe's Pub performance, May 27, 2007). She articulates for the audience a rage that is socially impermissible, thereby creating a space in which the disenfranchised are empowered, and their public and political foes are flayed.

This political aspect is a primary characteristic of Kiki and Herb and derives from Bond and Mellman's background in AIDS activism and political street theatre. Kiki and Herb are washed-up, ridiculously irrelevant lounge singers and perpetually on the comeback trail, but they were created within the context of the political turmoil caused by AIDS and the in-your-face theatrics of Queer Nation and ACT UP. In the guise of Kiki and Herb, their political message was potentially more palatable. Bond explains: "I found that as this 66 year-old alcoholic lounge singer, I was able to get away with saying a lot more political stuff without sounding too strident or too preachy. I could say all of these things that everyone was thinking or feeling; I could express all these things in this funny way that everyone could relate to, and I could have a political agenda without sounding like I was being self-righteous or dogmatic" (Wilson). Kiki, then, is the mouthpiece for the collective political anger of the audience, and she creates a space to vent that anger. Nonetheless, she does not let her audiences off the hook easily.

Shane Vogel describes Bond's combination of cross-dressing and political invective as "*terror* drag" in its ability to assail the audience "both physically and psychically" (Vogel 44). While the audience can find a certain amount of solidarity in the shared political views and consolation in the narrative with its inevitable ebbs, flows, and final deliverance, the performers do not allow the audience to get too comfortable in realistic dramatic structure and gender-bending performing traditions. With obvious age lines hastily drawn on their faces, making them look like high school actors in a production of *Arsenic and Old Lace*, and with no attempt at hiding their youthful physiques in their outdated costumes, Bond and Mellman continually remind the audience of the fiction of Kiki and Herb. The drag act does not tease the audience with a persuasive act of impersonation. Additionally, recalling Antonin Artaud's "theatre of cruelty," the act continually breaks down the barriers between spectator and performer. Artaud bemoaned the fact that theatre had become a passive, voyeuristic event that "limits itself to showing us intimate scenes from the lives of a few puppets, transforming the public into Peeping Tom," and he argued "that we need above all a theatre that wakes us up: nerves and heart" (Artaud 83).

Bond and Mellman deliver the kind of psychic and near-physical violence Artaud advocated. Performing in cabaret spaces like New York's Cowgirl Hall of Fame, Flamingo East, Fez, and Joe's Pub, Kiki often walked across the tables and climbed over the banquette while customers hastily moved their drinks. In some of the earlier shows, Kiki would stand on a table and command a patron to lick her fishnet-stockinged leg. Alex Ross writes, "When I first saw them, five years ago [1998], Kiki would climb on top of café tables and order the customers to lick her legs. If you tried to remove your drink out of the way, she might grab it out of your hand. Another night, she threw a tray of steak knives, fortunately causing no harm" (Ross 90). During their Christmas show, *Kiki and Herb: There's a Stranger in the Manger*, Kiki recounted the story of the Little Match Girl, while simultaneously tossing lit matches at the spectators (*Kiki and Herb: There's a Stranger in the Manger* played at Westbeth Theatre Center, November–December, 2001). The musical interludes provide no respite from the assault on the senses. When critics refer to the musical numbers, for instance, they often put quotation marks around the word *song*, to indicate that Herb's loud, pounding piano accompaniment and Kiki's screeching, over-amplified voice are emotionally jarring and *un*musical by conventional cabaret and theatre standards. Describing the performance of "Total Eclipse of the Heart," *Boston Globe* critic Louise Kennedy wrote, "Whatever it is, by the time the 'song' is over, there's only one singer who could do it. As the fawning Herb intones, with an almost invisible glint of malice in his eye: Ladies and gentlemen, Miss Kiki DuRane" (Kennedy C5). Ian Mohr writes, "When Kiki barks at the audience, 'Kiki loves you,' it sounds less a term of endearment than a rageful threat. And when she drunkenly loses her place in songs, any customary, uncomfortable la-di-da's are instead replaced with clenched, staccato growls—as if she's livid at those damned words for having escaped her besotted, aging mind" (Mohr 8). The sensory assault further moves the experience from conventional performance to political activism.

From the outset, Bond and Mellman recognized the possibilities of transforming the vacuous and irrelevant conventions of the cabaret lounge act as a space for political discourse and queer activism. While the environs sanction traditional theatrical elements, such as the elaborate characterization and dramatic backstory of the two personalities as well as a fictionalized context (i.e., the audience is in attendance to celebrate the comeback of these former recording artists), the cabaret venue also allows for experimental theatre practices. The cabaret and lounge act format offers an additional level of familiarity and a means of foregrounding the political content within an apolitical genre. In the 1980s and '90s, "pseudo-bad lounge acts," as Ben Brantley explains, had become "a comic staple" (Brantley, "Campily Serious Singing" C24). Television's *Saturday Night Live*, in particular, found much to mine from the form and featured several regular sketches, including Bill Murray as Nick the Lounge Singer (his last name changing from episode to episode), who specialized in a heartfelt version of "Feelings," and Jan Hooks and Nora Dunn's Sweeney Sisters, who scatted their way through old chestnuts like "The Trolley Song." The influences and replications of swinging Vegas acts of Frank Sinatra, Sammy Davis, Jr., and Steve Lawrence and Eydie Gorme had become calcified shtick. The cabaret lounge act, which was by the 1980s associated with suburban hotel lounges and terminally *unhip* middle-aged, middle-class heterosexuals, had become a catchphrase for bad art and represented the lowest rung on the show business ladder for a performer.

The venue itself, then, shaped the show, for as described by Shane Vogel, Bond and Mellman positioned "cabaret not simply as a genre or site of performance but also a mode of performance, characterized by fluidity and improvisation, intimacy and contact, immediacy and spectacle — a mode that confuses distinctions between performer and spectator" (Vogel 35). Incorporating components of transgender performance art, queer activism, and rock concert, they also created what Dereka Rushbrook calls a "queer space" (Rushbrook 201) through their transformation of a typically heterosexualized performance space (the rock nightclub or stand-up comedy club) and performance genre (the lounge act). The volatility of theatrical, musical, and narrative forms, and the play with gender, age, and socioeconomic identity contribute to the twisted, upturned world that the shows create. Attending a Kiki and Herb show can be like entering a carnival funhouse in which reality is viewed through bulging and concave mirrors reflecting upside down, elongated, squashed, and bloated visions of humanity. This technique epitomizes a notion of queer theatre where, as David Savran argues, "the boundaries between the traditional and the experimental have become increasingly porous and in which ostensibly stable meanings and identities (sexual or otherwise) are routinely displaced by notions of mutability, instability, and polyvalence" (Savran 58). The funhouse effect in which the performers distort reality can be both exhilarating and discomforting. Kiki's unflinching and politically incorrect diatribes, for instance, can make audiences confront and evaluate their own liberal points of view.

According to David Román and Tim Miller, a potential effect of queer theatre is its ability to make spectators question their own relationships to the larger community. Román and Miller argue in "Preaching to the Converted" that queer theatre may provide an opportunity for interrogating the ideologies of the queer community:

> On the one hand, the support of many lesbian and gay audiences for community-based theatre results from the desire to be in a crowd of other lesbian and gay people. This desire rests on the comforts of identity politics and easily adapts to the primacy of sexuality in identity construction. And yet, on the other hand, many spectators also attend community-based events in order to defy the politics of sameness. Rather than upholding an uncritical stance toward the notion of queer community, many queer spectators set out to put pressure on this concept. This desire never rests, but rather prefers to unsettle the comforts of identity politics in the very space of its enactment [Román and Miller 176].

Kiki's exceedingly dark humor extends beyond attacks on conservative viewpoints and zeroes in on liberal assumptions as well. She pokes fun at gay adoption of international babies— to Kiki, "white babies" are regarded as status symbols for successful gay male couples—and she casually uses racial stereotypes and epithets when describing her black lover Yasaweh and their "biracial" daughter Miss D. And while proudly proclaiming herself a "retard" ("Retard: We *own* that word!"), Kiki forces the audience to consider how identities are forged in exclusionary terms.

The act also explodes any attempt at countering gay stereotypes associated with presumed sexual deviance. Taboo subjects are mocked and drained of their power to be used as a weapon against lesbian, gay, and transgender people. Historically, these groups have been "diagnosed" as victims of sexual abuse and vilified for unconstrained sexual promiscuity and for supposedly preying on children for sex. Kiki revels in stories of rape and molestation. At a recent performance, she bemoaned the fact that young people don't dance closely anymore. "It made," Kiki philosophized, "the step to date rape much faster" (Joe's Pub performance, May 27, 2007). Additionally, a central part of her narrative is her sexual relationship with her father ("I was Daddy's little girl"), and one of her most often-quoted lines is, "I always say, if you weren't molested as a child, you must have been an ugly kid." (The line has been included in John Cameron Mitchell's film *Shortbus* [2006], in which Justin Bond has a featured role.) For this reason, Kiki has an affinity for Jon Benet Ramsey, with whom she can identify because she "too was loved inappropriately by men" (Joe's Pub performance, May 27, 2007). Kiki even overturns tragic notions of AIDS and the gay community, saying that it is a far preferable disease than humdrum cancer. In an exchange with Herb, she surmised, "AIDS is a good disease because at least you can have fun getting it. What's a boring disease, Herb? Leukemia?" (Joe's Pub performance, May 27, 2007). The references to rape and pedophilia highlight the hypocritical public disgust for sexual predators and the simultaneous salacious media attention they receive. In Kiki's world of hedonism and show business even disease and death are judged by their inherent entertainment value.

The act also takes aim at right wing evangelism, which in the 21st century remains the most powerful political tool in legalizing discrimination against lesbian, gay, bisexual, and transgender individuals. Kiki fights back at the religious oppression and Christian evangelical bullies (as Bond refers to the Jerry Falwells and Pat Robertsons of the world) by mocking their beliefs and pointing out their hypocritical use of the teachings of Jesus Christ. The titles of many of their shows (particularly at Christmas) have religious allusions, including *Jesus Wept* (2001), *There's a Stranger in the Manger* (2001), and *Second Coming* (2007). For Kiki, Christian evangelism and show business are inextricably linked. Both are primarily coupled with fame and materialism. In the 2003 Carnegie Hall performance, Kiki claimed that "greatest show business martyr of all time was our Lord and Savior, Jesus Christ, who died so that Mel Gibson could be a billionaire" with the making of *The Passion of the Christ* (Carnegie Hall recording).

In recent performances, Bond and Mellman have pushed the Christian references to the extreme and developed a corrective to the New Testament by claiming that Kiki and Herb were present at the birth of Jesus. Apparently, Daisy, a cow in the manger of the Nativity, ate hay that contained the afterbirth of Jesus, and received eternal life. Kiki and Herb, who were then itinerant performers known as Naomi and Ishkabibble, drank Daisy's milk; thus, they also have eternal life. One might argue, justifiably, that this is not an altogether positive direction for the narrative. The performers have shunned strict realism, but the mythical account seems out of place with the social and political realities into which the act tends to delve. Additionally, the supernatural elements undercut the impending sense of doom for the characters. Overcoming adversity and survival of the show biz fittest does not have the same urgency when the characters cannot and will not die. And while Kiki has never been noted for the factual consistency of her tales, the new wrinkle makes the backstory of Kiki and Herb meeting at the government-run institutional a lie or a delusion.

The Naomi and Ishkabibble story does, however, have some practical benefits in the continuing saga of Kiki and Herb. First, it opens up possibilities for expanding the narrative across centuries rather than just decades. Kiki has hobnobbed with the likes of Grace "Goodtime Gracie" Kelly and danced in a strip joint with Maya Angelou, and one's mind reels at the historical figures that Kiki might describe in future performances. Second, the implausibility of the story may make the character seem a bit crazier and even more off-balance. This could enhance the discomfort Kiki establishes with the audience if they regard Kiki as both drunk and insane. (Her last name is, after all DuRane, suggesting she may be "deranged" and "insane.") On the other hand, if the mythical quality destabilizes the reality and conventional narrative even further, then it might provide an optimal space for examining, using Brechtian distancing techniques, the issues and themes the act introduces.

Most importantly, the biblical chronicle provides an opportunity to queer the New Testament and make it more inclusive. In Kiki's version, for instance, homosexuality was a part of life in the first few decades A.D. In fact, Kiki explains that Herb and Jesus were lovers, and just for the record, Jesus, Kiki says, was a "very tender, sensitive lover" (Joe's Pub performance, May 27, 2007). And in this retelling of the New Testament, Mary Magdalene was not the only woman to celebrate the joys of the flesh and to blissfully give into sexual desires. Kiki claims that, in fact, Mary Magdalene was her biggest rival in those years, but the Crucifixion joined these adversaries in a common cause. She says, "Never did two bitches so opposed to each other come together." The two women stood by the cross, shouting and wailing to all who could hear, "Take Him down! Take Him down!" (Joe's Pub performance, May 27, 2007).

The attack on sacred cows (or in Bond and Mellman's version, attack *with* a sacred cow in the form of Daisy, the after-birth eating cow) has a subversive element, and many Christians would find the references to Jesus Christ offensive. Yet as Martha Greene Eads argues, the queering of religion can actually have a positive effect on Christian and non–Christian audience members. The engendered laughter can provide a "balm and a bridge" for the politically charged topics addressed in the show, and the use of religion also offers a chance to "explore broad, even universal questions about human nature, suffering, and religious experience" (Eads 181). For Bond and Mellman, this spiritual element is essential to the performances, and the effect is intended to embody their interpretation of the central tenet of Christian faith. In each show, Kiki descends further and further into despair and madness. The stories get darker and sadder as the character confronts memories of a dead child, lost lovers, and show business calamities. Alcohol consumption makes the singing and storytelling sloppier and less controlled. Yet there is always a redemptive climax in each show, and as Bond says, there is a conscious narrative "arc." Even when the show appears to be completely improvised and loose, the performers are working within a spiraling downward dramatic structure (Wilson). At the end of the show, Kiki is saved (usually by kind words from Herb), and she is resurrected. In the final moments, she often becomes a savior for the audience, and many of the shows conclude with their anthem of survival, "Total Eclipse of the Heart," with the added lyric, "Don't turn your back on Kiki/ Kiki loves you/ Kiki needs you/ Kiki would die for you" (Carnegie Hall recording). The redemption and benediction of Kiki are crucial elements of the performance, as these provide a release for the audience from the assault on the nerves and senses. There is a spiritual release as well, for Bond explains that if audiences "can love and forgive Kiki, then they can love and forgive themselves" (Wilson).

"One Last Chance to Blow"

In "Building a Theatrical Vernacular," Jill Dolan writes, "To be queer is not who you *are*, it's what you *do*, it's your relation to the dominant power, and your relation to marginality, as a place of empowerment" (Dolan 5). Bond and Mellman use queer performance to actively subvert mainstream autobiographical performance, and they use the rhetorical tools of religious oppression to fight back against evangelical Christians. In short, they *do* queer. Even still, if, as Alisa Solomon claims, theatre is the "queerest art" (Solomon 9), mostly corporate interests and white straight men control mainstream theatre production. Even community-based performance spaces often rely on public funding, grants from private organizations, and donations from wealthy patrons, who all, therefore, have a stake in the kind of work that gets presented. Is queer theatre still *queer* if its relationship with the dominant power and marginality is intertwined?

From the outset, Justin Bond's definition of queer theatre extended beyond the material he developed for performance. In order to wholly manifest a theory of queer theatre, he realized that the mode of production would also need to be overturned. In the early 1990s, he recognized that economic constrictions and conventional theatrical hierarchies limited the possibilities of a queer artist. His revelation came during a San Francisco rally for the NEA Four (Karen Finley, John Fleck, Holly Hughes, and Tim Miller), whose funding was withdrawn for their controversial performances, which explored issues of gender, sexual desire, and sexual orientation. Holly Hughes was at the rally, and, according to Bond, was "devastated" by the recent events. Bond recalls:

> And as much as I felt compassion for [Holly Hughes], I couldn't understand why she would be so upset that a government that would want us dead would want to fund art where we were speaking out against them. I knew they were fascist, so I thought, well, if you have to rely on government subsidies to make your artwork, then you're bringing your art to the wrong community [Wilson].

Bond says he has since changed his position because he feels that art needs to be funded by the State since this is the only way that it can reach larger audiences. At the time, though, he was not going to make art that relied on government subsidies. He turned to a funding source that was all but assured: "People's need for alcohol" (Wilson). Bars and nightclubs offered an alternative economy to the traditional performance venue that relies on advertisement, ticket sales, and often outside funding so that a person's work may be seen.

Bond and Mellman upended the conventional route for art funding and simultaneously tackled traditional theatre hierarchies. Bond envisioned a system in which the performers have complete control of their art. Producers, directors, and managers in mainstream theatre can potentially alter the vision of the artist, and Bond wanted total responsibility over his work. Some of his inspiration for this pursuit came from Eartha Kitt, the legendary Broadway performer and cabaret singer. Because of Kitt's famous confrontation with Lady Bird Johnson in the 1960s, Bond realized that it is "possible to be both glamorous and political." When he had the chance to meet Kitt, he discovered that she did not have a manager, and she resisted many of the constraining structures of mainstream theatre. Kitt offered a model of political forthrightness and artistic authority. In an age in which the director is king in mainstream theatre, Bond and Mellman have rejected the role of an outside director (except with their Off Broadway production of *Coup de Théâtre* at the Cherry Lane Theatre). This decision has resulted in the most consistent criticism against the act, claiming that the shows are too long and in need of a director's eye to shape them. Bond says that the protracted length is a deliberate choice of the artists and connects directly with the main point of a Kiki and Herb show. The duration of the show further eschews conventions of tightly structure dramatic theatre and contributes to the psychic hostility of the performance. Bond explains:

> For me, the choice for the show to be too long and for it to go on [and on], and for Kiki and Herb to wear out their welcome was definitely a choice because I am not there to make people comfortable. I am not there to fulfill people's expectations that A and B equal C. "What a great night." Clap, clap, clap. "Let's go." I want people to be sitting there thinking, "Jesus Christ, why don't they fucking get off the stage?" Because Kiki and Herb would not get off the fucking stage! So that to me maintains the integrity of the piece. So if you're looking at is as a theatrical purist, who believes in all these things, then you're going to be disappointed — no, you're not going to be disappointed, you're going to think it's bad because that's the way you look at things.

In a Kiki and Herb show, *Kiki* tells the audience when the show is over. In this alternative theatrical universe, the performer is sovereign and does not pander to the minions. Neither the audience nor a director has a say in the final shape of the show.

In recent years, Bond and Mellman's audience has grown, and the duo has performed in a number of mainstream venues, including two that represent the quintessential bastions of high culture: Carnegie Hall and Broadway. Bond says that their act varies depending upon the "architecture" of the venue, but the assault on theatrical conventions does not. If anything, the attack is stronger when the conventional rules of fourth-wall theatre are the norm as in a proscenium-structured Broadway house. The queering of a non-queer-identified space requires a bit more aggression.

Kiki and Herb: Alive on Broadway, which played the Helen Hayes Theatre for a limited run in August and September 2006, included many of the familiar pieces of Bond and Mellman's nightclub performances. The two-act show included tales about family members (dead and alive), show business anecdotes, and songs by Scissor Sisters, Public Enemy, and Bright Eyes. *Alive on Broadway* received mostly favorable reviews from the theatre critics. Ben Brantley of the *New York Times* called it "a hyper-magnified cabaret concert that has the heat and dazzle of great balls of fire" (Brantley, "The Road to Catharsis with Those Two Immortals" E1). Ian Mohr of *Variety* called it an "edgy, winning revue" (Mohr 8), and Joe Dziemianowicz of the *Daily News* described the show as a "downtown experience gone uptown" and praised it as "shrill, delirious and demented" (Dziemianowicz 35). Several of the critics, however, said that the show could have used a director because with a running time of over two hours long, the act became wearisome. Additionally, nearly all the critics warned that Kiki and Herb are not for all tastes and, according to Elysa Gardner of *USA Today*, not "safe for matinee crowds" (Gardner 4D). And Howard Shapiro of the *Philadelphia Inquirer* qualified his review by stating, "Kiki and Herb are not for everyone — I got a few unhappy emails after I wrote about how much I liked their Philadelphia tryout" (Shapiro E1). People expecting a tamer, less antagonistic Kiki and Herb on Broadway would surely have been dismayed.

When Bond and Mellman were offered the chance to perform their act in a commercial theatre, they consciously decided that they would forcibly challenge the midtown audiences with their genre-bending approach and that they would not soften their political positions and sensory onslaught. In fact, they intended to push these further and "open up the boundaries of [mainstream] theatre because" according to Bond, "it's pretty fucking boring in general" (Wilson). Physically, the show had all the trappings of what one might expect of a Broadway show. *Alive on Broadway* had a fairly elaborate set (compared with their nightclub performances, which include just a piano for Herb and a stool for Kiki). The set included a huge, glittering leaf upstage right behind Herb's piano and a large tree downstage left. The tree provided a perch for Kiki and had numerous holes and cavities to store highball glasses and bottles of booze. Ben Brantley described Scott Pask's set as a "bizarre sylvan landscape that suggests Salvador Dalí working in Las Vegas" (Brantley, "The Road to Catharsis with Those Two Immortals" E1). Jeff Croiter's lighting, inflected with blue and green accents, highlighted the moody Las Vegas lounge quality, and Marc Happel's costumes were a throwback to the 1970s and paid homage to designer Bob Mackie. Broadway accoutrements ended there, and the show's content was decidedly adult and queer. The evening had some of the glittery frills of a Broadway musical, but there was a "We're-here-we're-queer-get-used-to-it" activist subtext. Because a queer audience perspective may not be assumed in a Broadway house, as it might be in a space that attracts primarily queer and queer-friendly audiences, Bond and Mellman accentuated this aspect. Bond explains, "When we went to Broadway, I made it a lot more gay oriented and a lot more queer and a lot more in your face because Kiki doesn't really talk about gay stuff in front of a gay audience or with a downtown audience so much. It's more of a worldview that makes it a queer performance than the actual subject she discusses" (Wilson). Identity politics move to the foreground when preaching to the *un*converted.

Audiences had mixed reactions to *Alive on Broadway*. The production attracted fans of Kiki and Herb from previous shows, and the many who were new to the act could find much to appreciate. (Justin Bond remarked that several people who thought they were "going to see a woman" in a variety show format left the show won over. He is always surprised that there are people he would not expect to "get" Kiki and Herb, but then are quite grateful for the experience.) There were, nevertheless, a substantial number of walkouts at intermission and before the final curtain. At one of the performances I attended, a large number of people left before the encore, affirming the critical complaint that the show wore out its welcome after almost two and a half hours. Billy Crystal, who was sitting across the aisle, was one of the people to make a beeline to the exit. (It is harder to make an escape in a tightly packed nightclub or cabaret). Justin Bond as Kiki did not take the mass exodus lightly. She hollered at the premature exiters, calling them "rude mother fuckers," and shouted, "I hope you get in a car accident on the way home!" After a pause, she offered a fatalistic shrug. "Well, that's up to God to decide," and she raised her glass of Canadian Club to the heavens (*Kiki and Herb: Alive on Broadway*, August 26, 2006 performance). On other occasions, she called the people who left early "cunts." When a friend told Justin Bond that a performer could not call Broadway audience members "cunts," Bond retorted, "Well, clearly you can because I just did" (Wilson).

The show closed in September 2006 after its scheduled limited run, but

Kiki and Herb: Alive on Broadway was nominated the following spring for the 2007 Tony Award for Best Special Theatrical Event. Bond and Mellman lost the award to ventriloquist and former situation comedy star Jay Johnson for his one-person autobiographical show, *The Two and Only*. The nomination, however, gave Justin Bond and Kenny Mellman an opportunity to attend the annual televised award show, and true to form, the pair used the event to assail the customs of mainstream theatre's rite of spring. Bond did not wear the Kiki drag to the show, but he certainly added a touch of the queer to the proceedings. Foregoing the typical tuxedo for men, Bond worked the red carpet in transgender formal wear. (Mellman wore a more traditional awards show outfit, a dark suit, white shirt, and tie.) Appearing in a black and silver, backless dress, a wristful of bangled bracelets, heavy makeup, and with his hair swooped over to one side, Bond was unapologetically queer. For television audiences accustomed to seeing strict gender roles acted out on highbrow awards shows, Bond subverted their expectations. For those eagerly waiting to see manifestations of standard award-show drag — high-class men in tuxedoes and glamorous women in gowns on the red carpet and in the audience — Bond's appearance seemed to shout, "Don't get too comfortable!"

BIBLIOGRAPHY

Artaud, Antonin. *The Theater and Its Double*. New York: Grove Press, 1958.
Bailey, Jim. "A Conversation with Jim." www.jimbaileyweb.com/index.htm
Brantley, Ben. "Campily Serious Singing." *The New York Times*, November 3, 1995.
_____. "The Road to Catharsis with Those Two Immortals." *The New York Times*, August 16, 2006.
Cheng, Meiling. "Highways, L.A.: Multiple Communities in a Heterolocus." *Theatre Journal* 53:3 (October 2001).
Cocker, Jarvis. *Jarvis*. Rough Trade Records, Ltd., 2006 [compact disc].
Cripps, Charlotte. "Cabaret: Confessions of a Boozy Battle-Axe." *The Independent*, December 8, 2005.
Dolan, Jill. "Building a Theatrical Vernacular: Responsibility, Community, Ambivalence, and Queer Theater" In *The Queerest Art: Essays on Lesbian and Gay Theater*, edited by Alisa Solomon and Framji Minwalla. New York: New York University Press, 2002.
Downie, Stephen. "Songs in the Key of Controversy." *The Daily Telegraph* (Sydney, Australia), February 3, 2006.
Dziemianowicz, Joe. "So Good at Being Bad: A Chanteuse Act Camps up Broadway." *The Daily News*, August 16, 2006.
Eads, Martha Greene. "Conversion Tactics in Terrence McNally's and Paul Rudnick's Gay Gospels." *Modern Drama* 48:1 (Spring 2005).
Gardner, Elysa. "'Kiki and Herb' Drags It Out a Little Too Long." *USA Today*, August 16, 2006.

Gates, Anita. "Taste, Schmaste! The Holidays Can Be a Drag." *The New York Times*, December 11, 2001.
Harrah, Scott. "In Her One-Woman Show, Mary Pat Gleason Uses Humor to Heal." *The Villager*, June 7–13, 2006. http://www.thevillager.com/villager_162/inherone womanshow.html.
Kennedy, Louise. "Beyond Fabulous: A Cabaret Parody with Kitsch, Glitter, and Pop." *Boston Globe*, June 15, 2007.
Kiki and Herb. *Kiki and Herb Will Die for You: At Carnegie Hall.* Produced by Julian Fleischer. Evolver Entertainment, 2004. [compact disc]
McKinley, Jesse. "Another Actor Is Flying Solo." *The New York Times*, March 1, 2002.
Mohr, Ian. "Theatre Review: Kiki and Herb: Alive on Broadway." *Daily Variety*, August 21, 2006.
Román, David. *Acts of Intervention: Performance, Gay Culture, and AIDS.* Bloomington, IN: Indiana University Press, 1998.
———, and Tim Miller. "Preaching to the Converted." *Theatre Journal* 47:2 (May 1995).
Ross, Alex. "Grand Illusions: Down Memory Lane with Kiki and Herb." *The New Yorker*, May 19, 2003.
Rushbrook, Dereka. "Cities, Queer Space, and the Cosmopolitan Tourist." *GLQ: A Journal of Lesbian and Gay Studies* 8:1–2 (2002).
Sandahl, Carrie. "Queering the Crip or Cripping the Queer? Intersections of Queer and Crip Identities in Solo Autobiographical Performance." *GLQ: A Journal of Lesbian and Gay Studies* 9:1–2 (2003).
Savran, David. *A Queer Sort of Materialism: Recontextualizing American Theater.* Ann Arbor, MI: University of Michigan Press, 2003.
Shapiro, Howard. "Kiki and Herb Storm the Great White Way." *Philadelphia Inquirer*, August 16, 2006.
Solomon, Alisa. "Great Sparkles of Lust: Homophobia and the Antitheatrical Tradition." In *The Queerest Art: Essays on Lesbian and Gay Theater*, edited by Alisa Solomon and Framji Minwalla. New York: New York University Press, 2002.
Veltman, Chloe. "Has Success Spoiled Kiki and Herb?" *San Francisco* (July 2007) http://www.sanfranmag.com/archives/view_story/1719/).
Vogel, Shane. "Where Are We Now? Queer World Making and Cabaret Performance." *GLQ: A Journal of Lesbian and Gay Studies* 6:1 (June 2000).
Will Die for You: Kiki and Herb at Carnegie Hall (Evolver Records, 2005) Two-disc set.
Wilson, James, Interview with Justin Bond, 13 September 2007.

Notes on Contributors

David Cregan is an assistant professor of theatre at Villanova University where he also teaches in the Irish Studies Program. David received a Ph.D. in drama studies at the Samuel Beckett School of Drama at Trinity College Dublin and has an M.A. in Irish studies from the Catholic University of America, an M.Phil. in Irish theatre and film from Trinity, and an M.Div. from the Washington Theological Union. David has published in *Modern Drama*, the *Australasian Journal of Dramatic Studies*, *New Voices in Irish Studies*, as well as a chapter in *Out of History: Essays on Sebastian Barry*. His research interests include the Irish playwright Frank McGuinness, Irish theatrical practice, and contemporary Irish culture. David is a theatre director at Villanova and a theatre critic for a Philadelphia newspaper.

Leslie Atkins Durham is an associate professor in the Department of Theatre Arts at Boise State University. She teaches courses in theatre history, dramatic literature, and dramaturgy. Her first book, *Staging Gertrude Stein: Absence, Culture, and the Landscape of the American Alternative Theatre*, was published by Palgrave Macmillan in 2005. She is currently working on a new book chronicling alternative approaches to the construction of American character since 2001.

Sean F. Edgecomb is a doctoral candidate in the Department of Drama at Tufts University. He has presented his research in the United States, Canada, Finland, and Croatia. Most recently his article, "A History of the Ridiculous Theatre 1960–1987," was published in the *Gay and Lesbian Review Worldwide*. He is currently completing his dissertation "Still Ridiculous: The Legacy of Charles Ludlam and the Ridiculous Theatre Movement in America, 1987–2007."

James Fisher is professor of theatre and head of the Department of Theatre at the University of North Carolina at Greensboro. He was the 2007 recipient of the Betty Jean Jones Award for Excellence in the Teaching of American Theatre from the American Theatre and Drama Society. Fisher, who has published numerous essays and reviews, previously edited *Tony Kushner: New Essays on the Art and Politics of the Plays* (McFarland, 2006) and is the author of several books, including *Understanding Tony Kushner* (University of South Carolina Press, 2008), *The Historical Dictionary of the American Theater: Modernism* (with Felicia Hardison Londré; Scarecrow, 2007), *The Theater of Tony Kushner: Living Past Hope* (Routledge, 2001), *The Theatre of Yesterday and Tomorrow: Commedia dell'arte on the Modern Stage* (Mellen, 1992), and three bio-bibliographies (Al Jolson, Spencer Tracy, and Eddie Cantor) for Greenwood Press.

Annie Giannini is a graduate student in theatre research with a specialization in theatre for youth at the University of Wisconsin–Madison. She completed her thesis, *Young, Troubled, and Queer: Gay and Lesbian Representation in Theatre for Young Audiences*, in the spring of 2008.

Robert F. Gross teaches theatre at Hobart and William Smith Colleges. He is the author of *S. N. Behrman: A Research and Production Sourcebook* and the editor of volumes on Christopher Hampton and Tennessee Williams in the Garland/Routledge "Casebook on Modern Dramatists" series. He has published essays on a wide range of texts, from Henrik Ibsen's *Rosmersholm* and Gerhart Hauptmann's *Fuhrmann Henschel*; to plays by John Guare, Harry Kondoleon, and Len Jenkin; the film *Malice*; and the television series *Six Feet Under* and *The Rockford Files*.

Joe E. Jeffreys teaches at New York University's Tisch School of the Arts Department of Undergraduate Drama and Stony Brook University's Theatre Department. He has published in various encyclopedia and anthologies including *Extreme Exposure* (Theatre Communications Group), *Out of Character* (Bantam), and *Art, Glitter and Glitz* (Praeger) as well as academic journals including *The Drama Review*, *Theatre History Studies*, *Theatre Journal*, and *The Journal of New York Folklore*. In addition, he has worked as a dramaturg for productions at PS 122, La Mama, and Dixon Place. His documentary *Drag Show Video Vérité* premiered at the New York Public Library for the Performing Arts at Lincoln Center and also played the Fire Island Film and Video Festival.

Jacob Juntunen dropped out of high school and had his first play produced by Edward Albee at Stages Repertory Theatre in Houston. Since then, his plays have been produced in Chicago, Austin, Minneapolis, and Portland, Oregon. He is an Artistic Associate at Chicago's Jeff Award winning company Infamous Commonwealth Theatre, a Network Playwright at Chicago Dramatists, and the Resident Playwright at Uptown Chicago's only theatre for development, Scrap Mettle SOUL. His play *Kantor! Kantor!* is currently being considered by Tadeusz Kantor's Polish state archive for publication. *Under America*, his latest script, was one of five selected by the Driehaus Foundation for potential workshops by the Sundance Institute. His chapter "Repairing Reality: The Media and *Homebody/Kabul* in New York, 2001" appeared in *Tony Kushner: New Essays on the Art and Politics of the Plays* (McFarland, 2006) edited by James Fisher. Jacob currently teaches at the University of Illinois, Chicago (UIC) and the School of the Art Institute. For more information, go to www.jacobjuntunen.com.

Charles Eliot Mehler is pursuing his Ph.D. in theatre at Louisiana State University. His published articles include "*Brokeback Mountain* at the Oscars" in the anthology *Reading Brokeback Mountain* and "*Fiddler on the Roof*: Considerations in a new age" for the journal *Studies in Musical Theatre*. As a playwright, composer and lyricist, Mehler is the author of the musical plays *Poster Children* and *Wealth, and How Not to Avoid It*, a musical adaptation of Shaw's *Major Barbara*. In his forthcoming dissertation, Mehler explores the connection between commercial musical theatre and the mainstreaming of marginalized populations.

Paul Menard is a theatre professional, critic, and journalist living and working in New York City. He currently works at HERE Arts Center, a cutting-edge, hybrid-performance space in downtown Manhattan and is a columnist with *Back Stage*; his criticism has also appeared in the *Village Voice* and *The Brooklyn Rail*. A former panelist and presenter for the International Federation of Theatre Researchers, he is currently a judge for the New York Innovative Theatre Awards. Paul received his M.F.A. in dramaturgy from Columbia University.

Jordan Schildcrout is assistant professor of theater history, criticism, and dramaturgy at Ohio University. He earned his B.A. in literature from Yale University and his Ph.D. in theatre from the Graduate Center of the City University of New York, where he also worked for the Center for Lesbian and Gay Studies. He has been published in *Theatre Journal, Theatre Topics, Columbia Encyclopedia of Modern Drama,* and *Journal of the Pirandello Society of America,* and he regularly presents new scholarship at the Association for Theatre in Higher Education and other national conferences. His article "The Performance of Nonconformity on *The Muppet Show*—Or How Kermit Made Me Queer" appeared in *The Journal of Popular Culture.* As a literary manager and dramaturg he has worked for Manhattan Theatre Club, Adobe Theatre Company, and Wash & Fold Theatre Project.

Manon van de Water is an associate professor in theatre research and director of the Theatre for Youth program at the University of Wisconsin-Madison. She has published widely on theatre, drama education, and theatre for young audiences in national and international journals. Her book *Moscow Theatres for Young People: A Cultural History of Ideological Coercion and Artistic Innovation, 1917–2000* was published by Palgrave Macmillan in 2006.

James Wilson teaches at LaGuardia Community College and the Graduate Center of the City University of New York. His articles have appeared in *Urban Education, Teaching English in the Two-Year College,* and *Theatre History Studies.* His writing has also been published in anthologies ranging from *Staging Desire: Queer Readings of American Theater History* to *Reclaiming the Public University: Conversations on General & Liberal Education.* He is currently working on a book about lesbian and gay theatre and performance in the Harlem Renaissance.

Index

Abbey Theatre 125
Abingdon Theatre Company 179
ACT UP 20, 27, 201
Acting Gay: Male Homosexuality in Modern Drama 22
Adams, Neile 180
Aeschylus 64
African-Americans 1, 7, 29, 88
Agamemnon 64
The Agony and the Agony 100, 101
AIDS (HIV) 1, 2, 3, 7, 8, 9, 12, 14, 16, 17, 18, 19, 20, 22, 23, 24, 25, 27, 28, 32–55, 63, 93, 94, 95, 97, 98, 99, 100, 158–176, 196, 201, 205
AIDS and Its Metaphors 93
AIDS Medical Foundation 36
AIDS Resource Center 36, 37
A.I.D.S. Show (San Francisco) 34
Akalaitis, Joanne 151
Albee, Edward 11, 96, 177
Alfaro, Luis 104
Alford, C. Fred 91
Algonquin Hotel 194
All About Eve 72
All My Hopes and Dreams 143, 146, 149
An Almost Holy Picture 199
American Ballet Theatre 178
American Buffalo 79–89
American Civil Liberties Union (ACLU) 93
American Conservatory Theatre (ACT) 156
American Red Cross Home Attendant Program 36
Amos and Andy 88
And the Band Played On 20, 45
And Things That Go Bump in the Night 23
Anderson, Robert 10
Andreach, Robert J. 164
Angelos, Maureen 142, 143
Angelou, Maya 206
Angels in America 1, 3, 4, 7, 9, 22, 26–30, 158
Anspacher Theatre 36
Aristophanes 57
Arsenic and Old Lace 202
The Art of AIDS 20
Artaud, Antonin 57, 72, 202
Arthur, Bea 198
As Is 3, 18, 26, 34
Association for Theatre in Higher Education (ATHE) 101n, 184n
Astor Library Building 151

At Liberty 198
At Stake: Monsters and the Rhetoric of Fear in Public Culture 92
Athens by Night 197
Augé, Marc 141
Auntie Mame 165
Avant-Garde-Arama 147

Babuscio, Jack 131, 133
Bachelard, Gaston 141
Bacon, Kevin 199
Bailey, Jim 196
Bailey, Pearl 180
Baker, Rob 20
Ballard, Kay 180
Ballet of the Dolls 178
Barnes, Clive 42
Beautiful Child 100, 101
Beauty and the Beast 188
Belle Reprieve 188, 190
Bennett, Susan 34
Bent 18
Bergman, David 48, 50
Berman, Shelley 182
Bersani, Leo 94
Beyond the Valley of the Dolls 178
Big Hotel 72
The Big Three at Yalta 18
Bilandic, Michael 84
The Birdcage 17
Blagojevich, Rod 85, 86
The Blonde in the Thunderbird 199
Bloolips 191, 192
Bluebeard 187
Bond, Justin *see* Kiki and Herb
Borne, Bette 191
Bornstein, Kate 196
Boston Center for the Arts 70
Botticelli, Sandro 66
Bowles, Norma 104
Boy Bar 178
The Boy in the Basement 11
The Boys in the Band 2, 3, 7, 8, 11, 18, 25, 26, 27, 29, 82
Brando, Marlon 181
Brantley, Ben 148, 156, 203, 209, 210
The Breadwinner 161
Brecht, Bertolt 22, 27, 46, 51, 52, 67, 69, 196
Bright Eyes 209
Brokeback Mountain 4, 30, 79

217

Index

Bronski, Michael 93
Bull, John 33
Bumiller, Elisabeth 93
Busch, Charles 71, 75, 195
Bush, George W. 77, 93, 95
Bush, Kate 195
Butler, Judith 58, 105, 106, 107, 185
Butterfield 8 182, 183
Bybee, Jay S. 95
Byrne, Jane 84

Café du Nord 197
Caffe Cino 12
La Cage aux Folles 17, 18, 24
Callas, Maria 24
Callen, Michael 50
Callow, Simon 199
Camhe, Pamela 142
Camille 12, 56, 76
Cannibals Just Don't Know Better 12
Can't Stop the Music 180
Cantone, Mario 199
Care Bears 89
Carey, James 33, 38
Carlson, Marvin 39
Carlyle Hotel 194
Carol's Speakeasy 83, 84
Carrie 182
Cart, Michael A. 106
Case, Sue-Ellen 191
Centers for Disease Control (CDC) 21, 32, 38, 46
Certeau, Michel de 141
Chapman, Jennifer 103
Charles, Andre 195
Chaucer, Geoffrey 179
Chekhov, Anton 61, 62, 127
Cheng, Meiling 200
Cherry Lane Theatre 208
Cherubini, Luigi 64
Chesley, Robert 34
Chester Mystery Plays 92
Chicago Gay and Lesbian Hall of Fame 85
Chicago Gay Pride Parade 85
Chicago Log Cabin Republicans 83
Chicago Transit Authority 85
Children and AIDS 36
The Children's Hour 10, 104, 107
Children's Theatre of Charlotte 104
Children's Theatre of Maine 110
Chinatown 183
Chiola, Tom 85
Christine Jorgensen Revealed 72
Christine Jorgensen Reveals 68, 69, 70, 71, 76
A Christmas Carol 199
Circle Repertory Theatre 23, 34
Clítoris, Clitóris 61
Club 57, 178
Club Chandelier 178
Clum, John M. 22, 48, 49, 51, 135, 139

Clytemnestra 66
Cocker, Jarvis 194
Cody, Gabrielle 59, 74
Cohn, Roy 27, 28, 29
Como, Perry 145
The Complete Works of Charles Ludlam 59
Confessions of a Farceur 62
The Conquest of the Universe 179
Cook, Barbara 199
Cootie Shots: Theatrical Inoculations Against Bigotry for Kids, Parents, and Teachers 104
Corpus Christi 25, 26
Cowgirl Hall of Fame 202
Coward, Noël 14, 164
Cox, J. Robert 52
Crawford, Joan 179, 181, 183
Croiter, Jeff 210
Crowley, Mart 2, 3, 7, 8, 12, 23, 82
Crystal, Billy 199, 200, 210
Cunanan, Andrew 90
Curran, James 38
Curtis, Jackie 179

Daley, Maggie 85
Daley, Richard Joseph "Dick" 86, 87
Daley, Richard Michael "Richie" 83–89
Dalí, Salvador 210
La Dame aux Camélias see *Camille*
Dame Edna: Back with a Vengeance 199
Dame Edna: The Royal Tour 199
A Dancer's Life 199
David, Jacques-Louis 63
Davis, Bette 196
Davis, Sammy, Jr. 203
Davy, Babs 142, 143
Davy, Kate 143, 191
Dawson's Creek 110
Day, Doris 180
The Death and Resurrection of Mr. Roche 126, 127
Democratic Party 79, 80, 83, 84, 85, 86, 87
Dennis, Charles 147
The Destiny of Me 23
Deveare-Smith, Anna 151
Dial "M" for Model 178
Diamond, Lisa 106
Dibbell, Dominique 142, 143, 155
Divine 195
Dixie McCall's Patterns for Living 196
Dodger Stages 70
Dolan, Jill 192, 207
A Doll's House 161
Dolly West's Kitchen 128–139
Donohue, Denis 137
Doubt 156
Douglas, Lord Alfred "Bosie" 80, 81
Dovima 177
Dublin Gay Theatre Festival 70
Dumas, Alexandre 12, 56
The Drag 9

Dress Suits to Hire 191
Dry Bones Breathe: Gay Men Creating Post-AIDS Identities and Cultures 173
Dublin Theatre Festival 126, 134
Dunaway, Faye 183
Dunn, Nora 203
Durang, Christopher 4, 96
Dziemianowicz, Joe 209

Eads, Martha Greene 206
Ebb, Fred 24
Edelman, Lee 94, 165
Edinburgh Fringe Festival 70
Eichelberger, Ethyl (James) 56–78, 179
8 B.C. 178
Elbe, Lili 67
Elliott, Kenneth Yates 58
Emergency! 196
Eminem 195
An Enemy of the People 41
epic theatre 27
Epperson, John *see* Lypsinka
Erikson, Kai 163
Esslin, Martin 134
Eureka Theatre Company 26
Euripides 64
European Union 137
Evans, David T. 174
Everything in the Garden 11
Extreme Exposure 62

The Fabulous Lypsinka Show 179
Faggots 18, 19, 20
Falana, Lola 143, 149
Falwell, Jerry 93, 201, 205
Far from Heaven 79
Fat Men in Skirts 96
Fauci, Anthony 23
Federal Theatre Project 59
Feingold, Michael 41, 167
Feinstein's 194
Female Trouble 72
Fences 88
Fez 202
The Field of Drama 134
Fierstein, Harvey 3, 4, 12, 13, 14, 15, 16, 17, 22, 24, 30
Fifth of July 11
59E59 69
Finley, Karen 207
Finnegan, Brian 134
First Year Born 68
Fitch, Clyde 9
The Five Chinese Brothers 143
The Five Lesbian Brothers 142–157, 192
Flaming Creatures 186
Flamingo East 202
Flanagan, Hallie 59
Flatbush Tosca 12
Fleck, John 207

Flower Drum Song 88
Foley, Helene 63, 64, 73
Foucault, Michel 141
Fowlkes, Martha R. 163
Franks, Bobby 100
Freaky Pussy 12
Frechette, Peter 158
Free Will & Wanton Lust 96
Freud, Sigmund 96, 101, 159, 163
Friel, Brian 127, 128
Fringe Benefits 104
Fugue in a Nursery 13, 14

Gardner, Elysa 209
Garland, Judy 196
Gay and After 173
Gay Games 85
Gay Liberation Front (GLF) 128
Gay Men's Health Crisis (GMHC) 20, 21, 32, 34, 35, 36, 38, 48, 49
Gay-Straight Alliance 117, 119
Gellar, Samantha 104
gender-fuck 76
Genet, Jean 94
Gentle Island 127, 128
The Gentleman's Agreement 88, 89
The Geography Club 115, 116, 117
Gibson, Mel 205
Girvin, Brian 132
The Glass Menagerie 161, 162
Gleason, Mary Pat 200
Glengarry Glen Ross 79–89
Goldstein, Richard 95
Goodman, Lizbeth 32
Gormé, Eydie 194, 203
Gossett, Lou, Jr. 88
Gottlieb, Michael 44
Grace, Rob 59–78
Gramercy Theatre 158
The Grand Tarot 59
Gray, Dolores 177, 181
Gray, Spalding 156
The Great Depression 59
The Green Bay Tree 10
Greenberg, Richard 4, 5, 30, 158–176
Gregory, Lady Augusta 124, 125
Grene, Nicholas 126, 128
Grey, Joel 52
Grey Gardens 72
Grisham, John 167
Gross, Gregory 46, 47, 51
Guare, John 158
Guess Who's Coming to Dinner 88
Gussow, Mel 41, 42
Gusto House 178
Guthrie, Tyrone 127
Guthrie Theatre 127

Hagedorn, Jeff 34
Hagedorn, Jessica 151

Hamlet 60, 179
Hammerstein, Oscar 88
Happel, Marc 210
Happy Everything 179
Harris, John F. 93
Hart, Bill 52
Hartinger, Brent 115, 116, 117
"The Hawaiian Wedding Song" 145
Hay Fever 164
Healy, Peg 142, 143, 148, 155
Hecht, Josh 69
Helen Hayes Theatre 209
Hellman, Lillian 10
Hello, Dolly! 17
Henry, Ann 180
Hepburn, Katharine 96
HERE Arts Center 67, 74
Herman, Jerry 17
Hesse, Hermann 45
Hidden: A Gender 196
Hines, Mimi 180
Hinkley, John 201
Hirschfield, Magnus 67
Hitler, Adolf 179
Hoffman, William 3, 18, 34
The Holocaust 18
Hooks, Jan 203
Hopwood, Avery 9
Hot Peaches 187, 191, 192
Houdyshell, Jayne 152, 156
The Hours 79
House Un-American Activities Committee 27
How I Learned to Drive 4
How to Have Sex in an Epidemic: One Approach 50
Hudson, Rock 20, 35, 44
Hughes, Holly 104, 190, 192, 199, 207
Hugo, Victor 72
Humphreys, Laud 82
Humphries, Barry 199
Hurrah at Last 5, 158–176
Hush, Hush, Sweet Charlotte 183
Hwang, David Henry 88

I Am My Own Wife 72
I Could Go On Lip-Synching 179
I Saw What You Did 183
Ibsen, Henrik 41
In a Garden 161
In Search of the Cobra Jewels 12
Independent Voters of Illinois/Independent Precinct Organization 85
Inge, William 11
Ingebretsen, Edward J. 92
The International Stud 13
Ireland and the Second World War 132
Irish Literary Theatre 124
Irish Republican Army 124
Italian Renaissance 67
Ivanov 60, 61

Jackson, Jesse 87
Jarry, Alfred 57
Jeffrey 26
Jeffreys, Joe E. 63
Jenkins, Christine A. 106
Jessel, George 182
Jesus Christ 205
Jesus Wept 205
Jews 27, 88, 170
Joan Crawford Live at Town Hall 72
Jocasta 66
Joe's Pub 194, 202, 205, 206
Johnson, Jay 211
Johnson, Lady Bird 208
Jones, James Earl 88
Jones, LeRoi (Amiri Baraka) 11
Jongh, Nicholas de 48, 49
Jorgensen, Christine 56, 67, 68, 69, 70, 75, 76
Judy Speaks 72
Julius Caesar 179
Just Between Friends 198, 199
Just Say No: A Play About a Farce 21, 22

Kabuki theatre 74
Kander, John 24
Kane, Sarah 64
Karam, Stephen 118
Kass, John 85
Kaufman, Moisés 3
Kazin, Alfred 9
Kelley, Clifford 83
Kelly, Grace 206
Kennedy, Louise 202
Kennedy's Children 12
Kershaw, Baz 33, 37
Kierkegaard, Søren 73
Kiki and Herb 5, 194–212
Kiki and Herb: Alive on Broadway 209, 210, 211
Kiki and Herb: Coup de Théâtre 198, 208
Kiki and Herb: It's Not Unusual 198
Kiki and Herb: One Last Chance to Blow 198
Kiki and Herb: There's a Stranger in My Manger 202, 205
Kiki and Herb: Whitey's on the Moon 198
Kiki and Herb Will Die for You: At Carnegie Hall 198
Kilroy, Thomas 126, 127
King Tut's Wah Wah Hut 178
Kinsley, Michael 1, 4, 8, 9
Kinzer, Craig 51
Kiss of the Spider Woman 24
Kissel, Howard 39, 46
Kitt, Eartha 208
Klein, Melanie 91, 173, 174
Klytaemnestra's Unmentionables 62, 66, 67, 71, 73, 74, 76
Kmart 155
Knocker's Up 72

Knowles, Ric 33
Koch, Ed 21, 38, 40, 46
Kramer, Larry 4, 5, 18–21, 27, 30, 32–55
Krim, Mathilda 19
Kroll, Jack 43
Kron, Ann 152, 153, 154
Kron, Lisa 5, 104, 141–157
Kucinich, Dennis 87
Kushner, Tony 1, 3, 4, 6, 7, 8, 9, 13, 22, 26–29, 47, 104, 151, 158

The L-Word 79
LaChapelle, David 70
Lady Bunny 178
The Laramie Project 3, 104
The Last Hurrah 87
Laugh Whore 199
Laurents, Arthur 17
Laurie, Piper 182
Lawrence, Steve 194, 203
Lawson, D. S. 51
Lee, Eugene 46
Lefebvre, Herni 141
Leguizamo, John 199, 200
Leopold, Nathan, Jr. 100
Lepore, Amanda 70
Lesbian in Herstory Archive 144
Lesko, Nancy 108
Limbo Lounge 178
Lindsey-Hogg, Michael 46
Lips Together, Teeth Apart 24
The Lisbon Traviata 24
Little Women 166
Living Newspaper 39
Loeb, Richard 100
London, Julie 196
Longacre Theatre 156
Los Angeles's Highway 199
Louryk, Bradford 56–78
Love! Valour! Compassion! 4, 7, 25, 27, 29
Lowe, Donald M. 174
Lucas, Craig 4
Lucrezia Borgia 66, 67, 71, 72
Ludlam, Charles 3, 5, 12, 18, 56–78, 179, 187, 188, 190, 192
Lyne, Sister Sheila 84, 85
Lypsinka 5, 71, 177–184, 195
Lypsinka! A Day in the Life 179
Lypsinka! As I Lay Lip-Synching 179, 181, 182, 183, 184n
Lypsinka Must Be Destroyed 179
Lypsinka! Now It Can Be Lip-Synched 179
Lypsinka! The Boxed Set 179, 181, 184n

M. Butterfly 88
Mack and Mabel 17
MacKenzie, Gisele 180
Mackie, Bob 210
Magnuson, Ann 178
Magritte, Rene 152, 154

"Make Believe" 23
La Mama Experimental Theatre 17
Mame 17
Mamet, David 5, 79–89
Manhattan Theatre Club 25
Manny and Jake 17
The Many Moods of Lypsinka 179
Marat, Jean-Paul 63
Margolin, Deb 188, 199
Mark, Jordi 142
Mark Taper Forum 26
Marlowe, Christopher 179
Martin Short: Fame Become Me 199
Martyn, Edward 125
Mary Magdalene 206
Mason, Patrick 128
Mast, Jane *see* West, Mae
McCarthy, Sen. Joseph 27, 94
McGuinness, Frank 123–139
McKay, Fay 181
McKeon, Larry 85
McKinley, Jesse 199
McNally, Terrence 4, 23–26
Medea 64, 66, 77, 179
Mee, Charles 64
Mell, Deborah 86, 87
Mell, Richard 85, 86, 87
Mellman, Kenny *see* Kiki and Herb
Mendelssohn, Felix 145
The Merchant of Venice 87
Merman, Ethel 180, 182
Meyers, Kevin 135
Miguel, Gloria 187
Milhous, Judith 101n
Miller, Arthur 11
Miller Neil 95
Miller, Tim 147, 199, 204, 207
Mitchell, John Cameron 204
The Mobile Theatre 151
Mohr, Ian 202, 209
Mommie Dearest 183
Monroe, Marilyn 75, 76
Moore, Joseph 85
Moossy, Joan Marie 184n
More, Thomas 192
Mormons 27
Morris, Libby 180, 181
Morrow, Karen 180
The Most Fabulous Story Ever Told 26
Mostly Sondheim 199
Les Mouches 64
Moulton, Charles 147
Müller, Heiner 64
My Deah 179
The Mystery of Charles Dickens 199
The Mystery of Irma Vep 12

Nader, Ralph 87
National Endowment for the Arts (NEA) 207

National Institute of Health (NIH) 23, 32
National Theatre of Ireland 125, 128, 139
Nazis 133
Nefertiti 66
New Conservatory Theatre 107
New World Stages 70
New York City Theatre Ensemble 12
New York Public Theatre 20, 32, 35, 36, 37, 38, 40, 41, 44, 46, 50, 51, 52, 53, 151, 152, 153, 156, 194
New York Shakespeare Festival *see* New York Public Theatre
New York Theatre Workshop 26
Newhart, Bob 182
Newton, Esther 58
Nietzsche, Friedrich 91
No Future: Queer Theory and the Death Drive 94, 165
Non-Places: Introduction to an Anthropology of Supermodernity 141
The Normal Heart 4, 5, 7, 18–21, 23, 32–55

Observe the Sons of Ulster Marching Towards the Somme 135, 136, 137
An Officer and a Gentleman 88
O'Hara, John 87
Ojeda, Perry 134
Olympia Theatre 126
O'Mason, Patti "Cupcake" 180
On Tidy Endings 17, 19
Onassis, Aristotle 198
101 Humiliating Stories 146, 148, 150, 153, 154, 155
O'Neill, Eugene 9, 10
Orr, David 86
Orton, Joe 96
The Other Side of the Closet 107, 110, 111, 112

Papp, Gail 151
Papp, Joe 39, 41, 45, 151
Parents, Families & Friends of Lesbians and Gays (PFLAG) 94
Parker, Mary-Louise 104
Parks, Suzan-Lori 4, 151
Pask, Scott 210
The Passion of the Crawford 179, 181
Pati, Sebastian 85
Patrick, Robert 12
Phaedra's Love 64
Philadelphia, Here I Come! 127
Phyllis Diller Laughs 72
Picnic 161
Pierce, C. S. 90
Pierce, Charles 195
Pink Flamingoes 195
Pirandello, Luigi 152
The Play About the Baby 177
The Playboy of the Western World 125, 126
Pleasure for Pleasure 61
The Pleasure Man 9

Poiret, Jean 17
Poitier, Sidney 88
The Politics of Irish Drama 126
Polyester 195
Poole, Mary 51
Pope Benedict XVI 201
Presidential Advisory Council on HIV and AIDS 93
P.S. 122, 146, 147, 148, 150, 194
Pterodactyls 90, 95, 96, 97, 98, 99, 100, 101
Public Enemy 209
Puig, Manuel 24
Pyramid Club 178
Pytka, Meghann 53n

Queer as Folk 79, 88
Queer Nation 27, 201

Rabkin, Gerald 57
Radiohead 195
Raised in Captivity 5, 100, 101, 158–176
Ranson, Rebecca 34
Raywood, Keith 46
Reagan, Nancy 22
Reagan, Ronald 20, 21, 22, 27, 201
Republican Party 20, 84, 173
Rich, Frank 38, 39, 41
Rich, Richie 70
Richards, David 24
Ridiculous Theatrical Company 3, 5, 12, 56–78, 187, 188
Ridiculous Theatre, Scourge of Human Folly 56
The Ritz 23, 24
Rivera, Chita 199, 200
Rivera, Jose 151
Roach, Joseph 52
Roberts, Brian 158
Roberts, Geoffrey 132
Robertson, Pat 205
Rodgers, Eileen 180
Rodgers, Richard 88
Rofes, Eric 173
Román, David 32, 35, 37, 50, 196, 204
Roman Catholic Church 62, 84, 125
Rose, Peter 147
Rosencrantz and Guildenstern Give Head 61, 62
Rosenthal, Mark E. 104
Roundabout Theatre 119
Royal National Theatre of Great Britain 26
Rudnick, Paul 4, 26
RuPaul 178, 195
Rushbrook, Dereka 203
Russell, Mark 147
Russell, Nipsey 68, 69, 75

Safe Sex 17, 18
St. Augustine 92
Salvato, Nick 101n

Samuel French, Inc. 179
Sandahl, Carrie 200
Sartre, Jean-Paul 64
Saturday Night Live 203
Savin-Williams, Ritch C. 105, 106
Savran, David 101n, 103, 203
Scissor Sisters 209
Seattle Children's Theatre 110
Second Coming 205
The Secretaries 146
Sedgwick, Eve 81
Senelick, Laurence 74
The Sensuous Woman 72
A Service for Jeremy Wong 107, 112, 113, 114, 115
700 Sundays 199
Sex, John 178
Sexaholic 199
Shabad, Peter 164
Shairp, Mordaunt 10
Shakespeare, William 60, 87, 127, 144, 151, 179
Shapiro, Howard 209
Shatzky, Joel 46
Shaw, Peggy 142, 187, 188, 191, 192
Shepherd, Matthew 3, 26
Sherman, Martin 18
Shilts, Randy 20, 40, 44, 45
Shklovsky, Victor 51
Short, Martin 199
Shortbus 204
Show Trash 179
Showboat 88, 89
Silver, Nicky 4, 5, 90–102, 158–176
Silver, Warren 84, 85
The Silver Cord 161
Simon, John 42, 47
Simone, Nina 181
Simonson, Robert 156
Sinatra, Frank 203
Sinfield, Alan 173
Sissies' Scrapbook 18
Six Feet Under 79
Smith, Dan 53n
Smith, Jack 186
Soja, Edward 141
Solomon, Alisa 101n, 142, 207
Somers, Suzanne 199
Sommers, Michael 47
Son, Diana 151
Sontag, Susan 93, 130, 186
Sophocles 64
South Coast Repertory Theatre 158
Southern Fried Chekhov 62
Speech and Debate 118, 119
Split Britches 5, 185–193
Split Britches 188
Spookhouse 17
Stanislavsky, Konstantin 74
Stein, Gertrude 184

Stewart, Patrick 199
Stonewall Inn (and riot) 3, 27, 128, 141, 165, 179, 185, 190
Strange Interlude 9
Street Scene 161
A Streetcar Named Desire 71
Streisand, Barbra 196
Stritch, Elaine 198
Suddenly Last Summer 183
Sugar and Spice 72
Sullivan, Andrew 171, 172, 173, 174
Sundance Theatre Laboratory 72
"Superstitious" 154, 156
Syna, Sy 39
Synge, John Millington 125, 126

Take Me Out 4, 7, 30, 79
Talburt, Susan 115
The Talented Mr. Ripley 72
Tamburlaine 179
Target store 155
Tarzian, Charles 147, 150
Taylor, Elizabeth 182, 183
Tea and Sympathy 10, 104, 107
"Tea for Two" 181
Thacker, Jerry 93
Theatre Laboratory 72
Theatre of Cruelty 72
Theatre Offensive 70
Theatre Rhinoceros 199
"There's No Business Like Show Business" 180, 181
The Thin Blue Line 72
This Is Not a Pipe 154
"This Nearly Was Mine" 23
Thompson, Kay 180
Tian, Min 51
The Tiny Closet 11
Titus Andronicus 179
The Toilet 11
Torch Song Trilogy 3, 7, 12–20, 24, 26, 29
Tracers 45
The Tragedy of Hamlet, Prince of Denmark 60, 62
La Traviata 24
Tunney, Tom 85
Twain, Mark 87
The Two and Only 211
Two Loves 80
Tzara, Tristan 57, 72

Upwardly Mobile Home 188

Vaccaro, John 187
Valley of the Dolls 178
The Ventriloquist's Wife 73
Versace, Gianni 90
Verushka 177
Vietnam War 12

Vietnam Veterans Memorial 46
A View from the Bridge 11
Vineyard Theatre 96, 100
Vogel, Paula 4
Vogel, Shane 201, 203
Von Trapp Family Singers 89
Vortex Theatre 96
Voyage to Lesbos 142–157
Vrdolyak, Ed 84

Waking Life 72
Walker, Nancy 180
Wallace, Naomi 4
Wallach, Allan 39, 40
Wallenberg, Christopher 76
Wandor, Michelene 80
Warhol, Andy 186
Warner, Sara 101n
Warren, David 158
Washington, Harold 84
Waters, John 72, 195
Watt, Douglas 39
Weaver, Lois 142, 187, 188, 191, 192
Weaver, Sigourney 148
"The Wedding March" 145
Weir, John 173
Weisman, Wendy 156
Well 151–157
West, Mae 9

What Evil Means to Us 91
Wherry, Kenneth 95
Widows and Children First! 13, 15, 16
Wilde, Oscar 9, 80, 81, 96, 185
Wilder, Laura Ingalls 148
Williams, Tennessee 2, 10, 11, 27, 30, 71, 161
Wilson, August 88
Wilson, Julie 180
Wilson, Lanford 11, 12
Wolfe, George C. 151, 152
Women in Love 18
Women Who Survive 66
Wonder, Stevie 154
Wong, Jeremy 107, 112
Woolly Mammoth Theatre 96
World AIDS Conference 172
WOW Café 142, 143, 144, 146, 147, 148, 188, 190, 191, 192, 199
The Wrestling Season 107, 108, 109, 110, 112

X, Y and Zee 182, 183

Yates, Andrea 64
Yeats, William Butler 124, 125
You Can't Take It with You 165
Youth, Education, and Sexualities 105

Zaytoun, Constance 101n
Zeifman, Hersh 80–89

www.ingramcontent.com/pod-product-compliance
Lightning Source LLC
Chambersburg PA
CBHW032051300426
44116CB00007B/686